Revelation and Planet X

The Kolbrin Bible Indigo Connection

Revelation and Planet X

The Kolbrin Bible Indigo Connection

Marshall Masters
Your Own World Books
Nevada, USA

Knowledgemountain.org
Yowusa.com

Copyright

Revelation and Planet X: The Kolbrin Bible Indigo Connection

No part of this book may be reproduced or transmitted in any form or by any means, graphic, electronic, or mechanical, including photocopying, recording, taping, or by any information storage retrieval system, without the written permission of the publisher.

Copyright © 2024 by Knowledge Mountain Church of Perpetual Genesis, NV, USA.
All rights reserved.

Your Own World Books
An Imprint of Knowledge Mountain Church of Perpetual Genesis, NV, USA
Author: Marshall Masters, Founder and Chief Steward

Paperback
First Edition — January 2024
ISBN-13: 978-1-59772-201-8
Knowledgemountain.org
Yowusa.com

Notice: Every effort has been made to make this book as complete and as accurate as possible, and no warranty or fitness is implied. All of the information provided in this book is provided on an "as is" basis. The authors and the publisher shall not be liable or responsible to any person or entity with respect to any loss or damages arising from the information contained herein.

Fair Use: This book contains copyrighted material and is made available for educational purposes, to advance the understanding of preparedness research and related survival issues, etc. This constitutes a "fair use" of any such copyrighted material as provided for in Title 17 U.S.C. section 107 of the US Copyright Law. In accordance with Title 17 U.S.C. Section 107, the material in this book is made available for non-profit research and educational purposes.

Trademarks: All terms mentioned in this book that are known to be trademarks or service marking have been capitalized. Knowledge Mountain Church of Perpetual Genesis cannot attest to the accuracy of this information and the use of any term in this book should not be regarded as affecting the validity of any trademark or service mark.

Table of Contents

Dedication..xiii

Introduction..xiv

1 – Look Up..15

    The Phoenix..16

    Fear is the Mind Killer...17

    Why I Wrote This Book...18

    Dawn of the Riselings..19

    Dear Riselings..21

    Alphas and the Indigo Path...21

    Dear Riseling Parents..23

    Teach Your Riseling Well..26

    Lights of Hope..29

    Teaching Tools...30

2 – Planet X System..33

    Nibiru / Planet X...35

    Blue Kachina / Red Kachina..36

    The Nemesis Cloud..37

    Teaching Tools...38

3 – Previous Planet X System Flybys..43

    The First Decode Clue...44

    Eyewitness Observers...44

    A Great Light..47

    December 26, 2012..47

- Noah's Flood and Exodus..49
  - Deluge Flyby..49
  - Exodus Flyby..50
- The Kozai Mechanism..51
- Poor Phaeton...53
- Teaching Tools...54

4 – Indigo Riselings..57

- To Be an Indigo...58
- Indigo Children..58
- We are Spectral Beings...59
  - The Indigo Aura...61
  - Color System..63
  - God's Favorite Color..64
- What Am I?..64
  - Star Seeds..65
  - Riselings..66
  - Indigo Children...67
  - Crystal Children..69
  - Day of the Riselings..74
- Teaching Tools...76
  - Kiri and Lo'ak..76
  - The Way of Water...77

5 – Revelation River...79

- Indigo Construct...80
- Good vs. Evil..80
- Time Canoeing..82
  - Soul Mates...84
  - Chutes and Oxbows..85
  - Clarity Mantra...86
- River's End...87

- Teaching Tools 88
  - Survival Comms 89
  - HAM Cram 90

6 – Revelation 8:8-9 – The Mountain 93

- Anunnaki Invasion 95
- Act of War 97
- Cycle of Empire 99
- Teaching Tools 101

7 – Revelation 8:10-11 – Wormwood 103

- Revelation 9 Alien Invasion 104
- Preemptive Strike 105
- Revelation 8 Review 106
  - Metaphors 107
  - Fountains 109
  - Wormwood Mud Flats 110
- Blue Kachina 111
- The Great Winnowing 112
- Teaching Tools 114

8 – Revelation 8:12 – Pole Shift 117

- Lithosphere Lock 118
- Solar Sprite - Killshot 118
- Nibiru Eclipse 119
  - Revelation 8:12 119
  - The Kolbrin Bible 120
  - Carlos 120
- Ferrada Impacts Venus 122
- Pole Shift 123
  - Pole Shift Effects 124

       Earth Post-Shift... 125

   Teaching Tools.. 126

9 – Prophecy Timeline 129

   2024 – Revelation 8:7 131

       Midwinter 132

       Late Winter 132

       Spring 133

       Fall 134

   2025 – Women and Gold 134

       Late-Winter 134

       Summer 135

       Early Fall 135

   2026 – Revelation 8:10-11 135

       Mid-Winter 135

   2027 – Revelation 8:12 136

       Mid-Winter 136

       Early Summer 137

   2028 – Killshot Event 137

       Late Spring 137

   2029 – Final Warning 138

       Early-Summer 138

   2030 – Pole Shift 138

       Summer 138

       Late Fall 139

   2031 – New Lands 141

       Mid-Winter 141

       Summer 142

   2032 – Solar Calm 142

       Mid-Winter 142

       Summer 142

   2033 – Earth Settles 142

       Mid-Winter 142

Summer	142
2034 – Cleansing Rains	143
Mid-Winter	143
Early Winter	143
2035 – Blue Skies	143
Mid-Winter	143
Early Spring	143
2036 – Sweet Waters	143
Mid-Winter	143
Summer	144
2037 – Our New Earth	144
Mid-Winter	144
Spring	144
Universal Constants	144
Teaching Tools	145

10 – Indigo Construct 149

Guidelines	149
Incarnation	150
Awareness	151
The Void	152
Theory of Everything	153
The Big Bang	154
Path of Discovery	156
Ascension Trigger	160
The Plan	161
Waking Dreams	163
Teaching Tools	166

11 – We Are a Hunted Species 169

A Few Good Seeds	170

We are a Hunted Species...171
Indigo Freedom Tools...173
Language is a Weapon...174
    Subliminal Programming..174
    Paralinguistics...175
    Effective Listening...176
    Less is More..177
Channeling...178
Remote Viewing...180
Out-of-Body...183
The Great Winnowing..184
Teaching Tools...186

12 – Perpetual Genesis...**189**

Follow the Photon...190
Poetry of Evil..192
Source..193
Goals..196
Lexicon...197
The Void...199
I Am..201
Creator and Creation...203
Heaven...204
    co-Creators...205
    Life Force Energy...206
    Our Home..208
Reincarnation...210
Redemption..211
    Soul Scaring..212
    Lost Souls..213
    Death Eternal..215

    Reach for Freedom...217
    Creator's Plan...219
    The Great Winnowing..221
    Your Role..224
    Teaching Tools...225

13 – Shawheylu 229
    Ascended Species..230
    John and Sally...232
    Spirits and Souls..233
    Weddings...234
    Making the Bond..239
    Teaching Tools...241

14 – Call to the Nation 243
    Good News – Bad News..244
    Can You Handle the Truth?..245
    One in Three...246
    Flight Insurance...247
    What Creator Wants...248
    Turbo Redemption..250

Epilogue...255
    Share Day..256
    Amelia..257
    Pathfinders..259

Appendix A – Affirmations..265

Appendix B – Cinema List..273

Appendix C – Library List..275

Alphabetical Index..279

Dedication

Chilean Astronomer Carlos Muñoz Ferrada (1909 - 2001) calculated the existence of the Planet X System as we call it today, and he announced his findings in 1940.

His discovery was not by observation; instead, he employed a reliable method first used to discover Neptune using mathematics, and he was right!

He carried the burden of this knowledge for the better part of his life. If he had lived just a few years longer, he could have seen Nibiru, the outermost major planet in the systems, just as I did on December 26, 2012, thanks to a live university webcam feed from the mouth of the Turrialba volcano in Costa Rica.

On that day, one could say Carlos passed the baton on to me, and perhaps it was more fitting this way because Carlos is not a quitter, and my readings with him in *Being In It for the Species: The Universe Speaks*. Several excerpts from those readings are in this book.

His selfless love and passion for the survival of humanity burn brightly on both sides of the veil. That is precisely why this dedication is not by me.

Instead, it is our collective acknowledgment of his achievements and sacrifices because:

We always honor our heroes, creators, thinkers, and those who inspire us. *This is the way.*

Introduction

How can the prophecies in Revelation and other great wisdom texts survive the long march of time?

The answer is, penned with love and hope for the future, their warnings to us living today express the most extraordinary form of love possible—the love of your kind.

These ancient authors were in it for the species, and their prophecies converge from many directions and times.

Take heed, for should we fail, every human who has ever walked the earth will have no story to tell and no songs to sing.

In such a final silence, it will be as though we never were nor could ever be again. The death eternal of a species.

For this reason, regardless of source, these ancient prophecies all share the same silent plea woven between the lines, which has echoed throughout time.

Do you hear it?

"Please, dear children, save us all."

–Marshall Masters

1

Look Up

Look up. The Destroyer has returned. Long live humanity. Look up. The Destroyer has returned, and our species is on the verge of genetic extinction.

The last to know will be among the first to die, and this warning was passed on to us by the ancient Egyptians thousands of years ago.

> **The Kolbrin Bible: 21st Century Master Edition**
> Book of Manuscripts
>
> 3:1 Men forget the days of the Destroyer. Only the wise know where it went and that it will return in its appointed hour.

Rejoice. You now hold the knowledge of the wise in your hands, so do not despair; this is the time to prepare. Yes, the Destroyer has been here before, but this time is different.

This time, humanity will eventually win its freedom as a species and thrive in a peaceful world for whatever time remains for our beautiful blue-green planet. That is good news, but getting there will be hard.

The bad news is that woe and wonder are upon us in the coming fifteen or more years, and a good portion of humanity will perish, primarily by resignation.

You are about to learn all this and more, but in the meantime, why will people die from resignation during this Planet X Tribulation?

It is because they will only look up once it is too late, and by then, they will realize that their denial has decided their fate. A few will redeem that unfortunate choice with the help of good people, but most will choose to go quietly into the night.

Dear Reader, the proposition is simple. Are you ready to look up, and if so, what are you prepared to do about it? If you are unwilling to do anything, I can offer you nothing of value except this.

You are not yet ready to fight for your life, and reading this knowledge will only push you deeper into your denial, thereby setting you on a path of failure, and you will likely die badly.

As one human to another, I implore you. Please close this book now and place it back where you found it. When you are ready to open your mind, it will be there.

Take your time deciding this, that is, what little of it you have left. I say this with patience and love because I've spent most of my life waiting for people to look up.

The Phoenix

In 1962, the City of Phoenix, Arizona, commissioned a triptych for the Sky Harbor Airport Terminal 2 lobby. In those days, there were no security checkpoints, and you could walk straight from the curb to the gate.

As a sixteen-year-old with a freshly minted driver's license, I had this inexplicable, constant urge to burn gas for any reason imaginable, and thankfully, it was pretty affordable at the time.

Of course, someone is always flying in, and I always volunteered to pick them up at the airport.

I would get there early so I had time to sit in the lobby and watch passengers streaming down from the gates. Most rambled past me to the baggage pickup without looking up or sideways and would typically pass right by the triptych's center panel with a glazed look.

Those were the dull masses, and I blurred them out because I knew one would occasionally look up, and that was when the magic happened, time and again.

Captivated by "The Phoenix," as it was named, they studied this wonder of colored tiles, 75 feet wide and 16 feet high, and a magnificent Phoenix bird rising in the center panel. It was a feast for the eyes, with a color and design that were uniquely bold, engaging, and gifted, if not daring.

The few who did look up would step aside from the others, often setting their carry-on down. Their expressions were childlike with delight and wonder; this was an amazing and unique piece of art.

I always wondered which area of the triptych fascinated them the most. After a few years of observations, I saw that it was the wing root and center neck area of the Phoenix.

Depicted as a fire bird, the plumage of the Phoenix was fiery but soft; however, the area of focus featured the color indigo. It was this color that people focused on in this area, but why is it so special?

It is because cinnamon is God's favorite scent, and indigo is God's favorite color. It is His sign that humanity will overcome horrific obstacles in the coming years and prevail as this sick civilization dies away in the coming Planet X tribulation.

Are you ready to look up? If so, this book aims to show you how to rise out of the fiery ashes of this coming tribulation. To not only survive but to thrive with purpose and meaning.

You will know what to expect when to expect it, and how to survive it in the Indigo way because survival is less about holding onto things and more about holding on to each other with love–not fear.

Fear is the Mind Killer

What will happen in the coming Planet X Tribulation years ahead? Terrible impact events, tsunamis, fires, near-global defoliation, earthquakes, eruptions, and all things we dare not imagine. And yes, a zombie apocalypse.

It will happen over the next fifteen years or so, and so we wonder, after years of tribulation, what shall remain of humanity and our world?

Those who survive this will be magnificent and free and shall peacefully lay the foundations of a new and enlightened civilization. What do I call this future post-tribulation period?

Over the years, I always signed my books "CYB, Marshall." It stands for "I'll catch you on the backside."

We will discuss the backside at length later on, but for now, it defines a future time when, after the last tremblers, the last meteorite falls, and Earth has cleansed itself with years of rainstorms. Then, stouthearted survivors will see blue skies and taste sweet waters again.

Why I Wrote This Book

After more than twenty years of researching, authoring, and writing on Planet X, I've learned that fear is a mind-killer, so this book's purpose is not to provoke fear and despair but to defeat it. I do this because I am a psychic, an Indigo Elder, and a Mensan, and I have seen future timelines, and all this has come with a lifetime price.

A man of three score and ten years, I am divorced, childless, and have no family. It is the price of my calling, which I received shortly after getting my driver's license, and why I would later choose to love all the innocent of the Earth, even though I could not possibly imagine this in my sixteenth year of life.

My calling came on a lovely Sunday afternoon; all the stores at the local mall were closed, and I drove slowly because of the speed bumps. The world was quiet, and I was alone, so at the age of sixteen, I began pondering my future and what would come of me, as we all tend to do around this in our lives. I did not expect the answer to come so quickly as I asked aloud, "God, what will my future be?"

To my surprise, God answered, clear as a bell.

My life would be difficult, with many twists and turns, after which I would write a spiritual book late in life.

It turns out that God was spot on about the twists and turns, and it's not the years; it's the miles. But what about that spiritual book he mentioned? That stuck with me.

Over the years, I've written several on surviving the coming Planet X tribulation, and after each one, I asked, "Is this the one." Each time, the answer was "No."

Here's a tip. God is not blabby; this time, He finally told me this is the book.

Please remember that We all talk to God in unique ways that comport with our world paradigm and naturally resonate with us. For me, God's personality is easy. All you need is two words. Pleasant persistence.

God tends to cut to the chase, and when we help to take a big step, He helps us. Some call this a heavenly nudge in the right direction, but for me, it usually feels like being shot out of a cannon. Either way, you'll eventually get there, powder burns and all.

It sure took long enough, and like all other books, you must know your intended audience before you put pen to paper.

No matter who you are, you've got a dog in this fight. Humanity is teetering on the brink of an artificial genetic extinction as mRNA vaccines have turned billions of homo sapiens into homo synthetics. Life as we know it will not end as in the future tense; it already has.

Dawn of the Riselings

Because I am a psychic, an Indigo Elder, and a Mensan, the reading level of this book is for 13-year-old and older Indigo Children and Crystal Children.

However, a new generation of Indigos has emerged from within the ranks of the Alpha generation children (Born after 2010).

Unlike previous Indigo generations, they are on the Indigo path but, unlike previous generations, were not born fully realized because this generation is being assaulted as none before by sick and demented monsters who have entirely lost their humanity.

I call this new generation Indigo Riselings, or just Riselings for short, and they represent the most precious generation in the history of our species since Adam and Eve.

Our Riselings are our glorious phoenix generation, and they will never falter or fade because when things are at their worst, we are always at our best, and Riselings are among the best of our best. They will rise bravely from the ashes of a sick world to answer the call, so let's cut to the chase. We need to circle the wagons around these precious Riselings and their families.

I know this with every fiber of my being, and the only way for them to fail us in preserving our species, as God made us, is for the rest of us to fail them first.

If we dawdle and dither, as is our nature, the end will be of personal consequence to every human soul who has ever walked the Earth since the dawn of humankind.

Dawdle and dither, we shall become another fossil layer oddity with no past and no future. Then, our species will end in an eternal nothingness, where in the stillness, nobody will be left to sing songs, hug a child, or build a rocket ship to the moon.

With this in mind, dear readers, what are you prepared to do?

Are you prepared to come together with like-minded others to do whatever it takes to save our precious Riselings and their courageous families?

Or will you accept eternal nothingness for our species because you despise yourself? If so, you are a sick soul and need to know the one law of survival for all sentient species.

> **The one law of survival for sentient species: if you are stupid, you deserve to die.**
> *This is the way.*

Good luck with that, and please remember to return this book where you found it until you are ready to walk humbly with your God and to fight for your life and the love of others.

Now, I will only talk to those who agree, "OK, winners never quit, and quitters never win, so tell me more?" If so, I'm calling out to you, my dear Riselings and Riseling families.

Dear Riselings

If you are of the Alpha generation, healthy and unvaccinated, you are a Riseling, and we will discuss this at great length throughout this book. You are on the Indigo path of awareness to open your third eye.

Those born with a fully open third eye have incarnated on this world often enough to be born with a fully open third eye. This process typically takes several lifetimes for reasons we will discuss later.

For now, what you need to know, my dear Riselings is that most of you were born with partially open third eyes, and here is the good news. If you want it, you can go flame on, totally open in this lifetime.

I am an Indigo Elder and a Mensan, and I was born flame-on and knew it when I was seven. It was in early 1960 in Phoenix, Arizona, and my older sister was not old enough to vote but was a volunteer in the campaign to elect John F. Kennedy.

As she dressed me for school, she asked, "If you could, would you vote for Kennedy?"

Without hesitation, I answered, "No. They'll kill him."

She laughed at me, and that was that for her. For me, it was my first flame-on moment.

Alphas and the Indigo Path

Indigo is a word, and most Indigos do not know its meaning, but every indigo knows one thing, usually early in life. You're different, and it has nothing to do with popularity or other shallow measures. You're just different.

That said, my prediction about Kennedy was not different, as people make predictions every day. What was different was my knowing.

I knew it as though I had traveled through time and witnessed it myself. This is the power of knowing, and this was the moment I knew I was different and not some freak of nature.

When your third eye is open or begins to open, you know things and can see through deception long before others perceive the poetry of evil. The more open your third eye is, the more you see and with greater clarity.

Here is the part nobody wants you to know. Everyone is an Indigo. It is a universal genetic trait embedded within the human genome, and something extraordinary is happening.

Imagine you're making popcorn the old-fashioned way. Put a pot on the stovetop, add oil and popcorn, then shake the pan while heating it. In time, the magic happens—a pop here and a pop there until the popcorn goes flame on and sounds like a hailstorm.

This is that popcorn hailstorm, and my dear Riselings, you are popping up everywhere. It is glorious to behold and makes me feel like the luckiest Indigo Elder alive because I'm seeing as God always knew it would happen. Oh, dear ones, you are magnificent, and the force of freedom is on your side.

Is this knowledge for you? Look to your thoughts for the answer because the miracles we all need to survive this tribulation are within us. God made it so, and we'll explore this later, but for now, here's a quick Indigo self-test.

All of the books and websites about Indigos are about Indigos. They're all people who see us from the outside in. As an Indigo Elder, I see it from the inside out.

With that, let's get down to the business of survival, and the first test is to see if you are somewhere along the Indigo Riseling path.

1. Are you having prophetic dreams, visions, or premonitions?
2. Do you sometimes know a future outcome with absolute certainty, and more often than not, it happens that way?
3. Do you suffer in popularity amongst your friends because when you see them planning something reckless, you choose not to participate?

If you answered yes to one or more of the above, you are on the Indigo path, and here is a friendly tip using horse racing terminology.

> When your friends are watching, win by a nose. When the world is watching, win by a length. This is the way.

If you cannot answer yes, there is only one test, and the same holds for those who can. A maxim is a proposition serving as a rule or guide. Throughout this book, you will see several, and each will end with "*This is the way.*"

Later, I will teach you the Indigo way of centering, but now, only one truth matters. It is a truth that resonates within you because you and you alone put it there.

If this resonates with you, I can help you, and this chapter and each after that will end with what I call teaching tools.

The knowledge is for everyone but is for the benefit of the healthy, unvaccinated, heterosexual Alpha Generation children I call Riselings—humanity's last hope.

Now, a word to you, 13-year-old Riselings. You will find the concepts in this book challenging, which is why I am writing this book for 13-year-old Riselings and Crystals. Their need is immediate, and this is their time, but as you grow older, my dear Riselings, remember the timeless adage. "When the student is ready, the teacher will appear."

When you are ready, this book will be waiting for you, and in the meantime, if you're up to a challenge, you will need the help and the love of your parents to master the content in this book.

Dear Riseling Parents

To have and raise healthy children these days is an onerous burden. I see fathers being handcuffed and dragged out of school board meetings because pronoun-males are in women's sports and bathrooms.

Or maybe he opposes the grooming of his child in the classroom by dancing transvestites with repulsive bearded princess fantasies.

I also see the moms who stand with their defiant husbands and take upon themselves the added burden of homeschooling. The emotional carnage of it is a horror to behold, but yet, is this not the stuff of true heroism?

For those parents who went to great lengths to keep their children healthy and away from the vaccine bioweapon, I stand in awe of you. You are unsung heroes and precious.

So very, very precious. More than you could ever know because whatever made you what you are is why your Riseling children represent the most precious generation since Adam and Eve.

History is on your side, Riseling parents, because people have always survived better in groups, and the family has always been the most basic foundation of group survival for eons. Consequently, families that emphasize the "creation" of the family, in every possible respect, survive far better than those in denial.

The bottom line is this. What do I want for your child? The same thing you do. A good, healthy, long, productive, and joyful life.

As I said before, I am childless. While this was not my desire, it was my responsibility. It was a tough choice, and all business about the miracle of invitro fertilization and how women can safely postpone having children until their 30s proved to be an expensive disappointment. Perhaps this is why we only hear about the less frequent successes.

My wife's first round of invitro was challenging for her, only to end in a miscarriage. To go a second round had risks, and she was prepared to do it but left the decision to me because she knew I still mourned a child I lost to an abortion when I was in college.

It had to be my choice, and I knew she would take the risk if I asked. I loved her even more for giving me that choice, and I decided we would not go through another round. It wasn't a decision. It was a knowing, and it presented me with two options.

The first option was to feel cheated and waste my life railing at God. Yuck.

The second option was that if I cannot love my own, then I shall love and do what I can to be in service to all innocent lives, and it matters not if they know me. It would not be until 2021 that I learned the truth.

I have several sources feeding me leads all the time, and one sent me a link to BitChute and said it wouldn't last. The link was to a dark web disclosure video of a body harvesting in what appeared to be the Philippines or somewhere else in that region.

The clip begins with men offloading the bodies of men in their 20s. They toss them off the back of a truck like firewood.

Now, whoever is making this video is a person of authority or under the direction of one, and all of the workers in this processing area step back.

The camera tilts down on a young toddler with a stilted walk, such as when they're just getting their legs. She is a beautiful child. Her dress and hair showed me that she was very much loved.

She was in a place she did not expect to be, and the camera followed her into the processing center as she continually cried out, "Mama Dada," with desperate hope of finding her parents. All this while she is walking past two rows of gurneys upon which are the bodies of these 20-something-year-old men in some stage of processing.

The intestines of each body were draped over the sides of the gurney, spilling onto the floor. It was a horrible thing you could not unsee or unhear.

The child was processed long before I watched this horrible video. Harvested for adrenochrome and whatever other commodities of interest. Nonetheless, for the rest of my life, the memory of watching this precious child racing past a cascade of human intestines to both sides and calling out for her parents haunts me.

As my source said, it would not last, and BitChute pulled the video. After reading their terms of service, I understood why.

Nonetheless, I published an article on my website, yowusa.com, where I described this dark web video and said of these monsters, "God's judgment upon them will be heard through the voices of children."

After that, it started raining anvils all around me as Google, YouTube, and Facebook began crushing me with vicious fury. It's not like I'm the only one because the result is the same. There is no defense against a government that harms all who dare refuse the official narrative.

Consequently, when government agencies use social media to make war on your right to free speech, you typically wind up in bankruptcy, as I did, and all because I dared to say, "God's judgment upon them will be heard through the voices of children."

Well, I just repeated it twice. Some could say I'm too stupid to quit; get in line.

As for me, I'm here, so this brings me to you, dear Riseling parents, and your urgent mission.

Teach Your Riseling Well

Throughout history, knowledge has always been passed down from generation to generation. From father to son, mother to daughter, master to apprentice, and so forth.

Things are different now. There is no time for this natural process; even if there is, we're all up against something entirely new, and we do not have the luxury of time to sort it all out.

What happens without this book?

You and everyone you know will be blindsided by most catastrophic events, and this is terrible juju because the first to die are usually the last to know. This sad outcome is serious, and here is why.

> **Never underestimate the power of human denial.** *This is the way.*

Conversely, what happens with this book?

I hope this book helps your family receive global support for your efforts to ensure the continuity of our species as God made us.

My mission is to use over twenty years of research and publishing to help you survive what comes, and neither Creationism nor Darwinism can explain what is coming.

Before Darwinism, there was Catastrophism. The scientific community's previously held belief theory explains the coming tribulation with perfect clarity.

It describes that Earth goes through long periods of relative quiescence punctuated by brief moments of global cataclysm that will reorder life on the planet.

Before you doubt that, consider this. Darwinism bypassed review and was generally accepted because it offered a clean break with Church doctrine. Ergo, the rapid adoption of Darwinism was a sociopolitical event with unforeseen consequences.

The problem with Darwinism is that it sidesteps the need to be mindful of events that can and will reorder life in our lifetimes.

With this in mind, my dear Riseling parents, here is what you must be mindful of. We're on the upslope of a brief moment of global cataclysm, and if you can see that coming, you are a survivor.

As a Riseling family, here is your mission.

Survival is less about holding onto things and more about holding on to each other.
This is the way.

My calling as an Indigo Elder is to give you knowledge tools to help you survive the awful times and to thrive and prosper.

Yes, I see the terrible times ahead, but after that, I see a clean slate for humanity, and upon it, your descendants will build a Star Trek future. As they set their hands to it, they will sing songs to honor you for being in it for the species.

Listen. Can you hear it? I do, and what I hear them singing is, "Our family is our fortress. Built upon the courage of our ancestors, we are one. We are one."

Now that we have the theory let's focus on the application. For Riseling fathers and mothers, I created the global heading of Teaching Tools, which appears at the end of each chapter. The knowledge tools are for everyone, and I made two types—one for moms and one for dads and with that, ladies first.

Moms, imagine saying to your children, "OK, kids, it's time to do your catastrophism homework," what will they likely do:

A. Begin jumping up and down in an enthusiastic frenzy.
B. Start moonwalking backward.

If you answered "A," whatever you are doing, keep doing it, and please write a book about it. Otherwise, "B" is the safe bet.

So, how do we turn this lemon into lemonade? Let's make the homework a fun family affair.

Watching movies together is something families enjoy, and for you, Moms, in each chapter, I introduce a cinema teaching tool. I'll give you the name of the film and the elements within it you can use as teaching moments.

As I said before, the reading level of this book is suitable for 13-year-olds or older, Indigo or Crystal children. Therefore, Mom, this is your call because you know your kid down to the genetic level, and well, you should because the activated Indigo trait typically follows the mother's bloodline.

Mom. You will know when your child is ready for this knowledge. Before that, use the cinema teaching tools to begin creating awareness.

That way, one day, when you feel it is the right time, you hand this book to your Riseling and hopefully say something like, "I can't say I agree with everything, but it's a good read." Do that, and I'll begin jumping up and down in an enthusiastic frenzy.

Now, Dad, for you. If you're still alive, have you wondered why you still managed to survive after all the stupid things you've done? I have–frequently.

The point is it is about teaching our children to handle themselves and how to pick their battles. It is usually not an everyday thing that gets you. Instead, the consequences of a reckless choice will blindside you. So here is the drill.

While Mom uses cinema tools to create awareness, you can use the Indigo affirmations in this book. Affirmations describe things declared to be true, and in this book, each ends with, "*This is the way.*"

All of them are in Appendix A - Indigo Affirmations. Use them as you see fit and add your own—one suggestion. There are lists, and there are tax codes. Keep it simple because the goal is to reinforce a critical survival concept or message, and with that, here is your teaching mission:

> Survival is about learning enough about what works before what hurts kills you.
> *This is the way.*

As protectors, there is nothing you would not do for your child, so help them to remember what works because *this is the way.*

What do you want to hear from your Riseling child?

The very same thing God wants to hear from each one of us. "Father, you can take the trainer wheels off. I got this now."

Imagine the two of you are watching your happy Riseling wheeling about with a new sense of freedom. Where will this first step lead your family? Towards a light of hope.

Lights of Hope

Your Riseling children will know when to flee the cities and will push for it. Prepare for that because you may underestimate how young Riseling could change anything, let alone convince a doubting family of the need to adopt an entirely new pioneering lifestyle to survive what is coming.

News flash… they can. Oh yes, and I've seen it with my own eyes.

Years ago, I taught English as a second language to Russian immigrants after the fall of the Soviet Union. My students were typically Russian intellectuals and professionals who had emigrated to America with their children.

Not because they want to do it. Even with the difficult times in Russia, they were typically at the height of their careers and enjoyed a wide circle of friends and colleagues. They all led satisfying lives, and after emigrating to America, that became take a number, please.

Why sacrifice so much? They did it for their children, and emigrating the whole family always began with one or more of their children driving it. I saw it repeatedly, and the draw of a beloved child reaching for life and freedom is irresistible for the parent.

As you and your children read this book, you will learn about awakening possibilities, preparing you to act as one with common sense and compassion.

Parents, this will be your Riseling's time to step forth as their light of hope, and they will help guide your families to safety.

Riseling families, I am only an old man who treasures you for what you mean to the future of our species. All that I can do, I will do, and I know you do the same. Together, let us be in it for the species because:

If we cannot love our own species, who in the universe will? *This is the way.*

Teaching Tools

In the Indigo way, we use mentorship to share life experiences and knowledge. It is typically a young Indigo and an older Indigo. Observation, visualization, and contemplation are the primary teaching tools.

Indigo Mentor Maxim

To teach is an honor.
To mentor is a greater honor.
To learn is the greatest honor.

This is the way.

Usually, we would be face-to-face while doing this, but as the Marines say, "Improvise, Adapt, Overcome," here is what we'll use. Movies with a helpful teaching tool message, and the first will be the film Rocky (1976).

It was a low-budget underdog fight film that took the country by storm, and the next thing we knew, all the fellows were going around saying, "Yo, Adrian."

I chose this as the first lesson tool because of the scene in Rocky's apartment when Mickey offers to be his manager for the fight against Apollo Creed.

ROCKY (1976)
Written by Sylvester Stallone

MICKEY and ROCKY
Rocky's Apartment

An' now I got all this knowledge, I wanna give it to ya so I can protect ya an' make sure ya get the best deal ya can!

There are two critical relationships for Rocky in this movie, and they balance his need for support. Rocky finally accepts Mickey as his manager, and what grows between them is similar to what happens with Indigo mentoring relationships. Mentors support and protect.

In my mind, Mickey is saying what I feel for you right now, my dear Riselings. I have all this knowledge and want to give it to you.

At the film's end, Apollo Creed wins the fight by a decision; however, the crowd cheers for Rocky. Rocky has won the day, but all Rocky is thinking about is the love of his life, Adrian, and she weaves her way into his arms for a magnificent film finale.

As you watch the film, observe the character development of Rocky and Mickey and Rocky and Adrian because it is a unique dual track. Observe how the relationships evolve and contribute to Rocky's success. For best results, view with another Riseling.

Most important. The night before the fight, he had a moment of honesty and made his call. Rocky had heart, went the distance, and won Adrian's love and the day. Not bad for losing a fifteen-round fight.

The point here is that you'll need to learn how to choose your fights, and whatever you do, never give up and never surrender because the Destroyer has returned.

Today, it is called the Nemesis Constellation, or more informally, the Planet X System.

2

Planet X System

Nemesis is a brown dwarf star in orbit around our Sun. Several times the size of Jupiter, it lacks the mass to burn brightly like Sol. Instead, it is more like a charcoal briquette in a backyard grill, so it must be within our system before it appears in visible light, suitable for the human eye. At all other times, it is only visible in the infrared range, where it is pretty noticeable.

One of the unspoken reasons for launching the Pioneer 10 deep space probe in 1972 was a first step to determine the possibility of Nemesis, and that was confirmed when the probe detected its magnetic fields.

The next step was to image it, and so on January 25, 1983, NASA launched the Infrared Astronomical Satellite (IRAS), which spent the next ten months performing an infrared sky survey. Google Sky and similar programs still use the survey results today to provide an infrared sky view. However, there are missing panels in the survey, and for good reason.

The mission was well along when Nemesis was imaged. Shortly after that, the image data suddenly stopped, and our government announced that the cryogenic cooling system onboard the satellite had failed, disabling the infrared imaging system.

Why the data from the payload computer system had stopped, the command-and-control telemetry continued. Such was the cover story, and it was mainly disbelieved elsewhere.

What happened, according to reliable whistleblowers, is that the IRAS mission changed. The new profile was to track Nemesis through the sky for as long as possible to establish an ephemeris. IRAS continued this mission until its onboard store of hydrazine fuel for navigation gave out.

An ephemeris is an astronomical table that gives astronomers the positions of Nemesis as it flies through the core of our system. One could imagine it like a train schedule. The route is fixed, and the schedule tells you where the train will be and when.

Today, Nemesis is known as a brown dwarf star. Previously, astronomers called it a "Black Star" because they could not be found in the visible light spectrum.

Today, government astronomers secretly use the IRAS ephemeris to help them track Nemesis, including three major planets: Helion, Arboda, and Nibiru.

According to the Guides, these are the names given by the inhabitants of that system. Also, I personally named two moons, Harrington and Ferrada, as explained below.

Surviving the Planet X Tribulation: There Is Strength in Numbers
Major Objects of the Planet X System (Excerpts)
Marshall Masters (2021)

At the center of the Planet X System is the small brown dwarf star called Nemesis. Around Nemesis orbit planets, and some of them have moons that orbit in ways that seem haphazard when compared with the planets and moons of our own solar system.

HELION: The innermost major planet to Nemesis, and it has one moon approximately the size of our own moon. This moon is named Harrington in honor of Robert Sutton Harrington, the U.S. Naval Observatory chief astronomer, who many believe was assassinated in 1993 for sharing his work on Planet X.

It is a bright, gaseous planet approximately 3 1/2 times the size of Earth which makes it somewhat comparable in size to Uranus. If we were to see it from another one of the planets orbiting Nemesis, it would look like a smaller second sun in that system.

ARBODA: The second innermost major planet to Nemesis and has no moon. Arboda is a rocky planet approximately 2 1/2 times the size of Earth."

NIBIRU: A rocky planet made famous by the translations of the Sumerian texts by Zecharia Sitchin. Nibiru translates to 'place of crossing' or 'planet of crossing,' which is an apt title because Nibiru is the outermost major planet from Nemesis in the Planet X System.

At six times the size of Earth, it is the largest major planet in orbit around Nemesis. Its moon, Ferrada, named after Chilean Astronomer Carlos Muñoz Ferrada, is approximately the size of our own moon.

Nibiru / Planet X

Nibiru is the best-known planet and appears in modern reporting, ancient wisdom texts, and the folklore of several cultures, where many names know it:

- **Planet X:** Term created in about 1905 by astronomer Percival Lowell to describe an unobserved object through its interactions with observable objects. It does not mean Planet 10.
- **Hercolubus:** Latinos
- **Red Dragon:** Chinese
- **Destroyer:** Egyptians and Hebrews
- **Frightener:** Celts
- **Blue Kachina / Red Kachina:** Hopi
- **Bluebonnet:** Marshall Masters 2013 Turrialba Observations

It is important to note that Planet X is often cross-linked with Planet 9 by search engines. Planet 9 is a government propaganda red herring. Do not be distracted by it and never forget:

Hell is about being right. Heaven is about getting it right. *This is the way.*

The first time I observed Nibiru with my own eyes was through a live HD webcam on top of the Turrialba Volcano in Costa Rica on December 26, 2012.

Any object near or close to the Sun can only be observed before sunrise or sunset. This is because the atmospheric lensing removes enough solar glare for the object to be seen for a few minutes.

At the time, I named it Bluebonnet because its color reminded me of my favorite flowers from Texas. I formed a team of seven observers, and for nearly four months, we recorded several hundred sightings.

Using this observation database, we created a basic functioning trajectory for the Nemesis Constellation, which has held true since. My book, *Surviving the Planet X Tribulation: There is Strength in Numbers*, explains it in detail.

Blue Kachina / Red Kachina

It is also important to mention something often overlooked when discussing the Hopi Blue Kachina / Red Kachina prophecy: the assumption that they are two separate objects. This is false. Both describe the same object.

The reason for the confusion is that the Hopi are describing the Doppler Effect. Simply, it represents a change in the frequency of sound or light waves moving toward the observer and away. Visually, there are two effects:

- **Blueshift:** As the Nemesis Constellation approaches Earth's orbit, the distance closes, compressing the light waves. This effect will hold true for Nemesis and its planets and moons. This explains why I named Nibiru "Bluebonnet": it appeared blue due to this compressed wavelength of light.

- **Redshift:** Once Nemesis crosses above Earth's orbit, it will be descending back into the Southern Skies somewhere between Mars and Jupiter. Outside of Earth's orbit and going away, the wavelength of light increases, resulting in a Redshift effect.

In other words, the Blue Kachina, which the Hopi tell us precedes the Red Kachina, will be blue due to the Doppler effect Blueshift.

When we see the Red Kachina, we'll know the object has passed above Earth's orbit and now will be red due to the Doppler effect Redshift.

There is a more disturbing aspect to all this, with what we will see in our sky over the coming years.

Due to Blueshift and the sunlight of its large companion, Sol, the ruddy, dark, and muddy colors of Nemesis will turn into pleasant pastels, and if the Deep State is in control, what will we hear on the fake news:

They'll lead with the truth. What we see will pass overhead without hitting us, so enjoy the show with beautiful, unique celestial wonder. Later, beauty will bring the beast, and its hot breath will smell like the iron of the Nemesis Cloud.

The Nemesis Cloud

The Oort cloud was first theorized in 1950 by Dutch Astronomer Jan Oort. It is a vast theoretical ball of debris left over from the formation of our system that encapsulates our solar system as a whole and routinely sends comets our way.

It is vast, so a simple way to think of how far away it is is to take the distance from Earth to the Sun and multiply that 10,000 times. Do that, and you will be well inside the cloud.

Nemesis is also a sun and has its own version of the Oort cloud; we call it the Nemesis Cloud, and we began publishing our research in our Signs series at Yowusa.com; in 2017, we introduced the Nemesis Cloud.

> **Yowusa.com, June 28, 2017**
> Signs No. 15 – The Nemesis Cloud
>
> We first began tracking Fireball observations since publishing Planet X Signs — Update No. 1 by J. P. Jones on February 20, 2015. In the subsequent Signs articles and videos, we've reported a relentless statistical uptick in fireball observations reported to the American Meteor Society (AMS).
>
> Founded in 1911, the AMS is a reliable source for observation data and we have now amassed enough data to support the proposition that the Nemesis brown dwarf, a smaller and dark sister to our Sun, has something in common with it. It

> not only has an asteroid belt, but of even greater concern is a more menacing cloud that lies beyond.

After publishing Signs 15, our focus shifted to finding a data-driven model to define the makeup of the Nemesis Cloud. Using reliable AMS fireball observation reports, researcher J.P. Jones employed database mining techniques to find a telltale pattern.

Since 2017, it has yielded a reliable statistical view of the cloud surrounding the Nemesis brown dwarf companion star to Sol, with its multiple bands and gaps.

Thanks to this discovery process, we can see that Revelation describes the bloody misery that will rain upon Planet Earth with such impeccable prescience that everything connects–perfectly.

However, such clear connections are not always possible with other prophetic scriptures. For example, a widespread concern that Revelation 9 describes CERN being used to open a cosmic portal through which demons descend upon us like locusts in a horrific alien invasion.

What is noteworthy about that is that the prophecies of Revelation 8 must occur before those of Revelation 9 can begin.

Teaching Tools

Dear Riselings, this has been a gut punch, and more are to come. But as you saw with Rocky (1976), winning the day is about going the distance. He went all fifteen rounds, and so must you, and your victory will be glorious; later, I'll show it to you.

More importantly, after reading this book, you cannot say bravely and confidently, "I can do this," then I will have failed you, and this, my dear Riselings, will not happen, thanks to the wisdom of Corporal Harold Stark.

In the fall of 1976, I was a student at Arizona State University in Tempe, Arizona, and graduated with a B.S. in communications the following year. One project was writing a human-interest story for the school newspaper. I chose Harold Stark, a fellow on Dean's List student, and was delighted when he accepted my request.

Harold was a blind man in his late 50s and was often seen going about campus between classes carrying a portable reel-to-reel recorder. These were the days of analog, and things were heavy.

These were the days before wheelchair access, so his wife went with him everywhere to help him navigate the stairs and hallways. They were a beautiful couple together.

I began by taking photographs of Harold and his wife, and then we went to his house for the interview. Harold had a small audio work room that was impressive. A pegboard with painted outlines and everything being where it needed to be.

He organized an editing suite where he pieced together audiotape clippings from the lectures he studied for the exams. He was a 4.0 student and carried a full course load.

As we began the interview, I wanted to start with his disability, so I asked him about his blindness. Here's what he told me.

During World War II, he was Cpl. Harold Stark, a motorcycle courier carrying dispatches between command posts a few days after the Normandy invasion. As he was driving down the road, his Harley-Davidson motorcycle struck a German anti-personnel mine known then as a "Bouncing Betty."

When triggered, the mine would pop up a few feet into the air, and the charge was designed to send the shrapnel sideways to emasculate the soldiers. Castration was the intent of the weapon, but this time, the shrapnel peppered Harold's upper back and neck.

Harold told me the surgeons could remove all the shrapnel except one piece embedded in his neck. He was told that any attempt to do so would kill him and that he recovered and was returned to duty. After the war, he became an engineer and had a good life until that last piece of shrapnel began to move.

Surgery was not an option as before, and after a few years, the shrapnel caused Harold to go blind. We always say to wait for the miracle of science to catch up with you, and that didn't work out too well after I said it.

That was when Harold told me that the shrapnel was moving again, and this time, his doctor was telling him that in addition to being blind, he would also become deaf.

That news devastated me. This kind and humble man was doing his best and doing it well, and then this awful misfortune. I was so overwhelmed that I began crying a river of tears. I'm serious; it was like two rivers of tears on my face.

Embarrassed, I struggled not to make any noticeable sounds, which became pointless after the nose joined in. At that point, I felt like an idiot because I knew Harold could hear it. He probably could've counted every tear that fell to the floor.

That was when he reached out, put his home on my knee, and patted it, saying, "It's okay. It's okay. Winners never quit, and quitters never win."

Over the years, I have had numerous times where fate was unkind, and I was in a spot where I was beaten down and unsure about what to do. Should I fight or walk away?

Every time I hit that low point, I remembered sitting in Harold's audio editing room and hearing him say:

> Winners never quit, and quitters never win. *This is the way.*

As a Riseling, you must be a light of hope, but there will be days when it is challenging to keep it lit.

The cinema teaching tool for this chapter is Million Dollar Baby (2004).

Clint Eastwood is an American film icon, and his movies often include very spiritual, touching narratives. Such is the case with this movie, where Clint plays Frankie, a boxing manager and club owner. Hillary Swank brilliantly plays Maggie. A poor white girl from the South with a burning ambition to become a champion boxer.

There are two essential teaching tools in this film. The first is Frankie's first rule.

Throughout the film, Frankie asks Maggie, "What's the first rule?"

Each time, Maggie replies, "Always Protect Myself."

Then, the one time she does not, a mean-spirited boxer with a sick soul shatters her life and her dreams.

As a Riseling, you must be a light of hope for others and be wise, for you will be a little vulnerable that way. Always remember. Where am I? I am in the moment. *This is the way.*

All it takes is one brief moment of carefree, joyful distraction, and there you are. You're Maggie, and it's fly there, drive back, and it's not theatrical. It's your life, and in the days ahead, few safety nets will be left. Remember:

I always protect myself. *This is the way.*

In the Indigo way, this maxim is paramount for mentors. Intellectually, Indigos of all types are equals. However, the primary watch-over role of the Indigo mentor is to teach self-protection. The secondary function is to help Riselings formulate their own options and constructs and to provide moral support.

In the film Avatar (2009), James Cameron gave us a brilliant view of Pandora, and there are some helpful teaching tools here. We will discuss this in greater depth later, but I want to introduce you to a word I invented.

The Indigo tool for this chapter is a term I created. It is "Shawheylu." The eternal bond of unconditional trust.

It borrows from the word Tsaheylu, introduced in the film as a Na'vi word meaning "bond" or neural connection. I like the alliteration but wanted something more reflective of Indigos. I chose "Shaw.." because Shaw is another word for grove.

When I lived in the hills of the Santa Cruz Mountains in Northern California, I spent many at the Henry Cowell Redwoods State Park, walking through its 40-acre grove of towering old-growth redwood trees.

The redwoods are magnificent trees. What is fantastic about the grove is that underneath is where the heart and soul of the grove beats. All of the trees are interconnected and share water and nutrition.

They are also compassionate because there will be a small albino redwood that cannot sustain itself, so the other trees feed it for as long as it lives. The grove was a magical place for me, so it is "Shawheylu."

It is an eternal bond of unconditional trust between two souls that is so nurturing that they will weave together in subsequent incarnations. It's always nice to get the band back together.

We come to Shaweylu in many ways. We will use this movie to see one such way.

Frankie has "Mo Chuisle" embroidered on Maggie's silks in the movie in time for her first overseas fight. The crowds enthusiastically chant it, though Frankie never tells Maggie what it means until the movie's end.

The scene in Maggie's hospital room is a powerful testament to Eastwood's genius as a storyteller. Before that, Frankie visits a priest who warns him that if he does as Maggie asks, he will lose himself.

The problem is that the priest does not understand the nature of Frankie's relationship with Maggie. They shared Shawheylu, the eternal bond of unconditional trust between two souls. Her pain was his pain, and an awful accommodation was called for.

Maggie was the first to offer the bond, so as you watch the film, look for the moment that Frankie accepted. Then, carefully watch how it develops. There is a lot to learn here.

Next, we will examine the previous flybys of the Planet X System (Nemesis Constellation).

3

Previous Planet X System Flybys

There have been many attempts to reconcile Bible prophecy with Planet X science, and the result has always been akin to square pegs and round holes. Always short of a good fit.

Revelation 8 offers us a perfect view of what is coming, but once again, we must address the first concern of any mindful cynic. Is there corroboration? If not, no matter how convincing Revelation sounds, without corroboration, it's still a one-trick pony. This is crucial because relying on one source makes everything a matter of faith.

Therefore, neither the Bible nor science is the problem. Instead, it is the agenda-driven assumptions folks used to reconcile the two.

This is how things have always been, but now, thanks to the Egyptian accounts of the Exodus in *The Kolbrin Bible*, we can corroborate Revelation 8 as a matter of science.

Imagine this combination as a pair of binoculars. One lens barrel is the Holy Bible, and *The Kolbrin Bible* is the other. When used together, a stereoscopic view emerges. One with much greater depth and detail than either alone.

This was not readily apparent until, by chance, we discovered the first decode clue.

The First Decode Clue

In the summer of 2023, researcher J.P. Jones and I discovered keys vital to scientifically decoding Revelation scriptures based on what is being described by the authors.

Exodus and Revelation collectively describe the Nemesis Cloud's dust, meteors, and asteroids consistently and with scientific clarity. However, there is a hitch.

Assuming one is an honest researcher, the need for multiple sources is imperative, and science holds the same. Here, cynics legitimately say that any single source finding is a one-trick pony. However, this is not the case because another ancient text, *The Kolbrin Bible*, corroborates Revelation 8.

Both wisdom texts present eyewitness accounts of the same phenomenon penned at about the same time and offer unequivocal correlations between Revelation prophecy and our research on the Nemesis Cloud and *The Kolbrin Bible*.

This is powerful because the Exodus accounts in both texts were made by corroborating eyewitness observers.

Eyewitness Observers

Exodus was a global event that occurred during the last flyby of the Planet X System, which caused the plagues of Exodus. At this time, Earth entered the Nemesis Cloud, encountering vast patches of debris with iron oxide and Schreibersite (an iron nickel phosphide mineral), resulting in devastating micrometeorite and meteorite showers.

This flyby event was documented by Moses and contained in the Old Testament. At about the same time, Egyptian scribes were writing their Exodus accounts, now in *The Kolbrin Bible*. This means that we have corroborating eyewitness observers who penned both Bible narratives.

With that in mind, let us set aside the issue of divine guidance and focus on what these ancient wisdom texts share in common:

- **Origin Concurrence:** The first part of *The Kolbrin Bible* and the Old Testament from the Holy Bible was written at approximately the same time. Likewise, the second part of *The Kolbrin Bible* was written about the time of the New Testament.

- **Historical Narratives:** The Holy Bible is often described as an allegorical work because it uses symbolic representation. Many tend to chaff at that explanation, so it's better to say both are laconic historical narratives rich with pithy metaphors and analogies.

- **Last Planet X Flyby:** The Hebrew Exodus from Egypt occurred in the previous flyby of the Planet X system through the core of our system. As Moses created the Torah, the Hebrew Bible's first five books, the new Pharoh of Egypt created The Great Book, the remnants of which became the first part of *The Kolbrin Bible*. According to it, the Pharoh of Exodus died at the Red Sea while leading his troops against the host.

- **Similar Accounts:** Both offer parallel narratives for The Flood, Exodus, and Jesus. In fact, *The Kolbrin Bible* has the unique distinction of being the only ancient wisdom text featuring the extrabiblical biography accounts of Celts who met Jesus, his family, and his followers. These biographical accounts were kept in the Glastonbury Abbey in England. Much was lost in the fire of 1184, and many Celtic priests lost their lives.

- **Multiple Authors:** Concerning the Holy Bible, another reason folk chaff at allegory is that there is a better term ideal for both works: the voices. Hence, the best term is anthology. Here is where many authors gift us a rich chorus of written voices, styles, and purposes. In both cases, we have the remaining compilations of those original voices today.

- **Compiled Works:** Both works are an anthology, a collection of narratives chosen by a compiler. The Holy Bible was compiled by the Council of Nicea in 325 AD. Survivors of the 1184 Glastonbury Abbey fire fled to Scotland and secretly compiled the surviving texts of *The Kolbrin Bible* as they are known today.

For centuries, generations of this Celtic order secretly preserved this ancient wisdom text and passed it along. Gifted with generations of stouthearted men, the order has served a noble mission, which concluded in 1991 with the fall of the Soviet Union.

The event was foretold in *The Kolbrin Bible*, with an old Egyptian prophecy dating back to the days following the Exodus. Once they saw the prophecy fulfilled, they knew the time had come to release this excellent ancient wisdom text to the world, and it is good they did.

Both the ancient Hebrews and Egyptians call Nemesis the "Destroyer." In the Book of Manuscripts, ancient Egyptian scribes offer a brilliant eyewitness account of the last flyby, adding new dimensions to Exodus and Revelation narratives. Here are relevant passages.

> **The Kolbrin Bible: 21st Century Master Edition**
> Book of Manuscripts
>
> 3:2 It raged across the Heavens in the days of wrath, and this was its likeness: It was as a billowing cloud of smoke enwrapped in a **ruddy glow**, not distinguishable in joint or limb. Its mouth was an abyss from which came **flame, smoke and hot cinders**.
>
> 3:3 When ages pass, certain laws operate upon the stars in the Heavens. Their ways change; there is movement and restlessness, they are no longer constant and a great light **appears redly** in the skies.
>
> 3:4 **When blood drops upon the Earth**, the Destroyer will appear, and mountains will open up and belch forth **fire and ashes**. Trees will be destroyed and all living things engulfed. Waters will be swallowed up by the land, and seas will boil.

Given all that we've discussed about Exodus and Revelation, these passages from The Kolbrin Bible add a chilling dimension to what has been and will be. This is only a fraction of the narratives and prophecies it offers.

In MAN:3:1, the author describes an object with what astronomers call a long-period orbit, which, according to Zecharia Sitchin, is 3,600 lunar years. However, of particular note is "When blood drops upon the Earth."

Blood as a metaphor for iron oxide dust is applied consistently in the Holy Bible and The Kolbrin Bible to describe the same phenomenon. With the Exodus accounts, both the Egyptian and Hebrew were authored by eyewitnesses to the event.

A Great Light

Now that we've made the case for Revelation 8:7, the only remaining question is, when? According to MAN:3:3, it is when "a great light appears redly in the skies." But when is when in our time?

In my book, *Surviving the Planet X Tribulation: There Is Strength in Numbers*, we present a timeline based on my 2012 and 2013 observations of Nibiru via an HD webcam feed from a Costa Rica volcano. I wrote this book especially for faith leaders as a gentle and compassionate quick immersion into the Planet X topic so they can effectively gather and lead their flocks to safety.

My predictions are holding, and in 2024, Nemesis will reach perihelion, the closest distance to our sun. When it does, it's show time. After that, it will be the time to get busy living or to get busy dying.

How to create a safe place for families is the topic of my book, *Win-Win Survival Handbook: All-Hazards Safety and Future Space Colonization*. The plan is simple.

> Find a safe niche in the world where history can mostly pass you by and go to ground. *This is the way.*

This book shows you how to do it, step-by-step, with a complete pro forma plan for non-profit and faith-based survival communities.

December 26, 2012

The number one question I get from folks has always been, "When will we see it?" This translates to: When will I be standing out in the street and pointing up with everyone else?

I began dealing with that question after I published Did Planet X / Nibiru Kill The Dinosaurs? in January 2002, and from that point forward, our best offer was always a rough estimate.

That changed on December 26, 2012, when I observed Nibiru, the third major planet in orbit around Nemesis, via a live HD webcam feed from atop the Turrialba Volcano in Costa Rica at 10,000'. It was the Planet Nibiru, though I did not know that initially and named it Bluebonnet.

We observed the object appearing each day near sunset for approximately fifteen minutes and then disappear as quickly. This is what happens when you view objects near or behind the sun.

I formed a new observation team, and we observed Nibiru live each day for nearly three months. Once we began publishing our findings, the US government ruined the Turrialba feed, ending our efforts. However, by then, we already had enough data to extrapolate the orbit of Nemesis using our observations of Nibiru.

In 2015, I published that orbit in my book, *Surviving the Planet X Tribulation*: There Is Strength in Numbers. As we track current observations via social media sites, that 2015 orbit stands to this day. We got it right the first time.

The second time I observed Nibiru was on September 9, 2018, in Warden, Washington.

Returning from a geological outing, a friend and supporter she was driving. It was near sunset, and we were motoring alongside wheat fields when she suddenly shouted, "I see it!" With that, she spun onto a side road and brought us to a screeching halt, after which we both jumped out and looked at the sun setting behind the wheat.

We both observed Nibiru with our naked eyes just above the sun at 1:30 relative to the sun, moments before sunset. I knew it when I saw it; my heart sank.

It also altered the nature of my mission. I could see that humanity's house would be on fire and that we would need to save as many children as possible. This set me on a course to write my 1,000-page survival trilogy. *Surviving the Planet X Tribulation*, *Radio Free Earth*, and *Win-Win Survival Handbook*. We'll discuss them more later on.

Meanwhile, this brings us back to the question everyone asks: When will I stand out in the street and point up with everyone else?

Well, that depends on when everyone decides to look up because it's already here.

With that in mind, let's see survivor accounts of what the ancients witnessed and observed during the previous two flybys of Planet X, according to the Egyptian Texts of The Kolbrin Bible.

Noah's Flood and Exodus

The prophecies of Revelation 8 describe aspects of a star called Wormwood. It is called Wormwood because of the way it makes water bitter.

In *The Kolbrin Bible*, the ancient Egyptians called Wormwood the Destroyer and documented how it appeared during Noah's Flood and Exodus.

Remember that no two Planet X System (Nemesis Constellation) flybys are identical. With that in mind, let's begin with the flood accounts in the second book of *The Kolbrin Bible*, called Gleanings.

Deluge Flyby

This Egyptian deluge account corroborates the Genesis account of the Holy Bible, and in this part of the flood tale passage, King Sisuda and his host have just boarded the ark.

Here is what they witnessed in the sky:

> **The Kolbrin Bible: 21st Century Master Edition**
> Book of Gleanings
>
> GLN:4:24 Then, with the dawning, men saw an awesome sight. There, riding on a great black rolling cloud, came the **Destroyer**, newly released from the confines of the sky vaults, and she raged about the Heavens, for it was her day of judgement. The beast with her opened its mouth and belched forth fire, hot stones and a vile smoke. It covered the whole sky above and the meeting place of Earth and Heaven could no longer be seen.

In Scrolls, the third book of *The Kolbrin Bible*, the Egyptians predict its return after the deluge narrative described in the previous book, which did occur during Exodus.

> **The Kolbrin Bible: 21st Century Master Edition**
> Book of Scrolls
>
> SCL:33:9 The Rakima watches in silence; patiently it sits, waiting for the day of the **Destroyer**. It will come in a **hundred generations**, as is written in the Great Vault.

The Egyptians were very detailed in their narratives, and they knew the stars, which is why they predicted it would return in 100 generations, and that is precisely what the Destroyer did.

Exodus Flyby

One hundred generations following the Deluge, here is what the Egyptians and the Hebrews witnessed during Exodus as described in Manuscripts, the fifth book of *The Kolbrin Bible*:

> **The Kolbrin Bible: 21st Century Master Edition**
> Book of Manuscripts
>
> MAN:5:1 The Doomshape, called the Destroyer, in Egypt, was seen in all the lands thereabouts. In colour, it was bright and fiery; in appearance, changing and unstable. It twisted about itself like a coil, like water bubbling into a pool from an underground supply, and all men agree it was a most fearsome sight. It was not a great comet or a loosened star, being more like a fiery body of flame.

As with the Deluge, the Egyptians gave another prediction for the Destroyers' next return in Manuscripts, the fifth book of *The Kolbrin Bible*.

> **The Kolbrin Bible: 21st Century Master Edition**
> Book of Manuscripts
>
> MAN:3:7 Thus it was in the Days of Heavenly Wrath, which have gone, and thus it will be in the Days of Doom when it comes again. The times of its coming and going are known unto the wise. These are the signs and times which shall

precede the **Destroyer**'s return: **A hundred and ten generations** shall pass into the West, and nations will rise and fall.

Not only do the ancient Egyptians warn us of the Destroyer's return in our times, in what almost reads like an afterthought to the narrative, but they also tell us that Earth has endured numerous encounters with the Destroyer.

The Kolbrin Bible: 21st Century Master Edition
Book of Manuscripts

MAN:33:5 My land is old, a hundred and twenty generations have passed through it since Osireh brought light to men. Four times, the stars have moved to new positions, and twice the sun has changed the direction of his journey. Twice, the **Destroyer** has struck Earth and three times the Heavens have opened and shut. Twice, the land has been swept clean by water.

This tells us there are five known previous flybys thousands of years apart. Three were on the magnitude of Exodus, and two were far worse because they were pole-shift events. We'll discuss this more later in this series.

The point here is that the Destroyer is coming. Whether you accept that fact or not does not change what will be. Nor will it change the fact that this will be the last survivable flyby for Earth and all its inhabitants.

The Kozai Mechanism

In celestial mechanics, the Kozai mechanism describes the orbit of a small object with an unstable or comet-like orbit around a larger object, such as our sun. It was created in 1962 by Japanese astronomer Yoshihide Kozai.

In this case, Nemesis, the brown dwarf star at the heart of the Nemesis Constellation, or what we often call the Planet X System. It has several planets, moons, and various satellites.

The Nemesis orbit is complex. It has a clockwise comet-like orbit around our sun that tracks on two axes at a steep angle relative to the orbits of the other planets in our system.

The orbital duration on the horizontal axis is approximately 360 days, and the orbital duration on its vertical axis is currently 3,600 lunar years.

When the Kozai mechanism is applied to the Nemesis orbit, it is seen that the orbit will deteriorate in one of two ways. It will eventually be flung back into deep space where it came from or circle the drain around our sun, causing havoc.

The answer to which is the more likely depends on where it came from, and here we have an excellent description from the guide, Carlos, who explains the origin of Nemesis and how it interacts with our sun. After that, you'll understand and more readily accept what comes next.

Being In It for the Species: The Universe Speaks
The Planet X System (Excerpts)
Authored Channeling with Carlos by Marshall Masters (2013)

Eons ago when the sun was forming, an interloper from deep space was attracted to the gravity of a young sun and it ceased its wandering in the heavens to begin an unpredictable journey from whence it first greeted the gravity of sun to the inner system of those planets first formed in the creation of this system.

The interloper, now a companion to your own star was created in a distant realm of the galaxy and is very different and its behaviors are likewise strange. It is why it is unlike anything humanity has experienced or has ever known, for it is truly alien to the inception of your own.

At the heart of this small alien system within your own more expansive system is an object you call a brown dwarf star. Brown dwarf stars or, black suns as they are also called are prevalent throughout the cosmos in great number. Hatcheries produce them in great numbers and they often support life forms within their iron rich wombs. It may seem incongruous, but this is the nature of these alien systems, such as the one which orbits your sun.

In the years to come, these interactions of change between your sun and this alien system will result in tribulations and hardships for your species as such similar events have and always will, throughout the cosmos.

This brings us back to the Kozai Mechanism and our question about whether Nemesis will circle the drain or be cast out into deep space, as in good riddance.

Poor Phaeton

Atop 10,700-foot Mount Graham, in southeastern Arizona, is the Mount Graham International Observatory. It is ideally situated for the most prolonged possible observation of this Planet X flyby, and the Vatican is dug in there like a tick in a hound dog's ear.

Why such interest from the Church? They know orbital periods can change, and that became a huge concern in 1997 when Comet Hale-Bopp came within 1.315 AU of Earth.

Due to a relatively close approach to Jupiter, the comet's orbital period shrank from 4,206 years to 2,380 years.

That was disturbing when you consider the Asteroid Belt between Mars and Jupiter. Its origins are still debated, and some think it was a planet called Phaeton.

A hypothetical planet is said to have existed between the orbits of Mars and Jupiter. Something smashed it apart, and the planet's debris became what we now call the Asteroid Belt.

Here is the sad news. In the Planet X Timeline, Nemesis reaches the ecliptic, and the moon of Nibiru, which we named Ferrada, will impact the southern polar region of Venus.

We'll discuss this in more detail, but the pattern is clear should the prophecy hold true. Nemesis is slowly circling the drain, destroying poor Phaeton in a previous flyby, and next up is the Venus impact during this flyby.

There is only one conclusion. After this flyby, we can expect the obliteration of all life on Earth during the next flyby, as our planet becomes the next Venus—no doubt there will be consequences for the inhabitants of Nibiru in the Planet X System as well.

Therefore, our existential need is to create a clean slate for the Riselings to build pioneering, space-faring communities. This needs to be the highest concern for us alive today. Remember, the Riselings cannot fail us unless we fail them first.

Teaching Tools

Dear Riselings, this chapter has undoubtedly been a gut punch, and more are to come. But as you saw with Rocky (1976), winning the day is about going the distance. He went all fifteen rounds, and so must you, and your victory will be glorious; later, I'll show it to you.

More importantly, after reading this book, you cannot say, "I can do this," then I will have failed you, and this, my dear Riselings, will not happen, thanks to the wisdom of Corporal Harold Stark.

In the fall of 1976, I was a student at Arizona State University in Tempe, Arizona, and graduated with a BS in communications the following year. One project was writing a human-interest story for the school newspaper. I chose Harold Stark, a fellow on Dean's List student, and was delighted when he accepted my request.

Harold was a blind man in his late 50s and was often seen going about campus between classes carrying a portable reel-to-reel recorder. These were the days of analog, and things were heavy. These were the days before wheelchair access, so his wife walked beside him everywhere to guide him along the stairs and hallways. They were a beautiful couple together.

I began by taking photographs of Harold and his wife, and then we went to his house for the interview. Harold had a small audio work room that was impressive. A pegboard with painted outlines and everything being where it needed to be.

He recorded his class lectures and then edited and pieced together the audiotape clippings so he could study for the exams. He was a 4.0 student and carried a full course load.

As we began the interview, I wanted to start with his disability, so I asked him about his blindness. Here's what he told me.

During World War II, he was Cpl. Harold Stark, a motorcycle courier carrying dispatches between command posts a few days after the Normandy invasion. As he was driving down the road, his Harley-Davidson motorcycle struck a German anti-personnel mine known then as a "Bouncing Betty."

When triggered, the mine would pop up a few feet into the air, and the charge was designed to send the shrapnel sideways to emasculate the soldiers. Castration was the intent of the weapon, but this time, the shrapnel peppered Harold's upper back and neck.

Harold told me the surgeons could remove all the shrapnel except one piece embedded in his neck. He was told that any attempt to do so would kill him and that he recovered and was returned to duty. After the war, he became an engineer and had a good life until that last piece of shrapnel began to move.

Surgery was not an option as before, and after a few years, the shrapnel caused Harold to go blind. We always say to wait for the miracle of science to catch up with you, and that didn't work out too well after I said it.

That was when Harold told me that the shrapnel was moving again, and this time, his doctor was telling him that in addition to being blind, he would also become deaf.

That news devastated me. This kind and humble man was doing his best and doing it well, and then this awful misfortune. I was so overwhelmed that I began crying a river of tears. Embarrassed, I struggled not to make any noticeable sounds, which became pointless after the nose joined in.

At that point, I felt like an idiot because I knew Harold could hear it. He probably could've counted every tear that fell to the floor.

That was when he reached out, put his home on my knee, and patted it, saying, "It's okay. It's okay. Winners never quit, and quitters never win." This is the way.

With that thought in mind, it is time to get acquainted with the color Indigo and your following cinema teaching tool.

James Cameron created a color scheme for the film Avatar (2009) based on the following six colors:

Avatar Color Scheme
Name: Oxford Blue
Hex: #0F2347
RGB: (15, 35, 71)

Name: Rainbow Indigo
Hex: #1C3F6E
RGB: (28, 63, 110)

Name: Lapis Lazuli
Hex: #2E67A0
RGB: (46, 103, 160)

Name: Carolina Blue
Hex: #5AACCF
RGB: (90, 172, 207)

Name: Key Lime
Hex: #EFFC93
RGB: (239, 252, 147)

Name: Dollar Bill
Hex: #80C271
RGB: (128, 194, 113)

In preparation for the next chapter, use the photo editor on your computer to create a color pallet using the settings from above. Print that out and tape it to the wall beside your television for reference.

That being done, sit down and watch the film; this will be fun with another Riseling. Your mission is to see how the scheme is applied, mainly wherever the Rainbow Indigo color is used.

4

Indigo Riselings

In the first chapter, Look Up, I introduced "Indigo Riseling," a term I created to describe the Alpha generation (born after 2010) who are healthy, heterosexual, and unvaccinated.

If you are a Riseling, you are on the Indigo path, thanks to your parents. They have shielded you from the monsters defiling and decimating our species, and through them, you inherited the human traits you'll need to fulfill your destiny.

How will you know your destiny? When God touches you on the shoulder and says, "Tag, you're it." So, what does "it" mean?

Riselings are the future of humankind and are precious because they are as God made them, and all are somewhere along the Indigo path of awareness to open their third eye.

This chapter will be a deep dive, but before we do anything else, I am asking, no begging, that all you wonderful Riseling make a pledge to save yourselves for marriage. Or at least, until you've finished reading this book, because it will be worth the wait as you shall soon come to know.

In the meantime, girls, did you know an aspirin tablet is 100% effective for birth control when used as directed? Hold it between your knees. It works every time, and here is the best part. It's reusable. Other than that, cold showers are pretty much it.

You've undoubtedly gotten similar wise counsel from your parents, so let's get down to what you're likely wondering more about right now. What is this Indigo thing all about, and what does it have to do with you and your future?

To Be an Indigo

Search the Internet for the term "Indigo Children," and the results pages will offer up a cornucopia of websites attempting to explain a phenomenon that has been arrogantly dubbed pseudoscience in a compassionate way, primarily for the benefit of parents.

How useful are these websites for Riselings? To answer that, imagine that sitting before us is a delicious-looking indigo jelly donut with lots of yummy sprinkles.

These sites do a fantastic job of saying we can see the Indigo jelly on the side, so it has to be authentic. Then, they start picking at the little sprinkles one at a time to cobble together a profile of Indigo behavior.

They describe the tasty sprinkles with forceful terms such as defiant, headstrong, passionate, frustrated, focused, and creative. It sounds great until you realize that they are describing the better part of humanity.

Likewise, when they use terms such as questioning authority and wanting to overturn the system, OMG, it's the 60s all over again.

As an Indigo Elder, what is my thought on all of this? Forget nibbling on sprinkles. Let's bite into this plump Indigo jelly donut and savor the flavor. Get some!

Indigo Children

The world knows those born with a fully open third eye as "Indigo Children, Crystal Children, and Star Children," etc. Here are five quick criteria. Indigos are:

- Highly intelligent and creative.
- Naturally defiant and opposes subjugation.
- Curious, objective, and logical.
- Speak truth to power with logic and truth, not emotions.
- Spiritual with a strong sense of right and wrong.

Indigos are presented as being different from other folk because they possess unique, supernatural traits or abilities. Nothing could be further from the truth because everyone is an Indigo in some form or another. After all, the Indigo characteristic is universally present in the human genome.

For most of the world, the indigo trait is dormant at birth. Therefore, the difference is the degree to which the Indigo trait has been activated at birth.

If you are a healthy, unvaccinated, heterosexual of Alpha generation age, it is prima facia evidence that you are activated to some degree and on the Indigo path. After reading this chapter, you'll know where you are and your options.

That being said, dear Riselings, the first bite of our indigo jelly donut with sprinkles is why indigo is God's favorite color.

We are Spectral Beings

Ask printers and painters; they will all tell you that indigo is one of the most challenging colors to reproduce accurately, and for good reason. Some versions are shifted towards purples, some to blues, and others to deeper magenta-reds.

Technically, indigo is a secondary color made by mixing the primary colors, blue and red. The primary colors are red, blue, and green; they can be mixed in varying amounts to produce a broad range of colors. The colors you see on your smartphone display vary from the three primary colors.

What does a smartphone see? The primary colors that define human sight. In addition to that, they also capture infrared and ultraviolet spectrums, which, like book ends, limit our visible range. We cannot see them, though many other creatures can.

All this explains why God reveals to us His favorite color in rare and brief moments of wonder, made to touch our souls most beautifully.

Imagine it is close to sunset on a warm summer day, and you are setting up your campsite when a sweet summer rain comes upon you. When it passes, the sun reveals a beautiful rainbow, and there, towards the inside, is the color indigo.

After that, you finish setting up camp and heat a few tins of beef stew, and about the time, you sit down with a full plate. In the far distance, the sun is within a thin sliver of blue sky and the ridges of a mountain range to the west.

In the near distance are tall pines cutting sharp contrasts against the sky, and then, as the sun slowly begins to slip beyond the far ridgeline, you see the ubiquitous sky blue of the day fade into indigo.

Proudly, the pines stand tall through this transition, adding a magnificent sense that, like the giant soap bubbles we like to make, it will dazzle us for a moment and then vanish in the blink of an eye. Consequently, we dare not turn our gaze away for even a moment, lest it passes unnoticed.

With rainbows and sunsets, God shares His favorite color with us; here is how it works.

The six colors of the rainbow are red, orange, yellow, green, blue, indigo, and violet. They all have in common that they are spectral colors, making them very rare.

All of the spectral colors we mortals can behold in rainbows come from either a single (monochromatic) light source or a small band of wavelengths. This explains why violet and indigo are seen in the rainbow. They are spectral colors, whereas purple is a non-spectral color and is not.

In dog show parlance, spectral colors are purebreds, and non-spectral colors are mutts. In other words, the colors in the rainbow are God's best of breed.

That is why indigo is so selective. It is the color of spiritual connection. In the previous chapter, I asked you to watch the film Avatar (2009) and to note the color scheme used in both Avatar films. Of the six colors in this scheme, I asked you to pay attention to the color Rainbow Indigo.

Avatar was directed, written, co-produced, and co-edited by James Cameron, and by his use of Rainbow Indigo in the film, it is clear to see his intention.

Since the early days of drive-in movies, we've been entertained with one face-eating alien species after another.

Then comes Avatar; the aliens are the good guys, and we are the face-eating aliens. Go figure, but audiences happily ate it up (as did I).

Many have been puzzled by how easy it was for Cameron to flip the equation, even though the key to this strategy has always been in their faces.

It was his use of Rainbow Indigo in both films. He uses Indigo as the base color for the darker-toned forest people and the lighter-toned ocean people.

Simply put, the Pandora of Avatar is an Indigo world, and we are the Na'vi. Cameron's films are a spiritual reflection of what humanity is going through.

The films do a masterful job of showing how our species is driven by acquisition and entitlement and seeks to dominate those driven by appreciation and harmony.

In the Indigo sense, the color represents a deep and abiding appreciation of Creation and all Its majesty and the harmony of souls living good and spiritually satisfying lives in peace.

Up to this point, we've made the case for why Indigo is God's favorite color and how it connects with us in extraordinary ways.

This brings us to the question that is undoubtedly on your mind, my dear Riselings. Exactly how do we connect with it?

The Indigo Aura

Megan Michaela Firester (aka Mystic Michaela) is an aura reader and psychic medium, and when she sees an indigo aura, she associates it with a compassionate and empathic person. "When I see an indigo aura on a person," she said, "immediately I know they are someone who absorbs thoughts, feelings, emotions, and traumas of others."

So true. However, observing an aura often takes the Indigo narrative in the wrong direction towards the study of auras.

Depending on the source, the number of aura colors is between nine and eleven. The eleven are Red, orange, yellow, green, pink, blue, purple, indigo, white, black, and rainbow.

Consequently, one cannot find clarity as to the true nature of Indigos by discussing their indigo aura relative to the other aura colors because this is the wrong conversation.

The proper conversation is with another system.

The chakra system developed within the Tantric tradition of Buddhism in the first millennium. Both the aura and charka color systems reference Indigo and other spectral colors.

The seven main Chakras are the body's energy centers, beginning at the base of the spine and ending at the crown of the head. Each corresponds to a different need.

Chakra: Crown
Sanskrit: Sahasrara
Role: Spirituality, "I Understand"
Gland: Pituitary
Color: Violet

Chakra: Third Eye (Brow)
Sanskrit: Ajna
Role: Awareness, "I See"
Gland: Pineal
Color: Indigo

Chakra: Throat
Sanskrit: Vishuddha
Role: Communication, "I talk"
Gland: Thyroid
Color: Blue

Chakra: Heart
Sanskrit: Anahata
Role: Love, Healing, "I love"
Gland: Thymus
Color: Green

Chakra: Solar Plexus
Sanskrit: Manipura
Role: Wisdom, Power "I do"
Gland: Adrenal
Color: Yellow

Chakra: Sacral
Sanskrit: Svadhisthana
Role: Sexuality, Creativity, "I feel"
Gland: Adrenal
Color: Orange

Chakra: Root
Sanskrit: Muladhara
Role: Basic Trust, "I am"
Gland: Reproductive
Color: Red

For Riselings, we will discuss the following three chakras in this book:

- **Root:** This is the first chakra, the energizing force of what I call "Shawheylu," the eternal bond of unconditional trust.

- **Third Eye:** In the sixth chakra, the third eye pierces deception with awareness.

- **Crown:** All knowledge comes together in the seventh chakra, and here is where you hear the voice of God.

Suppose one wanted to think of these as parts of a smartphone. In that case, the Root is the rechargeable battery, the Third Eye is the communications module, and the Crown is the processor, memory, OS, and apps, and this pulls everything together.

Color System

This brings us to why the chakra color system and not the Aura color system is the correct one to use.

If you compare the above list of charka colors, you'll see that the spectral colors of the rainbow are red, orange, yellow, green, blue, indigo, and violet. These are also the same spectral colors used by the Charka color system.

Another misleading thing is the widespread use of "child," as in Indigo Child or Star Child.

When psychics perform an aural reading, they see an aura representing the individual's present state of being and is, therefore, variable.

When children are born with their Indigo trait fully activated, it's flame on. This is when they get the attention of their parents long before puberty begins, and this is when the researchers and psychics engage them. This explains the "child" emphasis.

After puberty begins, the aura for a flame-on Indigo can become, shall we say, "variable?"

God's Favorite Color

Indigo is one of seven spectral colors in rainbows and chakras. For this reason, they are all significant, but Indigo alone is the most favored by God because it is the color of awareness and connection.

Through the third eye, awareness leads us to the truth as it unmasks the deceptions of those who would take a spoil of us. When your third eye is open, you can access the knowing of things through what others call our sixth sense.

This is why Indigo is God's favorite color. It is the spectral light of our cosmic pathway to wisdom by which we nourish our soul for good.

Through our third eye, we intuitively grasp the inner workings of things in less time than it takes for a wall clock to go from tik to tok.

> Indigo is the color of awareness that connects us to God's love and wisdom so we may serve the greater good. *This is the way.*

Now it's time to enjoy another bite from our tasty Indigo jelly donut with sprinkles.

What Am I?

One of my pet peeves as an Indigo Elder is that popular literature paints us differently from others. A case in point is the term "Indigo Children" itself.

While it is helpful for normal parents to ascertain which planet their child was born on, it is of no practical benefit to the children.

Likewise, you do not need a psychic who can read auras, a clinical researcher, or a website publisher to tell you who you are because you already know or sense it.

Your Indigo abilities come from past and present karma. To open the third eye upon birth partially or all the way requires two things: A cumulative amount of good karma from previous incarnations, plus the gifts of psychic ability and intelligence from the birth parents. This is how it works.

With this in mind, let's create three broad categories for humanity to help you sort this out. Let's start by imagining a large cast iron commercial gas stove.

On the front is a large nob for each burner. At birth, the knob will be in one of the three following positions:

- **Star Seeds:** The nob is turned all the way to the left to the off position.
- **Riselings:** The nob is turned to the right, enough for a pot to simmer.
- **Indigos:** The nob is turned all the way to the right, as in flame on!

Please note I've added a new term, Star Seeds. Later on, we'll discuss this at length, but for now, here is a quick summary of the three categories.

Star Seeds

There are, at present, over eight billion souls incarnated on Earth. Of that, only two billion are native souls of Earth. They continuously reincarnate on Earth as native souls.

This population of native souls is mostly healthy, and the remaining are sick. The sick souls are the monsters; their days are numbered, and they know it. Why?

There is a warm welcome home for those who lead good lives and love God when they cross over. Conversely, there is only one fate for the sick souls: Death eternal in the darkness of the Void. This is why they are a deadly minority that always fights to the end.

Then there are the Star Seeds. Distant souls from countless other worlds in Creation who have traveled here to incarnate and here to help humanity achieve ascension. Many of them are the kind of folk who struggle to lead honest lives and would give you the shirt off their back.

Star Seeds lack the life experience of native souls, and it was easy for the monsters to deceive them into rolling up their sleeves with relative ease. Many got wise to them, but sadly, it was too late.

We are in the ultimate battle of good vs. evil; every Star Seed soul knew this would be their fate before they incarnated, in service to God's Plan.

Later in the book, we'll go more into God's Plan, but for now, the role the souls of the Star Seeds have volunteered to play is that of a statistical population push that boggles the mind.

During the 1929 Great Depression, the global population was two billion. At the close of WWII, it was two and a half billion. Developments in sanitation, nitrogen fertilizer, and antibiotics unleashed a massive population surge in the post-war years.

Born between 1946 and 1964, the Baby Boomers are the Children of The Greatest Generation. In terms of God's Plan, distant souls have always traveled to this world in relatively small numbers until the massive uptick in the post-war years.

They could really be called the Star Seed Generation because this is when the migration of distant souls to our world began.

In broad terms, the Star Seeds are healthy souls who rolled up their sleeves and willingly participated in medical tyranny. No matter the reason for submission to this horror, they have done what they incarnated to do.

Then, like a rising tide, the incarnation of Star Seeds from all across Creation pushed the global population up high enough to allow all of Earth's native souls to incarnate at this time, and they have. We will discuss this in more detail later on.

Riselings

Should there be assistance from other intelligent species during this tribulation, many Riselings and Indigo will tell them, "Take the Star Seeds, for they have kept the faith, and bless them what relief you can. As for us, we shall remain here. Earth is our home; Gaia is our Earth mother. We are prepared and shall stand together as one species here."

You may wonder, why were you born a Riseling, with a partially activated third eye, and not as an Indigo with a fully activated third eye? Do you really want to know? Remember.

When you are ready for the answer, ask the question. This is the way.

The reason is that humanity has been a hunted species for thousands of years by a range of inhuman predators and traitors to our species. It is why you should have been born a flame on Indigo or Crystal. We'll cover how this works later, but you can defeat the cheat and become a flame-on Indigo this lifetime.

Suffice it to say, for now, you were born and raised a Riseling thanks to your parents' sacrifices in protecting you from the horrors of the monsters seeking you out, plus their genetic gifts of high intelligence and creativity. Even if they might look at you like you were born on another planet, thank them and hug them anyway.

You may wonder. Would you have been born a flame on Indigo, with a different mix of parents or genes? No, because it's not about any of that. It is about how your soul grows through past life actions. Here is the driving rule.

The cumulative quality of incarnations drives soul growth, not quantity. This is the way.

In other words, it's not the years; it's the miles, so whatever is left, you can finish in this life, and here is the best part. You have more brothers and sisters out there than ever in the history of our species. I call it the "popcorn phenomenon."

Indigo Children

How do you know you are an Indigo Child? Frankly, you have no clue you're an Indigo Child unless you keep up with popular literature. What you do know is that you are different, and this awakening will occur before you reach puberty. I call it the "First Knowing."

For me, my first knowing occurred when I was seven years old. Democratic Senator John F. Kennedy was running for President, and my seventeen-year-old sister was a young Democrat and worked as a volunteer in his campaign.

While tying my shoelaces, she asked, "If you could vote for President, would you vote for John F. Kennedy?"

Without hesitation, I answered, "No, they're going to kill him." It wasn't a guess, hunch, or a joke. It was my first knowing at seven, and I knew I was different.

I knew he would be killed as sure as a sunset. This is a knowing, and despite the number of dead animal skins that adorn an expert's office wall, you know what you know, which is the long and short of it. This is what it means to be different.

Nonetheless, my sister laughed at my answer, and we said nothing further as she finished preparing me for school.

I gave it no more thought until November 22, 1963.

I ate lunch at home that day and was bicycling back to school when a postman called out to me, saying that President Kennedy had just been assassinated in Dallas, Texas. This was the first I heard of it, yet I nodded and said, "I know."

When I entered my classroom, all my classmates had their heads on the desks and sobbing. JFK and Camelot were dead in one fell swoop, making a tragically dark day.

What surprised me was the teacher. Our regular teacher was recovering from an injury, and he was our temporary.

During a routine duck and cover drill the week before, I remember how he just stood there looking at his watch while we all jumped out of our seats to huddle under our desktops.

I asked him why he wasn't huddling under his desk, and he said, "Why bother? We're between two large Air Force bases." He was right. In the event of a nuclear war, we, along with our desks, would be incinerated.

He was a formidable fellow, but I watched him weep uncontrollably on November 22, 1963. In fact, I watched them all like I was in a surreal Twilight Zone episode because I was the only one in the room who didn't cry. In fact, I was unaffected because of my knowing.

Here is a point to remember: my knowing prepared me to keep a level the day Kennedy was killed while everyone around me was blindsided and distraught.

As an Indigo, you have a knowing of things, and it will make you different. If you embrace this ability with calm responsibility, it will serve you and those you serve well in a crisis.

Crystal Children

When you read popular Indigo Child literature, you'll soon find yourself sorting through a prolific range of different types and generations, each with a unique set of terms. Hence, it is nearly impossible to reconcile all of them with a simple, universal lexicon of terms.

For me, this inability to reconcile is not by coincidence. It is by design, so let's look at this from the inside out.

On December 15, 2004, I published *Indigo-E. T. Connection: The Future of Indigo Children and Planet X*. It was an early effort but was popular.

In 2006, I drove to a large Central Valley town in California to give a talk on *The Kolbrin Bible* at a local bookstore. I arrived the night before and stayed with the owner, and when I first met her daughter, she seemed like the usual run-of-the-mill valley girl.

Late the following day, I went to prepare for my presentation and book signing, after which I planned to begin the drive home. What do they say? Life is that funny little thing that always seems to get in the way of all your plans.

Her assistant store manager was a lovely Native American in her mid-thirties, and she pulled me aside and quietly told me that she had read my book and asked if I could stay an extra day to have lunch with her and another.

Typically, that's a big ask, but when you know what you are, you see it in others as quickly, and I knew she was a Mentor and was not asking for herself. This was a divine appointment.

"Let's make it an early lunch," I answered, "Eleven works for me. You name the place."

She smiled brightly and gave me the address of a local family restaurant with a great breakfast menu. With that, she returned to the counter to serve the customers, who were now streaming in for the presentation.

I went to the podium and began organizing my materials, and another woman of about the same age approached me and said that she had read my book, *Indigo-E. T. Connection*.

Then she told me that she wanted to talk with me about Indigos and their role in the evolution of humanity. She invited me to join her for lunch at a fine dining restaurant in the indoor mall across from the bookstore after my book signing.

Given that I had just agreed to a stayover, why not? I accepted. After the book signing, I followed her to the restaurant, a cinema fourplex. The theaters had been built in a traditional style and were impressive, but America went the video tape rental route, and they fell on hard times.

The new owners converted it into a fine dining restaurant with three dining areas. She had reserved an entire auditorium transformed into a dining room. The lighting and interior designs were elegant; a large table with two lamps was in the center. It was impressive, to say the least.

We ordered and began talking about my book and a range of topics. After dessert, we settled in with our coffees for what I wanted to know. I loved the setting, but it seemed like something out of a James Bond movie.

Then she told me that she worked with the office of Vice President Dick Cheney and that he was very interested in protecting the Indigo Children because of the vital role they will play in the evolution of our species.

This got us to that ...and what moment. I appeared enthusiastic and appreciative.

She continued. "We are reaching out to you for help. You see, we're finding it very difficult to find the Indigos now, and we were wondering if you could help us with that?"

Moment of truth.

After watching the White House administration overseeing the intentional drugging of the flower of multiple generations of Indigo, my first impulse was to tell her I wouldn't pee in Cheney's mouth if his teeth were on fire. Bad idea. Glad I didn't.

Instead, I appeared to be flattered and began asking her confirming questions to buy time as I invented an appropriate response. Once it came to mind, I enthusiastically led her down the mother of all rabbit holes, and she bought it and thanked me for it.

We parted cordially, and I returned to the bookstore to collect a few things. The owner was there. She was delighted with the presentation and invited me to stay with her again. Behind her stood her assistant manager, and she gave me the nod, and I happily accepted.

That evening, I was sitting and chatting with the owner when her daughter entered, greeted me, and said, "Thank you for accepting my invitation. I look forward to lunch tomorrow," and went to her room.

Now, the dots are connected. The store owner's daughter was a Crystal Indigo; the assistant manager was her Indigo Mentor.

It is so good to see people caring for each other this way. It is also why Cheney and his fellow travelers could no longer profile Indigos and continue the horror of pushing psychotropic drugs down children's throats; we Indigos adapted.

To illustrate this, let's focus not on profiling data and colors. This is generational, so let's cover that before we move on to the second lunch meeting in this story.

Baby Boomers
Born 1946-1964
Indigo Elders

There have always been Indigos throughout history, but always in small numbers. That changed with the Baby Boomers. This was when there was finally enough of us to identify, and all Indigos of this generation are called Indigo Elders.

Largely left alone, we were surveilled and studied by the Deep State and used their Indigo profiles to launch a war on us with psychotropic drugs, which began with the following generations.

Generation X
Born 1965-1980
Latchkey Indigos and Crystal Indigos

I created the term Latchkey Indigos to describe Generation X and Generation Y Indigos. Many were from single-parent households and very easy to force into mind-numbing drug regimes.

Generation Y (Millennials)
Born 1981-1996
Latchkey Indigos Fade and Crystal Indigos Appear

Generation Y was a transitional generation. Because of the government's drug war on Indigos, a divine adaptation occurred that had been foreseen in God's Plan.

Mid-generational transitions began as Latchkey Indigos faded out as a new generation of Indigos called Crystals faded in.

In terms of worldview and ability, there is no difference between an Indigo Elder, Latchkey, or Crystal. What makes the Crystals different is that they are chameleons. It is how God defeated the profiling. He made kids who couldn't be made.

Generation Z
Born 1997-2012
Indigo, Indigo Mentors, and Crystals

In terms of temperament, Crystals are peacemakers by nature. They are not openly defiant like other Indigos. This is why that lovely lady from Vice President Dick Cheney's office asked me to essentially update their Indigo profile so they could go back to their evil business. And God said, "Go pound sand."

During this time, a new kind of Indigo appeared repeatedly by God's plan. They are Elder and Latchkey Indigos who have become Mentors to the Crystals.

A Crystal is the perfect chameleon. So much so that other Indigos cannot spot them. The Crystal will always seek an Indigo Mentor who will be an Elder or Latchkey, and when they bond, it is for life. The role of the Indigo Mentor is to shield their Crystals from harm and to help them understand how the world works.

Generation Alpha
Born 2010-2025
Indigos, Crystals, and Indigo Riselings

What is so unique about Generation Alpha is that it is the generation monsters like Cheney and his fellow travelers had waited in fear for this day.

It is the coming day of the Riseling Elders, and I foresaw it after that trip to the Central Valley. I call it "the popcorn phenomenon" because why are Riselings not presently fully mature Indigos or Crystals?

By the end of this tribulation, all Riselings will be Riseling Elders, and as fully mature Indigos, they will lead humanity into an enlightened Star Trek future. We'll discuss this later, but let's do that second lunch in our story for now.

Our Crystal was sixteen years old, and her Mentor was in her mid-thirties. I found them waiting for me at the restaurant. We had a lovely breakfast, my treat, and the conversation ranged across several topics.

After the waitress cleared the table, this got us to that …and what moment. This is when this girl amazed me. She told me she could sense the spirits of her future children and asked me if I could tell her anything about them.

We were sitting in a booth, me and her Mentor on one side, and she alone on the other. For a psychic, this kind of reading involves a combination of soft focus and peripheral vision, and you never do a reading like this without permission.

When I did the reading, I could see two souls just behind her left shoulder and a possible third behind them.

I told her so, and she and her Mentor got excited and blurted out, "See, I told you three."

I added, "Trust your Mentor, for you are bonded with her, and she can see more clearly than I can, so yes, it is three."

She and her Mentor wanted to know that, but it would not be the final word. We wrapped things up and headed for our cars, which just happened to be parked nose-to-nose.

As we were getting into our cars, I heard a clear, strong voice, and I immediately knew it was a Guide from the other side for the Crystal. The voice said, "Tell her that her children will be beautiful."

I never refused such an accommodation, so I stood next to my door and waved to them to do the same, which they did, and I looked at the Crystal and said, "I've been asked to tell you that your children will be beautiful."

She came to the meeting because of something she wanted to know. They could convey to her what she most needed to hear through me, and she lit up like a Christmas tree, and so did her Mentor.

This is what it is like to walk the Indigo path, my dearest Riselings. There is a lot of love here.

Day of the Riselings

After my lunch with the pleasant lady who worked with the office of Vice President Dick Cheney, I knew they were unable to profile the Crystals because they are chameleons.

That was good to know, but even better, I knew they knew what was coming and why they feared you. In a sense, my dear Riselings, I've been waiting years for the corn to pop, as I like to think of it.

Imagine we're making popcorn the old-fashioned way. Place a pot on a stovetop burner and add oil and corn. Cover and heat, and shake the pot. Eventually, you hear the first few pops. On an Indigo scale, it's been that way for millennia.

But then, with the Baby Boomers, the corn started popping faster and faster. This is what was happening in 2006 during my Indigo lunch meeting.

What did I see coming back then? I knew that Indigos and Crystals would somehow play a pivotal role, but I had no idea what that could be at the time.

Today, I see how it worked out. The Q movement is a White Hat psyop to trigger awareness in the population. They accessed the Black Hat intelligence on Indigos and have used it for good. Oorah.

Consequently, most Anons who follow and decode Q drops are Indigos and Crystals. While there are some questionable types, they never grow much of a social media following.

On the other hand, the social media messaging of the Indigos and Crystals resonates with the public, and they are gaining ground as tellers of truth.

What impressed me is that the Crystals are stepping forward to speak to the public. Being chameleons by nature, they must deal with an awful amount of stage fright before going public on social media.

One such is Crystal, which can be found on Rumble. He goes by the pseudonym SG Anon and maintains the QNewsPatriot channel.

If you start with his first show, *Audio File 1, Inside the Command Structure of the Alliance to Save the World,* you'll hear a very challenged Crystal coping with his stage fright. Other Indigos, including you Rieslings, are warriors for truth, so this is not an issue for the rest of us. But it clearly was for him, and he was pretty emphatic.

Hearing him speak about his Indigo Mentor, who passed away recently, is fascinating. I'm not sure he knows who he is, but as long as he knows he is different, it's all that matters. Watching him grow into his new mission role has been inspiring.

That's great, but that's not the totally cool stuff. It's you, my dear Rieslings.

In 2006, I wondered when the sound of corn popping in the pot would swell furiously, filling the pot with fresh, delicious popcorn. I call this the "Popcorn Phenomenon."

I'm seeing you pop up more and more on social media these days. In the words of my generation, groovy baby, let the corn pop.

No matter what the monsters have done to suppress your soul journey, you are Riselings and the generation that will keep coming.

Now, my dear Riselings, I will share an urgent, knowing you most likely are beginning to sense. Who will change during this tribulation, and who will be left standing?

All Riselings will change, and as their third eyes become fully activated, they will follow their inclination to either the Indigo or Crystal path. This is important because, at the end of this tribulation, nearly all those left standing will be flame-on, fully mature Indigos, Riselings, or Crystals.

This brings me to the urgency of the Riseling mission. All those left standing at the tribulation will be mature Indigos. Very few who suppress their gift will survive.

Therefore, not only must you become a fully mature Indigo within a short span of years, but you must also be a light of hope to your family to help them fully awaken their own Indigo abilities and thereby survive the tribulation.

The following are simple guiding principles:

> **Good lives make for good souls.** *This is the way.*
>
> **Be young in your heart and old in your thoughts.** *This is the way.*
>
> **To open your third eye, be humble, compassionate, and merciful.** *This is the way.*

Embrace these principles, and you shall become an unstoppable, committed light of hope during an awful time. Keep the faith, dear Riselings, and the future shall be yours, and it shall be well worth the having.

Teaching Tools

Previously, we learned how James Cameron created a color scheme for the film *Avatar* (2009) that used six colors, and the color of interest was Rainbow Indigo (Hex: #1C3F6E).

For this chapter, the cinema teaching tool is the second film, *Avatar: The Way of Water* (2022), for two reasons. The film presents families in crisis and how they stand together and rise to the challenge.

Kiri and Lo'ak

Of particular interest are Kiri and Lo'ak. These characters are near your age, and both know they are different, so here is a proposition. Kiri is a Crystal, and Lo'ak is an Indigo. Watch and see for yourself; as you do, see how they help their families. There is much to learn here, especially Riselings with vaccinated parents.

Common sense and compassion are needed because the vaccine bioweapon is passed through body fluids. The weapon targets the brain, brain stem, heart, lungs, and reproductive organs. It also passes through a mother's placenta and, eventually, her milk.

Much is being done to find natural solutions to disable the graphene and mRNA components of the bioweapon, and there is cause for hope, but thanks to shedding, a loving good night kiss from a vaccinated family member can literally be a kiss of death.

All family members, including the unvaccinated family members, especially the Rieslings, must be proactive with the Zelenko protocol and detox protocols as a prophylactic defense. Also, I present a lot of helpful information in my six-part yowusa.com video series, *The Jab with Marshall Masters*.

The Way of Water

The second thing you want to be mindful of in this second film is how a family from the forest flees to a coastal village and learns to adapt to an entirely new place and lifestyle.

I call this "busting a move" because you have to bust up your life to do it. I've done it, and Lord, it's tough. But dear Rieslings, you must do it because with what is coming, it is safe to assume that no above-ground structures will survive the coming tribulation without some degree of damage if not total obliteration.

This is why I spent seven years researching and writing my book, *Win-Win Survival Handbook: All-Hazards Safety and Future Space Colonization*. It is a complete plan for a community that will survive, thrive, and prosper throughout it all.

When I wrote it, I had no Earthly idea I was writing it for you, my dear Rieslings. Functionally, these are all-hazard, self-sustaining land arks with below-ground farming. In terms of beauty, they are homey, comfortable, airy, and bright—the perfect place for Riseling families.

And who shall call for such communities to be started? Riselings of course. Tag, you're it, so watch the movie and enjoy the way of water because it is the perfect metaphor for what comes next.

5

Revelation River

When souls grow wise in the ways of the world, they naturally seek wisdom, and this is not a convenient process because the universe works on a need-to-know basis. When you need to know, you will, assuming you look for it.

For this reason, our guides are careful about how much information they give us because there is always the concern that we will be overwhelmed, causing us to take one or more steps backward in our soul evolution.

This is why the Guides are always trying to give us tools to navigate the dangers of this world so that we will not only know enough to ask the right questions but also accept the answers.

The chapters ahead will be gut-wrenching because the prophecies of Revelation offer precise scientific clarity about several catastrophic events to come.

If you are curious but unprepared, you will likely be overwhelmed, and your denial will amplify. This is why, my dear Riselings, I am walking you slowly to the bad news so that I can first give you the tools to help you understand, adapt, and overcome. First is to understand the state of the world you've incarnated into.

Indigo Construct

Previously, we compared the Matrix concept with the Indigo Construct. The Matrix is an artificial world created by artificial intelligence programs to enslave humans for the purpose of power generation for the benefit of their machine world.

Human minds create an Indigo Construct to seek truth so we can break free from the shackles of slavery. This book reflects the Indigo Construct of its author, and you must create your own. Again, here are some helpful guidelines:

- Use imagination, observation, contemplation, and vision to build your construct.
- Your construct is always a work in progress; you alone are its artist.
- Assume everything you know is wrong and take nothing for granted.
- Trust only those truths that resonate within you because you and you alone put them there.
- Remember, hell is about being right, and heaven is about getting it right. Keep your ego in check.
- There is no right or wrong; there is only that which is useful or useless. Keep the useful and leave the useless in your wake.
- Everything is in motion, so the only absolute is that all things can and do change.
- Do not submit to fear. It is a mind-killer that robs you of distance and clarity.
- Always be mindful of prophecy, but never live in expectation of it.
- Begin your Indigo Construct with a SPOT—a single point of truth. Like the corner piece of a puzzle, everything will connect with it.

We will delve into this topic in much greater depth later on, but for now, I want to introduce imagination as a construct tool you can use to navigate the dark times ahead with calm resolve. I call it Time Canoeing, and this construct tool will help you and your families paddle around the worst of what is to come in the years ahead.

Good vs. Evil

Humanity is embroiled in a toxic mix of natural and artificial catastrophes called World War III. How led us here? People with no regrets.

There are only two kinds of people in the world who have no regrets: Psychopaths and vegetables. This brings us to the one immutable fact of history.

No matter the kind of governments humanity forms, they all inevitably morph into psychopath magnets. Relying on patience, deceit, and violence, the psychopaths eventually capture any government they wish, and the first thing they do upon taking control is to hire all the vegetables.

The reason is that acquisition is the driving force of our lives, and it's always been about I got mine; you get yours.

For this reason, my eternal hope is that after this tribulation, the survivors will evolve beyond acquisition. Those who survive the backside, as I call it, where we see blue skies and taste sweet waters once again, will have a clean slate for a new world.

In this new world, the driving force of our lives will no longer be acquisition. It will be harmony. Harmony within ourselves and everything about us. What would that feel like? Many who have experienced a near-death experience (NDE) will tell you about the magnificent sense of harmony they experienced while on the other side.

It is so beautiful that those who tell the tale will say they wanted to stay and not return but are sent back. When their souls reenter their bodies, they are profoundly changed.

Having seen themselves as eternal beings, they lose their fear of death, though none would want to die badly. Those who are materialistic and self-centered before their NDE return with a compassionate need to serve others and help make this a better world.

Now, imagine how our precious Riselings will live in a new world with this kind of harmony and how glorious it will be. This is the destiny God has chosen for humanity, and the only way to cheat ourselves of our rightful future is fear.

Creating fear through deceit and violence has always been the modus operandi of the monsters, and they are steadily refining it. An excellent way to see this is in how the nature of warfare has evolved over the years.

Warfare Generations

1. **Manpower:** Man-on-man Biblical combat.
2. **WWI Industrial:** Use of industrial weapons such as machine guns and tanks.
3. **WWII Combined Arms:** Began with the Nazi Blitzkrieg tactics.
4. **9/11 and Terrorism:** Media manipulation and endless wars.
5. **WWIII Narrative:** Present-day propaganda and society collapse.

The point of all these horrors is they are engineered to make you fearful because that is when your critical thinking shuts off, and you are no more intelligent than a dear caught in the headlights. Never forget:

> Wars are created by evil for evil and do only evil. *This is the way.*

We are in WW III, and the goal is to depopulate the species by half or more, and the aim of evil is simple to understand. The last to know are always the first to fall, and so shall it be for the better part of humanity in the years ahead.

As a Riseling, your mission is not to save the world as we know it because it is ending. It is to protect those you love and who love you.

How does a Riseling do this? The Indigo way to navigate future hazards is with an Indigo Construct.

Time Canoeing

In the following chapters, you will read disturbing prophecies and an even more worrisome timeline leading up to 2037. However, using the word "timeline" is a limited way to begin building a construct because the only place in Creation where one can find a perfectly straight line is in the mind of a sentient being.

Ergo, a more fitting phrase for this construct is "time is a river." This is also one of the reasons I asked you to watch the film *Avatar: The Way of Water (2022)* in the previous chapter.

This movie will help put you in a fluid state of mind to conceptualize time as a vast river flowing through Creation with many branches, rivers, streams, and channels all inevitably flowing to the same destination.

With Revelation and other prophecies, the Mississippi River is an ideal river system for this visualization. No matter how much it changes over the years, it always reaches the same destination.

In the days of Mark Twain, when paddlewheel riverboats plied the waters of this mighty river, they depended on local River Pilots to help them avoid dangers in given areas of the river. They are still doing it today, even with all our fantastic technology.

For this construct, we will imagine a vast river system like the Great Mississippi River called the Revelation River.

Between now and 2037, we will be navigating the troubled waters of the Revelation River, a cosmic timeline flowing across vast distances through Creation with many twists, turns, channels, and tributaries.

As with all great rivers within Creation, it will go where it goes, and when you navigate its waters, you are restrained within the breadth of its banks. Therefore, the wise thing to do is to learn how to navigate within it through good times and bad.

To get started, here is your first SPOT. It is the time-proven axiom:

There is strength in numbers. *This is the way.*

In this visualization, you will be canoeing in the future with your Indigo soul mate, with guys in the stern and gals in the bow. You both know that you're his gal; he is your guy, and there is nobody you'd rather be doing this with. Around are loving family and friends with a small flotilla of single-man kayaks and standard canoes loaded with kids, dogs, and gear.

It is summer, the water level is high, and the river flows more gently.

As you carry your time canoes down the boat ramp, happy families race around you down the ramp. It is a beautiful day and an excellent time to get acquainted with your craft's handling characteristics and go along with the flow as you enjoy the view.

Hold on to these precious memories, for in the march of time, a dark time comes. The water will be treacherously low, and once inconsequential, things are now deadly. With such challenging conditions, only a few canoers stand ready to ply.

They will know that riding with the current as though the water is high invites dire consequences, such as getting caught up in the overhang, running aground, or capsizing in the middle of a boulder field.

How will the wise navigate the river in these dangerous conditions?

With the mindful common sense of a time pilot, know your piece of the river from bank to bank and as far as the eye can see, and paddle in still waters whenever you can.

Do this alone, and you are the master of your fate, within limits. However, paddle with someone of a like mind, and you can raise the boundaries of what is possible—more than enough to make a difference.

Soul Mates

What happens when Riseling soul mates work together as a team? They become formidable, and here is why.

Balance is essential; Our gal is in the bow, and our guy is in the stern. His strengths are that he has a knack for land navigation and the upper body strength for bursts of speed.

Our gal in the bow is the perfect lookout because her Spidey sense for potential dangers is more sensitive than the typical man's. It gives her a natural advantage as a time navigator because she can sense what is yet to be revealed.

She will also communicate with the time canoers further ahead with simple red bandannas. Using simple semaphore patterns, she can pass the info on to our guy in the stern, and he'll know if someone needs help or to beach for the night, for example.

The point is that survival is not about roles. It is about strengths because teamwork is essential when navigating time. With practice, team members will learn to anticipate each other, and in decisive moments, the quickness of a knowing nod or look can mean the difference between life and death.

Survival technology is essential. Does the canoe used make a difference? A practical question, but let's be honest. A $6,000 handmade cedar strip canoe is a joy to handle, but you're not likely to see many of them, let alone own one.

You'll likely settle for a garage sale, with a polyethylene rental canoe costing $350—a scuffed-up scale model of the Queen Mary with similar sluggish handling and a deep draft.

So what? It makes no difference. Our guy and gal are an effective team, and here is what they are always looking for.

Chutes and Oxbows

The Revelation River is like any other river system with tributaries, branches, twists, turns, and so forth, and there will hazards along the way. Those with white waters and steep falls are the primary concern, and as a time pilot, you know that one way to avoid those hazards while within the river system is to be mindful of side channels called chutes and oxbows.

- **CHUTES:** A chute leaves the main channel before a big bend in the river and rejoins it on the other side of the bend. A chute gets you downstream faster and is sheltered from hazards in the main channel by a natural bank.

- **OXBOWS:** An oxbow leaves the main channel and bypasses an extended bend in the river. While Oxbows are the longer route, like a chute, they are sheltered by a natural bank from hazards in the main channel.

The whole point of this visualization is that you must be mindful of the river and where to look for ways to bypass catastrophic events to the best of your ability. With that, here is a quick time pilot review:

- Build team cohesion with like-minded others.
- Know the dangers ahead as best you can.
- Use chutes and oxbows to bypass catastrophic timeline events.

As for the rest, the universe operates on a need-to-know basis. When you need to know, you'll see if you bother to look. That's the basics, and in the coming chapters, what should you do? Look for ways to bypass bad times with chutes and oxbows because while we all will flow to the same destination, how we get there will decide who makes it.

Clarity Mantra

Each time you learn about a new catastrophic event on the timeline, do not retreat into fear or feel overwhelmed. If you begin to feel overwhelmed, do the Clarity Mantra.

Begin by finding a quiet place and clear your surroundings.

Take a knee, and bow your head down. When you feel comfortable, close your eyes and take three deep breaths. Each time you exhale, imagine the emotions of your thoughts being carried out. Then, breathe naturally for a few moments and calmly say:

Clarity Mantra

Who am I?
I am a Good Person.

Where am I?
I am in the moment.

What am I prepared to do?
To be a light of hope.

This is the way.

Once you have clarity, then finding the solution is a simple, three-step process as follows:

1. Assess your situation honestly and what you need to do.
2. Form options, make plans, and then select one.
3. Take decisive action on that plan, even if it is not optimal.

When you are ready, rise and immediately take action.

We will expand the construct later, but you have what you need for bad news ahead.

Congratulations, you are ready to launch your time canoe into the waters of the Revelation River. This is your silver lining in all this dark business, my dear Riselings, because now you know where to paddle, so let's go downriver for a glimpse of your future destination.

River's End

Like the Mississippi River, the Revelation River is a dynamic and changing river, and as time pilots, we all navigate our little area of the Revelation River.

When we do as bonded teams, we can affect our fate for the better in many ways. Then again, we must go where the river goes, and if that destination is a barren wasteland, it's all the worse for us; nonetheless, try we must.

To the river's end, we must go, but consider this: What can we do to help free our species from the depredations and exploitation of those who have long held us in shackles?

How could we, the little guys, throw off the shackles of slavery to become a free and enlightened species and be welcomed by other benign species? We Indigos do as God wants for us. To be lights of hope for others.

Riselings, changing the timeline begins with changing minds, and our Creator has put these challenges before us to teach us the power of choice and what we can do when we choose to do the same thing together.

We can change our destiny as a species, and interestingly enough, the Guardians of the Looking Glass saw that future timeline. I document this in my two videos Yowusa.com videos:

- Project Looking Glass: NYC 4/18 False Flag, Trump, Q, and Devolution

- Guardians of the Looking Glass: Fact or Fiction?

The Guardians also saw many negative timelines and were horrific to behold, but they did describe this one golden bright future, and here is an excerpt from their manuscript.

> **Guardians of the Looking Glass, Mar 17, 2022**
> The 2030 Singularity - Two Timelines, One Outcome
>
> The positive outcome, as it was shown, results in the total and complete destruction of the current power structure. Those in power saw their future in the positive timeline, and they were terrified of it. They would end up mostly

homeless, without money or power. All of it is stripped away. Once the positive timeline completes, and the cosmic event occurs, humanity by the year 2030 has almost entirely reversed course.

We could see that the economy had completely changed, as individual habits changed, as the positive outcome became more likely. Fast food companies went out of business, as did Wal-Mart, Apple, Netflix and Amazon, and countless other destructive, negative companies. Viewership of many network shows dropped to nearly zero. Use of Facebook and other social media platforms dropped to nearly zero. Billions of people stopped paying taxes, and stopped using banks. Governments were starved of finances. Individuals became rich in wealth, as new revenue streams emerged, completely disconnected from the fiat money system. Many people began growing their own food, and formed small, community governments, often no more than a few hundred people in size.

In the positive timeline, humanity, as whole, did not fight the system, they simply stopped participating in it entirely.

Each individual began to make a decision to reject negative habits, and the negative system in place, and instead began to make more positive choices in their lives.

Think about it, Riselings. You chose to be here for what God, the Creator of all, wants for us. To master our free will by learning to make better choices. To know that when the obstacles to freedom will not go away, you go around or over them. Never surrender.

I firmly believe that the prophecies are given to us so that we may live and were not cast in stone. God made us as co-creators, and if we are to be worthy children, we need to come together as brothers and sisters and change our world through the power of love and a commitment to making positive choices.

Teaching Tools

Another cinema teaching from writer and producer James Cameron is the film Titanic (1997). When you watch the movie, consider this. In those days, it was "women and children first," and save for a few cowards, the men went down with the ship.

Today, it is "women and children last," and when ships like the Costa Concordia ran aground in 2012, the captain and crew abandoned the passengers to their fate. Later, when help arrived, in the scramble down the rope ladders to the rescue boats below, grown men were seen shoving women and children out of their way.

The point of watching the film is to understand that a disaster is an unbroken chain of mistakes leading to a catastrophic failure. For example, the Titanic sailed without enough binoculars, so the men in the crow's nest were not equipped, and spotting icebergs in calm seas was tricky at night.

When you begin studying the Titanic, the story takes on a larger perspective with many different and troubling aspects. There are many lessons to learn here because there is a tremendous wealth of information on this unfortunate sinking.

When you watch the film, you will see what those people experienced that fateful night, yet consider the number of lifeboats. Especially Rose's question about it. It is a few lines in the movie, but crucial. Everyone who died that night did so because they refused to do the math as Rose had done. She divided the number of souls aboard by the number of lifeboats and knew there was a problem.

Another vital scene involves a new technology of the day. Wireless two-way radios and the long-range naval communication method of the day was Morse Code.

In the film, after learning the Titanic will sink, the captain goes to the ship's radio room and hands the telegrapher a message, saying, "That's right, CQD, the distress call. Tell whoever responds that we're going down by the head and need help immediately."

What you never see in any of the movies about the sinking of the Titanic is that as the women were getting into the lifeboats, the captain's CQD distress message was being picked up by many ships in that region of the Atlantic, plus land-based stations.

Survival Comms

When writing my *Radio Free Earth: The Complete Beginner's Guide to Survival Communications*, I found the complete radio traffic log beginning from the first distress message and ending with the Titanic going off the air. It is in the appendix, and it totals thirteen pages.

If you read that log, it will break your heart because even though they are talking in dots and dashes, the humanity of it is stunning.

The terrestrial Internet will be devastated during the tribulation and likely never return. In its place will be Starlink, but even that will be plagued with damaged and destroyed satellites. While it will remain in some fashion, there will be areas with floating coverage outages for years, including GPS satellites.

This is why I wrote *Radio Free Earth*. It is not for HAM enthusiasts and geeky experiments. It's a practical, straightforward guide for one step away from operating a baby monitor.

Who should read it first? Ladies. Yes, ladies, because the guys are good at the tech stuff, but ladies will need two-way communications to learn about friends and family, and when a child is gravely injured, a friend from afar can send messages describing how to treat the wounds.

Let me put it to your girls. One day in the future, you may have to bury a child, knowing you were too busy to learn how to operate a two-way radio. Could you live with that?

If not, here is what every Riseling needs to do. Learn how two-way radios work because once the prophecies of Revelation 8 begin to unfold, the only use for your smartphone will be as a grave marker with your final testament.

HAM Cram

What can you do today? Start looking in your local area for HAM radio groups and inquire if they offer "HAM cram" for the FCC tests.

The old-school approach was a few months of study before taking the first test for the Technician license. This is for beginners, and once you pass that and get your call sign, you want to work on the second, which is the General license. You want the General.

I used the HAM cram for Technician and General, passing both with flying colors.

Here is how it works. You do not study or prepare for the test. Just get a good night's rest and be ready to rock and roll.

The FCC publishes the questions and correct answers for each test, and during the HAM cram, a HAM will pass out the printed question and answer with a yellow highlighter.

The HAM will then read out the question and the correct answer only, and you will highlight the correct answer. This way, it is all subliminal, and when you take the test, you'll know the correct answers, so trust your first impulse.

Is this cheating? Certainly not. In fact, it is better than doing it the old-school way because you are learning what the FCC wants you to know. As for me, it was beneficial to comply with communication rules and protocols.

How much will it cost you to get your first license? About as much as you would spend on hamburgers for two. The same holds true for the second; your licenses will be good for five years.

Then, you should teach yourself Morse Code. You can use Morse Code to talk thousands of miles, and you use two-way radios to bounce Morse Code signals off the face of the Moon back to a third of the Earth. Why the analog two-way radios in the book? Because they are peer-to-peer. No middlemen to throttle your communications.

After you finish reading this book, begin looking around for local resources, and learn this now because, at your age, you will pick it up five times faster than an adult. Once you master it, it's like riding a bicycle. You never forget.

With that, Riselings, it's time to launch our time canoes because you now have the tools you need to go downriver and survive.

6

Revelation 8:8-9 – The Mountain

In the previous chapter, we used accounts from *The Kolbrin Bible* and other texts to corroborate Revelation 8:7 – The Blood, which was an easy one, relatively speaking.

From this point forward, guacamole hits the fan, and if you get it and want to live through it, you will need the power of love to survive. With this in mind, let's see where we've been and where we're going now with Revelation 8.

Young's Literal Translation 1898
Revelation 8

7 and the first messenger did sound, and there came hail and **fire**, mingled with **blood**, and it was **cast to the land**, and the third of the trees was burnt up, and all the green grass was burnt up.

8 And the second messenger did sound, and as it were a **great mountain** with fire burning was **cast into the sea**, and the third of the sea became blood,

9 and die did the third of the creatures that [are] in the sea, those having life, and the third of the ships were destroyed.

With Revelation 8:7-9 we see that Earth is entering the Nemesis Constellation Cloud, which surrounds this small brown dwarf star, a companion to our own Sol. The critical metaphors are:

- **FIRE:** This is due to the ablation of the meteorites as they enter and pass through the Earth's atmosphere. Also, the other elements within the meteorites, such as phosphorus, are likely why they burn all the way to the ground.

- **BLOOD:** This metaphor unlocks Revelation 8:7. Upon entering the Nemesis Cloud, we will encounter a lot of iron oxide. It is a blood-red pigment and water-soluble. It will turn surface waters red and poison life in the water and those creatures on the land who depend on them.

- **CAST:** We see the same use of this metaphor with "cast to the land" and "cast into the sea." Casting suggests that these objects appear to be thrown with force, so these are seen traveling at high speed, which confirms extraterrestrial origin. Also, something being cast is often aimed.

- **GREAT MOUNTAIN:** The term "great mountain" is used by climbers to describe incredibly challenging mountains, such as the Matterhorn in the Swiss Alps. Here, the Great Mountain is an impactor the size of a small mountain with similar features.

- **THIRD:** This metaphor gives us a sense of global scale. This significant saltwater deep impact event spans the Earth's ocean with a massive loss of sea life and shipping.

Revelation 8:7 is the initial benign event in this series of prophecies. At this time, the Nemesis cloud will pelt the Earth with fiery meteorites and iron oxide.

Like our Oort Cloud, Nemesis also has a leftover ball of debris created due to its inception, and we call it the Nemesis Cloud. It is inundated with iron oxide and other debris.

The "great mountain" of Revelation 8:8 refers to a massive asteroid. John describes a deep-impact event of such magnitude that it destroys a third of the sea life and a third of shipping in a global catastrophic event.

Now, the assumption for most folks is that this is an act of God, but remember. When building a construct, you begin with an assumption that everything you know is wrong. In this case, perhaps the mountain is not an act of God but, in fact, an act of war.

Anunnaki Invasion

In March of 2023, I created a 10-part video series titled *Anunnaki Invasion + Ground Zero and the Obliteration of NATO*. In that series, I explained a prophecy from my book, *Being In It for the Species: The Universe Speaks (2014)*.

Being is a channeled work, and the Guides gave us a harbinger event that precedes Revelation 8:7 by approximately one year. It will be a massive volcanic eruption in the Western Pacific one or after the Winter Solstice on December 21, 2024.

The winter of ash eruption will fill the skies with ash, and aviation and farming will be impacted. This harbinger event happens during the wintertime. Most will overlook it, but those who know of this prophecy will understand its meaning.

After this eruption and before Revelation 8:7, there will be an alien false flag invasion in the spring, and later that summer, Nemesis will reach perihelion—the closest distance to Sol. At this time, solar sprites (cosmic lighting) from the sun will begin and continue through 2030.

Below are excerpts of the reading with a Guide named Carlos in the book. However, I can now reveal his full name. He is Chilean astronomer Carlos Muñoz Ferrada (1909 - 2001), the man to whom this book is dedicated, and here is his prophecy for our times, which includes the mountain described in Revelation 8:10-11.

Being In It for the Species: The Universe Speaks
Destiny Comes to Those Who Listen and Fate Finds the Rest
Authored Channeling with Carlos, Page 28 (Excerpts)

> What remains to be seen for humanity are signs of momentous change. Occurrences so dire and unusual they command the focus of even the most reluctant souls.
>
> This event shall be volcanic eruption in the Western Pacific ocean region of the planet. It will send great plumes of ash into the atmosphere that will disrupt the weather and the comings and goings of humankind in profound and noticeable ways. Commerce and trade, along with air travel and security will be impacted as a consequence.
>
> In this time, visitations of travelers from other worlds will increase significantly. Friends and foes alike will see this unshackling of human spirits. Some will embrace it, others will not. Those who will not will seek to suppress it and to keep shackled a species, which serves their material and ecological interests.
>
> Of both kinds will come warnings of a calamitous event to befall inhabitants of Earth in the spring following the eruption in the Western Pacific. It will be an impact event in the eastern Atlantic that will lay waste to the shores of many nations bordering this great ocean. Spain, France and America shall bear the worst of this, though nations beyond the borders of these shall see consequences as well. Shorelines are devastated and major rivers will reverse and flood inland empires without mercy.
>
> The force of this asteroid will drive through the middle Earth into the Western region of the Pacific North of the islands of Japan and into the lands adjoining Russia and China. The force will turn southward reaching the shores of Antarctica and will rebound backwards into the region known as the Ring of fire. Day after day will see events helter-skelter along these Pacific shorelines, and inland for many miles as well.

When we researched this book, we worked with a team of Guides, and the others were very precise about the actual impact location of the asteroid and what would happen after that. All this is explained and illustrated in detail in my video series, *Anunnaki Invasion + Ground Zero and the Obliteration of NATO.*

The critical point of that series is that we first see a false flag alien invasion, followed by an actual alien invasion as described in Revelation 9:5.

This invasion is only given five months. This is consistent with the need for the invaders to return to their home world before Earth enters the Nemesis Cloud.

When the Guides gave us this prediction in 2013, it didn't make sense, but we did not judge the material and published it as given.

In the book *Being In It for the Species*, this is all explained in detail, bringing us to the question, is this impact event an act of war?

Act of War

When we did our research with the Guides for *Being In It for the Species*, the vector they gave us for the deep-impact event described by Carlos and Revelation 8:10 used two different cities.

I reviewed our notes from those readers and created a new vector for the purpose of this analysis using readily identifiable sites. The approximate vectors for the impact site are:

- 800 Miles due West of CERN
- 1200 Miles due North of La Palma

The Guides told us this impactor would travel from West to East before impacting in the Eastern Atlantic. Therefore, it can be concluded this is a multi-mission attack as follows:

- Eliminate American and European NATO powers with tsunamis.
- Impact ejecta pulverizes the industrial heartland of Europe.
- Direct hit on a subsea nexus point for terrestrial fiber communications.

This begs an obvious question. What are the odds of such a random asteroid impact creating devastation like this? Infinitesimally small.

Assuming this is a guided asteroid weapon, as I explain in my video series, Anunnaki Invasion + Ground Zero and the Obliteration of NATO, what would be the reason they use it, and what does that tell us about their intentions?

It will most likely be a first strike by the Anunnaki to soften up the NATO powers. They use it as a surprise attack. With one blow, they eviscerate NATO, and America gets hammered hard. Because Russia is primarily spared the consequences of this attack, it would appear the Anunnaki are coming in on the side of the Russians.

Nonetheless, the Anunnaki will have a free hand to seize as much gold as they need to repair their atmosphere, which will be severely affected during the pole shift event between 2028 and 2030.

Also, they will enslave Earth women for their off-world slave breeding programs. They will favor young European women of Nordic and Ashkenazi descent.

With that, let's summarize the possible sequence of events discussed so far:

- First Harbinger *Being*: Massive wintertime volcanic eruption.
- False Flag Alien Invasion *Being*: UFO activity. Good and bad.
- Nemesis at Perihelion *Being:* The closest distance to Sol. Solar sprites begin.
- Revelation 8:7: Iron oxide and meteorites from the Nemesis Cloud.
- Revelation 8:8 and *Being*: Anunnaki asteroid attack destroys NATO.
- Revelation 9: The Anunnaki plunder us for five months, taking women and gold.

This series of predictions begins with a volcanic eruption in the Western Pacific; we could be with months of these prophecies coming to pass. As you will learn later, the Winter Solstice is a critical time of celestial alignment for tribulation prophecies.

In the summer of 2024, Nemesis will be in Taurus when it reaches perihelion, and become a regular fixture in our sky.

> **The Kolbrin Bible: 21st Century Master Edition**
> Book of Manuscripts, Egyptian Texts
>
> 3:7 Thus it was in the Days of Heavenly Wrath, which have gone and thus it will be in the Days of Doom when it comes again. The times of its coming and going are known unto the wise. These are the signs which shall precede the Destroyers return: A hundred and ten generations shall pass into the west and nations will rise and fall. Men will fly in the air as birds and swim in the seas as fishes. Men will talk peace one with another; hypocrisy and deceit shall have their day. Women will be as men and men as women; **passion will be a plaything of man**.

When we started publishing *The Kolbrin Bible*, one of the signs described in this passage, "passion will be a plaything of man," piqued my curiosity, and I could not figure it out. When that happens, I put the mystery in a glass canning jar and set it on the memory shelf. Eventually, the universe will fax you a label, and this was a long wait.

I finally got the fax. AI sex robots, also called AI sex dolls, are sophisticated playthings, and this explains how "passion will be a plaything of man." The prophecy is fulfilled.

This brings us to the prophecies of Revelation and *Being In It for the Species*.

Remember the first rule of prophecy.

> **Always be mindful of prophecy, but never live in expectation of it.** *This is the way.*

Here, you must think. What if these prophecies do come to pass? What will that mean for you and your loved ones? The answers begin with what you are capable of doing.

Cycle of Empire

In 1998, Hollywood released two blockbuster science fiction asteroid impact disaster films: Armageddon and Deep Impact.

Armageddon is a classic Bruce Willis movie, a rip-roaring yarn about oil roughnecks saving the world. It's loads of fun, but you need to watch Deep Impact, which is a very sober look at what can happen during an impact such as this mountain prophecy.

The film offers a realistic view of how people will react during a tribulation event. Remember, Riselings, this America was before you and is not today's America.

In Deep Impact, our government is portrayed in a positive role. Compared with the America of today, we must wonder, was this film about another planet that is far away?

Let me frame it this way: I'm a boomer, and my generation grew up watching our heroes launch into space. After 9/11, everyone began watching victims leaping out of high-rise buildings to their deaths.

What's wrong with this picture? A lot because the America of today is woefully unprepared for what comes. The fabric of our society has been shredded, and our institutions are failing us. If we apply the cycle of empire to our present situation, we are an empire ripe for collapse.

The cycle of empire explains why all empires inevitably fail, and it comes down to resources. When empires are young and growing, there is enough booty for all their citizens to have a piece of the action. This phase needs plenty of low-hanging fruit to work.

Then, as the easy-to-plunder low-hanging fruit disappears, empires must go further and further into the field for new resources. During this time, the elites began to concentrate power and wealth into their hands at the expense of the ordinary person. At first, the body politic tolerates this abuse by the elites until things reach a point of no return.

After that, the nation's body politic became so weak that even a minor event the empire could easily overcome in its early days was a death flow. That's when the people cease to participate, and like Rome, the next thing you know, the barbarians are at your gates.

The simple explanation is that evil always overreaches; therefore, empires fail, much like one slowly squeezing a tomato. You can squeeze it to a point where you will have a useless mess on your hands if you do not relent.

The same holds true today. Like that poor tortured tomato, we're about to get messy.

How this all happens is described in detail with copious illustrations in my 10-part video series, *Anunnaki Invasion + Ground Zero and the Obliteration of NATO*, and my book, *Being In It for the Species: The Universe Speaks (2014)*.

Let's get to the key points. If you live in America, within a few miles of the East Coast or West Coast, and you let Revelation 8:7 pass you by without notice, what will be your chances of surviving Revelation 8:8-9? If, by the grace of God, you survive the initial tsunami events, your odds of dying from disease, injury, or starvation will be brutally high.

Let me put it more directly. If you are not prepared for Revelation 8:8-9 and you are in its path, you and two-thirds of everyone you know will die.

So, is the correct question at this point: what are you prepared to do? No.

It's what everyone around you is doing, as in, are they racing about like hysterical maniacs and saying clever things like, "I don't know what to do, but I do know I need to be the boss." (I'd bet good money that you already know someone like that.)

Teaching Tools

As you might suspect, the cinema teaching tool for this chapter is Deep Impact (1998) because this film presents the most realistic simulation of what will happen to the East Coast of America when the mountain of Revelation impacts the Eastern Atlantic.

It is filled with teaching moments about how America in 1998 would have dealt with a disaster such as the one depicted in this film.

In the film's climax, a remnant of the comet travels from West to East at roughly the same latitude as the mountain of Revelation. In the movie, people living along the Northeast shores of the country see it pass overhead. Then comes the impact, and a devastating tsunami wiping out the Eastern seaboard.

The movie's theme follows the adage: when things are at their worst, we're at our best. It shows us how good government and media people do their best to serve. It is a pleasant fiction.

The reality of today is not such a pleasant fiction because now, the government and the media are monsters, and they are bent on adding horrors to this tribulation.

A helpful way to frame the movie is this. It shows you how good people respond in this kind of awful situation. That is useful.

The important thing is that you watch the climax of the movie. Please focus on the congested freeways and how they only serve to put people in harm's way. Watch what happens to them and replay the climax. After that, you're ready to find your chutes and oxbows on the Revelation River.

As we learned previously, a chute helps you bypass a large river area, putting you further downriver in less time. An oxbow is a bypass like a chute, but it adds time and distance. The goal is to find safe areas of the river.

While researching my book, *Win-Win Survival Handbook: All-Hazards Safety and Future Space Colonization*, I spent five years searching the USA for the safest regions, and there is only one way to do that properly. Boots on the ground.

I crisscrossed the USA from East to West and North to South. If I were inclined to write a book about those travels, it would be titled *Airport Food Courts of America - Yuck!*

Nonetheless, I learned that most Americans are one tank of gas from a safe zone. For the rest, two tanks of gas, if they are lucky. Either way, let the wise words of Louis Pasteur guide you. "Chance favors the prepared mind."

With that in mind, dear Riselings, here is your first chutes and oxbows assignment.

Obtain printed maps of your local area and region and look for routes of egress that do not rely on heavily traveled roads and freeways. Instead, look for side streets, plot several routes to nearby safe zones, and keep all this in your bug-out bag.

Also, discuss this with your family and the need to create rally points where everyone can gather if they get separated—copies of personal ID, telephone numbers, addresses, etc. Do not make this a good idea for someone else to do. Take ownership and see it through.

7

Revelation 8:10-11 – Wormwood

The most pivotal prophecy in Revelation 8:10-11 is about a star named Wormwood. Some believe it will impact the Earth. In truth, it will not, but it will be fateful for billions.

A quick review. In Revelation 8:7, we see a harbinger event of "hail and fire, mingled with blood." these meteorite showers will strike in isolated patches across the globe. Their onset will happen quickly, like a summer rain, and fade away. Primarily viewed as an oddity by the mainstream, most will ignore this harbinger warning and woe to them.

Then, in Revelation 8:8-9 and Planet X – The Mountain, an asteroid impact creates death and destruction for many. This brutal, deep-impact event will affect many regions of the world. As with Revelation 8:7, some will be affected and others not.

However, 8:10-11 will be very different, and once it begins, everything changes.

Before we delve into that, we will insert Revelation 9:1-5 between Revelation 8:9 and 8:10 because this reflects the actual timeline.

Revelation 9 Alien Invasion

It may offend the sensibilities of some, but I found that the accounts of the fourth messenger in Revelation 8 and the fifth messenger in Revelation 9 are out of sequence. They need to be reversed.

What is critical to understand is that the scriptures are used as-is. However, the Holy Bible is a compilation published and translated by men. Ergo, the sequence issue could have occurred long after John penned these scriptures.

The reason is that the only part of the Holy Bible that is faithfully reproduced as it was written in the first five books of the Old Testament is called the Pentateuch. For Hebrews, the Five Books of Moses refer to the Torah.

The first five books of the Old Testament are called the Pentateuch. They are the first five books of the Hebrew Bible, referred to as Torah. The Torah is written in Hebrew, the oldest of Jewish languages. Letter-for-letter it is identical to the original given to us by Moses. All other scriptures in the Holy Bible are subject to 3rd party translation, editing, and publishing issues.

Does this in any way invalidate or impugn the prophecies of Revelation. Certainly not, and in fact, this lends even more gravitas. Here is why:

When John received these visions, he was time traveling, and as we see with our river analogy, time does not flow in a straight line. Hence, it is easy to lose your place.

This is common to time travel visions, and I learned this while writing my book, *Being in It for the Species: The Universe Speaks,* in 2013. The book is a channeled work with a group of guides, and I was blessed to have the help of psychic Adriana, Planet X researcher, and project archivist William.

When William and I first organized the effort, it was a typical two-dimensional project management flow chart. After conducting over half of our readings, William and I were lost in the data.

It occurred because we were jumping backward and forward in time, so tracking and building a coherent timeline often became impossible.

As both of us are retired systems analysts, we did the one thing we knew would eventually get us back on track. Here is the rule.

If you are doing it wrong, do it consistently wrong. *This is the way.*

We completed the remainder of the channel readings, knowing we'd have something usable or alphabet soup at the end.

With that done, the next step was to build a useful timeline from the readings, and here I had an advantage. Software I first acquired as a consultant for systems analysis, such as bin sorts, fencing, etc.

We expected all kinds of issues because our questions, which spanned numerous readings, bounced back and forth in time like a table soccer game. Yet, as we unpacked the data, what we discovered amazed us.

No matter how many zigs and zags we took with our questions, the Guides always had a clear heading and everything clicked. No exceptions, no gotchas, no maybes; it was perfect. They tracked everything perfectly, which made us feel like the gang that couldn't shoot straight, so I empathize with John in ways you could not imagine.

The point is, when John was given these prophetic visions of our future, he had no software tools or someone to collaborate with. Like us, he got lost in the data, which is why Revelation's fourth and fifth messengers are reversed.

To illustrate the point, let's begin with Revelation 8:8-9 and the asteroid "Great Mountain" deep impact event.

Preemptive Strike

In my 10-part video series, *Anunnaki Invasion + Ground Zero and the Obliteration of NATO*, I explain this event in detail, as given by the guides.

For now, the point is that the impact event Revelation 8:8-9 is not an act of God. It is an act of war by the Anunnaki as a preemptive opening strike against the NATO Colonial powers to soften the target for invasion.

The timing of this attack was critical because the Anunnaki had a small window of time to conduct their invasion to capture gold for repairing their atmosphere and women for slave breeding. Once they land, the clock is ticking because if they dally, they will not launch for home in time to make it back.

With this in mind, read Revelation 9:1-6

> **YOUNG'S LITERAL TRANSLATION 1898**
> Revelation 9
>
> 1 And the fifth messenger did sound, and I saw **a star out of the heaven having fallen to the Earth**, and there was given to it the key of the pit of the abyss,
>
> 2 **and he did open the pit of the abyss**, and there came up a smoke out of the pit as smoke of a great furnace, and darkened was the sun and the air, from the smoke of the pit.
>
> 3 **And out of the smoke came forth locusts to the Earth**, and there was given to them authority, as scorpions of the Earth have authority,
>
> 4 and it was said to them that they may not **injure** the grass of the Earth, nor any green thing, nor any tree, but — **the men only who have not the seal of God upon their foreheads**,
>
> 5 and it was given to them that they may not kill them, but that **they may be tormented five months**, and their torment [is] as the torment of a scorpion, when it may strike a man;
>
> 6 and in those days shall **men seek the death, and they shall not find it**, and they shall desire to die, and the death shall flee from them.

In Revelation 9:5, an invasion window of five months is all the Anunnaki have, and they must launch before Earth enters the main body of the Nemesis Cloud, and this is when the Great Winnowing begins.

Revelation 8 Review

Let's take a moment to review the metaphors used in Revelation 8, from 8:7-11.

YOUNG'S LITERAL TRANSLATION 1898
Revelation 8

7 and the first messenger did sound, and there came hail and **fire**, mingled with **blood**, and it was **cast** to the land, and the third of the trees was burnt up, and all the green grass was burnt up.

8 And the second messenger did sound, and as it were a **great mountain** with **fire** burning was **cast** into the sea, and the third of the sea became **blood**,

9 and die did the **third** of the creatures that [are] in the sea, those having life, and the **third** of the ships were destroyed.

10 And the third messenger did sound, and there **fell** out of the heaven a great star, burning as a lamp, and it did fall upon the third of the rivers, and upon the **fountains of waters**,

11 and the name of the star is called **Wormwood**, and the third of the waters doth become **Wormwood**, and many of the men did die of the waters, because they were made **bitter**.

These scriptures add four new metaphors to the list with 8:10-11, so let's review all the metaphors used so far.

Metaphors

With Revelation 8:7-11 we see that Earth is entering the Nemesis Constellation Cloud, which surrounds this small brown dwarf star, a companion to our own Sol. The critical metaphors in order of appearance are:

- **FIRE:** This is due to the ablation of the meteorites as they enter and pass through the Earth's atmosphere. Also, the other elements within the meteorites, such as phosphorus, are likely why they burn all the way to the ground.

- **BLOOD:** This metaphor unlocks Revelation 8:7. Upon entering the Nemesis Cloud, we will encounter a lot of iron oxide. It is a blood-red pigment and water-soluble. It will turn surface waters red and poison life in the water and those creatures on the land who depend on them.

- **CAST:** We see the same use of this metaphor with cast to the land and again with cast into the sea. Casting suggests that these objects appear to be thrown with force, so these are seen traveling at high speed, which confirms extraterrestrial origin. Also, something cast is often aimed at something.

- **GREAT MOUNTAIN:** The term "great mountain" is used by climbers to describe incredibly challenging mountains, such as the Matterhorn in the Swiss Alps. Here, Great Mountain describes a stony-iron asteroid the size of a small mountain with similar features.

- **THIRD:** This metaphor gives us a sense of global scale. This significant saltwater deep impact event spans the Earth's ocean with a massive loss of sea life and shipping.

- **FELL:** This metaphor differs from CAST in significant ways. Something cast will accelerate faster than the speed of gravity, whereas when it falls, the acceleration is due to gravity.

- **FOUNTAINS:** This metaphor describes underground aquifers as vast subterranean lakes. The metaphor **"fountains of waters"** refers to the natural springs and artesian wells known in those times.

- **WORMWOOD:** Wormwood is a bitter-tasting plant used for centuries for medicinal purposes and is widely available at health food stores and online in essential oils, pills, and liquid extracts.

- **BITTER:** Revelation explicitly uses the "bitter" metaphor and is consistent with similar metaphor usage in other scriptures.

It is important to note that Wormwood is also associated with the Project Wormwood Learmonth Solar Observatory on the North West Cape of Australia. Such an observatory could be credited with the discovery of Nemesis.

While this explanation is arguable, what is not is the pairing of two more meaningful metaphors, Wormwood and bitter.

Fountains

It is likewise vital to note that the fountain metaphor is used consistently in Genesis, Proverbs, and Revelation.

Young's Literal Translation 1898
Genesis 7

11 In the six hundredth year of the life of Noah, in the second month, in the seventeenth day of the month, in this day have been broken up all **fountains of the great deep**, and the net-work of the heavens hath been opened,

Note how this scripture from Genesis references the fountains and heavens metaphors together so one can understand them. Then, Proverbs 8.

> **Young's Literal Translation 1898**
> Proverbs 8
>
> 28 In His strengthening clouds above, In His making strong **fountains of the deep**,

Again, the fountains and heaven [cloud] metaphor connection. This is a critical metaphor, so keep it in mind. To illustrate the point, consider the coming plight of Las Vegas, NV.

Wormwood Mud Flats

Once Revelation 8:10 is fulfilled, Las Vegas will likely be the first major city to experience anarchy and cannibalism because it depends on Lake Mead for water and power. After Revelation 8:10-11 starts, it will be a foul and bitter mass of blood-red mud and ooze, and they will call it the Wormwood Mud Flats.

Assuming a return to good governance, what could a government for the people do for the people? In this case, how could they save the people in Las Vegas?

Forty-five miles South of Las Vegas in the high deserts of California is a small town called Nipton. Its claim to fame is selling California lottery tickets to Nevadans. A place you have usually passed through since the lockdowns.

However, something else is passing through Nipton. A working rail line and so happens, this minuscule curio pit stop in the high desert of California sits atop what could be considered a vast, deep, underground freshwater sea 400' down and all there for the pumping.

A benign government could build multiple pumping stations alongside the tracks in Nipton. Then, fill mile-long freight trains with tank cars with sweet, delicious water for all those poor, thirsty, suffering souls in Las Vegas.

That happens when a government works for the people. Nonetheless, the prophecies in Revelation 8 will begin to occur soon, and the suffering will last a decade or longer. And now it is about percentages of those who survive all the way through because the days of denial will be over with the appearance of a Great Star.

Blue Kachina

In Revelation 8:7, Earth has entered the leading edge of the Nemesis Cloud, with all its iron oxide and debris. With Revelation 8:10, Earth will be entirely inside the Nemesis Cloud and remain there for years.

Nemesis is the Great Star of Revelation 8:10 and the Blue Kachina and Red Kachina of Hopi prophecy. When people see it as described by John, the wise will be prepared. Sadly, the only hope for the unprepared is that fate is kind.

So, let's take a closer look at these scriptures.

> **YOUNG'S LITERAL TRANSLATION 1898**
> Revelation 8
>
> **10** And the third messenger did sound, and there **fell** out of the heaven a great star, burning as a lamp, and it did fall upon the third of the rivers, and upon the **fountains of waters,**
>
> **11** and the name of the star is called **Wormwood**, and the third of the waters doth become **Wormwood**, and many of the men did die of the waters, because they were made **bitter**.

What John is describing here is scientifically factual and also corroborates the Hopi Blue Kachina prophecy for this object. Here is why.

When Revelation 8:10 occurs, the Planet X System will be directly above Earth's orbit, and here is the point where the Blue Kachina turns into the Red Kachina.

Many have always assumed that the Hopi prophecy describes two objects, but it actually describes one object in two different segments of its orbit. After Nemesis, the Great Star reaches perihelion, its closest point to the sun; it will begin arcing downwards from overhead.

From its perihelion point to when it is directly above Earth's orbit, Nemesis the Great Star will appear as the Blue Kachina. After it passes over our orbit and until it disappears in the Southern skies, it will be the Red Kachina.

This is because its trajectory curves down more sharply after it passes over our heads as it aims to pass between the orbits of Mars and Jupiter back into the Southern skies.

How does this work? It's called the Doppler effect. When an object comes at you, it compresses the light waves with a resulting blueshift. Hence, Nemesis will likely be beautiful because it will benefit from the blueshift effect and the sun's light.

Then beauty will bring the beast, and once Nemesis the Great Star passes over our orbit, the blue shift effect will be replaced by the redshift effect as the light waves decompress. Then it will become a fearsome sight to behold, for with the coming of the Red Kachina comes the Great Winnowing.

The Great Winnowing

I use the term "backside" to describe the years after when we will see blue skies and the taste of sweet waters once again, and I am not alone. Life will continue, but every generation that survives this, like the ancients, will know the horror of the Destroyer and that it will return once again, as it has in the past.

When Revelation 8:10 begins, humanity will start a process of natural selection the ancients called "The Great Winnowing." As the term implies, the chaff is separated from the wheat during the Days of Doom.

My dear Riselings, once you behold the Red Kachina Nemesis Great Star, know the Days of Doom and the Great Winnowing will be upon humanity.

> **The Kolbrin Bible: 21st Century Master Edition**
> Book of Manuscripts
>
> MAN:3:5 The Heavens will burn brightly and redly; there will be a copper hue over the face of the land, 'followed by a day of darkness. A new moon will appear and break up and fall.
>
> MAN:3:6 The people will scatter in madness. They will hear the trumpet and battlecry of the Destroyer and **will seek refuge within dens in the Earth**. Terror will eat away their hearts, and their courage will flow from them like water from a broken pitcher. They will be eaten up in the flames of wrath and consumed by **the breath of the Destroyer**.
>
> MAN:3:7 Thus it was in the Days of Heavenly Wrath, which have gone, and thus it will be in the **Days of Doom** when it comes again.

MAN:3:11 Great God of All Ages, alike to all, who sets the trials of man, be merciful to our children in the **Days of Doom**. Man must suffer to be great, but hasten not his progress unduly. In the **great winnowing**, be not too harsh on the lesser ones among men. Even the son of a thief has become your scribe.

The events prophesied in Revelation 8:7 will affect some parts of the world while others remain unaffected. Some will see it as a fulfilled harbinger that precedes a decade or more of suffering and will begin organizing permanent underground survival communities.

After the Great Mountain impact event of Revelation 8:8, there will be a series of regional disasters, after which support for positive action will galvanize the survivors, primarily in the affected regions.

Those unaffected will assume the danger has passed and resume life as before. This assumption will be their undoing because Revelation 8:10-11 will be a slow grinding global hell for everyone living above ground, and only after enough have died will there come the worst of it.

Countless millions will lose the will to live and perish due to hopeless resignation, but what about you, my dear Riselings, and your precious families? What will be your destiny? Let me answer with my favorite passage from *The Kolbrin Bible*.

The Kolbrin Bible: 21st Century Master Edition
Book of Manuscripts

MAN:3:10 In those days, men will have the Great Book before them; wisdom will be revealed; the few will be gathered for the stand; it is the hour of trial. The dauntless ones will survive; **the stouthearted will not go down to destruction**.

This work is depressing but necessary, and this passage has always given me the strength to carry on. These eight words have always comforted my soul.

> The stouthearted will not go down to destruction. *This is the way.*

Resolve to be stouthearted, my dear Riselings, and you will find safe ways to navigate the troubled waters of the Revelation River.

Teaching Tools

When I began my field research for my book, *Win-Win Survival Handbook: All-Hazards Safety and Future Space Colonization,* the goal was to create an all-hazards community, as in earthquakes, floods, impact events, bombs, and radiation.

These communities will operate underground farms that produce no less than ten times the community's needs. Ten times need is a widely accepted number for farms to become profitable.

For the Win-Win designs in my book, I decided to use the Planet Mars as the benchmark, with the following qualifier. Earth-based Win-Win communities will be pioneers.

After Win-Win construction and design techniques prove themselves during the tribulation, we'll know how to pioneer space because our survivors will survive, thrive, and prosper.

Therefore, the goal is to develop solutions for Mars-based Win-Win communities, where there will be a fifteen percent or less difference in technology between the two planets. Hence, there is a chapter aptly titled "Feeding 1,000 Martians."

Granted, Mars is a hostile environment, to say the least, but it shares three things in common with Earth: water, soil, and basalt rock.

Plenty of water and soil in the northern regions of Mars offer the necessary elements for underground farming on Mars, save for one minor problem. The Martian soil has a high salt content, making it difficult to grow plants. However, scientists found one plant that thrives in such soil and will cleanse it through uptake.

Elsewhere on Mars are many basalt rock flows. This igneous fire rock comes from a planet's core and has all the minerals necessary for life. For farming, it can be ground finely and used as a potent fertilizer.

Also, basalt can be mined and processed into reinforcement for construction. How does basalt compare to steel for reinforcement?

A structure made with steel reinforcement will last 100 years, whereas one made with basalt reinforcement will last 1,000 years and be more durable.

Of course, there is the issue of water. While there is a lot of it in the polar regions, it must be treated as a scarce resource, and here is where the Win-Win communities on Earth and Mars will have a considerable advantage. They will be using aquaponics to grow crops below ground without interruption, and here is the best part.

A Win-Win aquaponics underground farm will use one-tenth of the water needed to grow plants raised in soil above ground. Plus, the plants will grow 25% faster, and crop yields will be 25% greater than conventional above-ground traditional farming yields.

With that, the cinema teaching tool for this chapter is The Martian (2015). It's about an astronaut who survives on Mars by growing potatoes and being given a literary license. It's a great movie about raising potatoes on Mars, and it helped inspire some of my thinking.

As you watch this movie, be mindful of three things:

- How the astronaut works the problems.
- See Mars as the ultimate acid test environment for a Win-Win on Earth.
- Imagine yourself living on Mars as a terraformer.

The bottom line is that if you can make a Win-Win work on Earth, it will work elsewhere in the galaxy.

My dear Riselings here is where you can be a true light of hope during a dreadful time. Assuming you're in a Win-Win while the world above is howling with torment and pain, the ground trembles beneath everyone's feet, and young children are frightened.

This is the time to calm their fears. You gather them together and calmly reassure them, "Do not worry. We are space pioneers and built this place to take much worse elsewhere in the galaxy. Remember how safe you are now because someday, you or perhaps your children will go to the stars and build places like this. So, let us join hands like brave pioneers and sing Old MacDonald Had a Farm." Remember:

Life is what you make of it. *This is the way.*

8

Revelation 8:12 – Pole Shift

The days of darkness come with the Fourth Angel, making this the pole-shift harbinger event. When Nibiru transits between Venus and Earth, it will create an eclipse prophesied in Revelation 8:12 and referred to as "The Days of Darkness."

The Days of Darkness is the third event in a related series of events leading up to the eventual pole shift event. The five events are:

1. **Lithosphere Lock:** Nemesis gains a gravitational foothold on Earth. It is a final warning.

2. **Solar Sprite - Kill Shot:** Ed Dames predicts a devastating solar sprite strike on Earth called the "Kill Shot."

3. **Nibiru Eclipse:** Called the "Days of Darkness" in Revelation 8:12, the pole shift sequence starts here.

4. **Ferra Impacts Venus:** Nibiru's moon, Ferrada, will strike the south-polar region of Venus with severe consequences for Earth.

5. **Pole Shift:** What we'll see and experience as the shift affects the globe.

Please note the term pole shift refers to three different types:

- **Magnetic:** Earth's magnetic poles reverse, and South becomes North and visa versa.
- **Crustal:** This is the most common use. Earth's lithosphere is its rigid, outermost rocky shell. Pulled by the gravitational forces of the Planet X System, Earth's outer shell will move relative to the core.
- **Axial:** The Earth is currently tilted 23.5° from the plane of its orbit. Any change will have a profound impact on the weather.

Of the three, the axial shift concerns me the most, as you learn below, which is not to downplay the other two.

When the Planet X System and its sun, Nemesis, achieve lithosphere lock on Earth, the jig is up if you're smart enough to notice.

Lithosphere Lock

During the Winter Solstice of 2026/2027, Earth will be at its close approach with Nemesis as the trajectory of Planet Nibiru, the outermost major planet of the Planet X System, will begin its transit between the orbits of Earth and Venus.

At this time, Nemesis will achieve a lithosphere lock on Earth, and this precursor will confirm that Earth is on the pole shift timeline.

Expect a sudden rise in earthquakes and volcanic eruptions during this time, which will already be excessive.

Solar Sprite - Killshot

Major Edward A. Dames, United States Army (ret.), is a remote viewing teacher and the creator of technical remote viewing. In 2004, Ed released a video predicting a devastating hit on Earth.

He calls it the "Killshot," and his mission is to help people use the technique of Remote Viewing to find their place of safety.

According to his 2004 video, Ed tells us the event will happen when a massive planet, five to seven times the size of Earth, passes between Earth and Venus.

What he describes is actually a solar sprite, or what is also known as cosmic lighting. This is a very concerning solar phenomenon, and as we discussed earlier, our sun will begin emitting solar sprites sometime in the spring/summer of 2024.

These solar sprites cause the "hail and fire, mingled with blood," events prophesized in Revelation 8:7.

What kind of damage can a solar sprite do to a planet?

Consider Valles Marineris on Planet Mars. Many times larger than the Grand Canyon, it is a system of canyons that spans 2,500 miles and is six miles deep in parts.

While scientists tell us that the Grand Canyon was created by water erosion, that explanation does not work for Valles Marineris. What does is a solar sprite.

When this happens, pray you are not on the daylight side of the planet when the "Kill Shot" solar sprite strikes. Next will be as bad, but in a different way.

Nibiru Eclipse

In the Spring of 2027 will come the "Days of Darkness" prophesized in Revelation 8:12, which John describes in this passage with brilliant clarity.

We will see the Planet Nibiru transiting between Earth and Venus and the sun's eclipses. Fortunately, we have three different sources to help us understand this event.

Revelation 8:12

John describes the beginning of the Days of Darkness, which, from our perspective on Earth, is when Nibiru begins to pass in front of the sun. This is when the obscuration starts to occur, creating a temporary dimming of the sunlight before cutting it off. Then, the process reverses.

When you read the prophecy, remember this is the onset of the event.

Young's Literal Translation 1898
Exodus 8

> 12 And the fourth messenger did sound, and smitten was the **third of the sun**, and the **third of the moon**, and the **third of the stars**, that darkened may be the third of them, and that the day may not shine — the third of it, and the night in like manner.

To put this perspective, a total solar eclipse of Earth's moon can last anywhere from 10 seconds to about 7.5 minutes.

However, an eclipse of a planet that is between five to seven times the size of Earth will require days, which is what *The Kolbrin Bible* maintains.

The Kolbrin Bible

There will be consequences to having a planet five to seven times larger than our own, passing within thirty to forty million miles of Earth. It has happened during previous flybys as described in *The Kolbrin Bible*.

> **The Kolbrin Bible: 21st Century Master Edition**
> Book of Manuscripts
>
> MAN:6:22 **There were nine days of darkness and upheaval**, while a tempest raged such as never had been known before. When it passed away, brother buried brother throughout the land. Men rose up against those in authority and fled from the cities to dwell in tents in the outlands.

Remember, this is how it happened many thousands of years ago, so it is logical to wonder what we will see during this tribulation event.

Carlos

As mentioned, I only named the Guide Carlos when I published this book. He is Chilean Astronomer Carlos Muñoz Ferrada, who first announced what we call Nemesis and Nibiru in 1940.

In this reading, Carlos tells us precisely what Revelation 8:12 will bring. The news is terrible, but his love for humanity is profoundly inspiring.

Being In It for the Species: The Universe Speaks
When the Earth Cries, So Shall We
Authored Channeling with Carlos

In the fullness of time one event will transcend the sands of time to be forever remembered by your species. This will be remembered as the days of darkness when the Anunnaki home world of Nibiru transformed your skies into an ink-stained night such as you have never known before.

Its coming will blot out the sun so effectively that all those who dwell on the surface of Earth will mourn the death of sunlight in a way that will be remembered and ceremonies and gatherings for generations to come. A time when fate embraces each soul on the planet in a way so profound that none can evade it.

This will be a time when many whose lives are plagued with fear and emotions of self-interest will perish in vast numbers. Going suddenly - they will fall to the Earth, as rags on the tattered shells of exhausted dolls. Falling where they stand, their hearts will give way as their bodies expire like the snuffing of a candle's flame.

The darkness of Nibiru will creep into view like an ominous ooze in the celestial night. Light from the sun will bleed away in retreat as the two planets form a perfect alignment with your sun, as its twin steals in behind you - slightly to the left and above the equator of your sun.

Earth will wail with trumpet cries that will torment the souls and steal sleep from even the most innocent of babes. The invisible shield that protects your world from the lurking radiation enveloping it will collapse inward upon itself, measure by measure, day by day. Some days are faster and others are reluctant pauses but in the scheme of things, it is an irreversible process exposing all manner of life upon the surface of your planet to the predation of nuclear particles seeking ground from the stillness of space.

Then will come sensations such as few generations in the history of your species have known before. A reversal of the Earth's rotation upon its own axis that begins with a halting gradual purpose. Mountains will grumble with discomfort and seas will boil with displeasure for this change in direction will subvert the very organization of the planet itself.

That which pressed in one direction now is pressed from another. That which was submerged beneath columns of water thrusts upwards through these waters to embrace an atmosphere, now electrically charged and violent in ways that few can remember or imagine.

Lightning will rise up from the Earth, spread through the atmosphere and stinging all those beneath it with random horrific strikes. The sounds and waves of radiation pelting the Earth will fall upon those who survived the past. Now huddled underground, their only hope is to live to see the return of a tranquil world no matter which shape or form it pleases - and to see that this cosmic madness has run its course - after which those who survive can rebuild.

When the ominous body of this alien world slips past the face of the sun, light will slowly return, as will hope. The dead, too numerous to count will rot for the most part like fish thrown up upon the shore by a great storm.

This event will be devastating for all those trying to survive on the surface of the planet, and it will come with a terrible loss of life. Yet, even worse is to come.

Ferrada Impacts Venus

After the Days of Darkness occurs in the Spring of 2027, we will have approximately two years to prepare before the final stage of the pole shift begins with a collision between Ferrada, the moon of Nibiru makes a glancing blow on the South Polar region of Venus.

We worked with many Guides in developing this book, and Adriana corroborated the prediction by Carlos with other Guides, and here it is.

> **Being In It for the Species: The Universe Speaks**
> As Venus Goes, So Goes the Earth
> Technical Readings with Adriana
>
> During her transit of the Sun, Venus receives a glancing impact from Ferrada in the extreme southern hemisphere. Venus's orbit will be perturbed as a result of this impact. It will become elongated with a more inclined orientation to the ecliptic.
>
> Not only does the Ferrada impact destabilize the rotational spin of Venus, it also triggers solar sprites as a result, some of which will be Earth-directed. Also, some impact debris will strike the Earth.

After the Ferrada impact, the lithosphere lock occurs when the Earth's magnetosphere is weakest. At this time, three objects of the Planet X System will align in a triangle formation. The subsequent result is a lock on Earth's lithosphere resulting in crustal displacements that will be felt by every soul on the planet.

A quick note on Adriana. As explained previously, when I was doing the channeling research for *Being In It for the Species*, fellow researcher and retired systems analyst William and I hopped back and forth on the timeline so much that halfway into the work, we lost our bearings.

This forced us to ask each other, "What do we tell Adriana?" the third team member. Adriana is one of the most talented, if not the most talented, psychics I've ever worked with.

After much discussion, we decided, "Never mind, she's on a roll." Truth be known, Adriana knew where she was going better than we did, and when push comes to shove, guys typically do not like to admit that.

Pole Shift

Revelation 8 clearly describes the event that launches the pole shift sequence of events. That is the Hebrew account, and the ancient Egyptians go beyond that with a more detailed prophecy of the coming pole shift.

> **The Kolbrin Bible: 21st Century Master Edition**
> Book of Manuscripts
>
> MAN:4:1 O Sentinels of the Universe who watch for the Destroyer, how long will your enduring vigil last? O mortal men who wait without understanding, where will you hide yourselves in the Dread **Days of Doom**, when the Heavens shall be torn apart and the skies rent in twain, in the days when children will turn grey-headed?
>
> MAN:4:2 This is the thing, which will be seen, this is the terror your eyes will behold, this is the form of destruction that will rush upon you: **There will be the great body of fire, the glowing head with many mouths and eyes ever changing**. Terrible teeth will be seen in formless mouths, and a fearful dark belly will glow redly from fires inside. Even the most stouthearted man will tremble, and his bowels will be loosened, for this is not a thing understandable to men.

MAN:4:3 It will be a vast sky-spanning form enwrapping Earth, burning with many hues within wide open mouths. These will descend to sweep across the face of the land, engulfing all in the yawning jaws. The greatest warriors will charge against it in vain. The fangs will fall out, and lo, they are terror-inspiring things of cold hardened water. **Great boulders will be hurled down upon men, crushing them into red powder.**

MAN:4:4 **As the great salt waters rise up in its train and roaring torrents pour towards the land, even the heroes among mortal men will be overcome with madness.** As moths fly swiftly to their doom in the burning flame, so will these men rush to their own destruction. **The flames going before will devour all the works of men, the waters following will sweep away whatever remains.** The dew of death will fall softly, as a grey carpet over the cleared land. Men will cry out in their madness, O whatever Being there is, save us from this tall form of terror, save us from the grey dew of death.

The message here is, if you're still trying to survive on the planet's surface, here is where your timeline ends, so let's take a closer look at how.

Pole Shift Effects

When we did our readings with Adriana, William and I asked a series of technical questions about the event, and here are the results:

Being In It for the Species: The Universe Speaks
Reading 06 with Adriana

Adriana and Marshall with live mics. William with muted mic. The following events may be anticipated on the current timeline.

Marshall asked the Guides detailed questions about the Three days of darkness [pole shift event]:

- We will feel the Magnetosphere Collapse.

- Lightning storms will blanket the Earth.

- Pulsing waves of static electricity will fill the atmosphere.

- The sensation of gravity will diminish.

- Earth's moon is not perturbed in its orbit during the three days of darkness. However, it is tilted on its axis. Our view of the moon will remain the same after the three days of darkness.

- Pole shift aftershocks will take two years to subside.

Please note that while the aftershocks will end sometime in 2032, post-flyby impact events will continue until 2036.

This raises a question. Depending on where you live on Earth, how will you fare?

Earth Post-Shift

During the pole shift event, another period of darkness will be shorter than the previous one. Interestingly, Ed Dames and I independently determined that after the shift, the USA will be approximately 12 degrees closer to the equator.

An excellent example of this degree of change would be the San Francisco area. It will look similar to Hilo, Hawaii, assuming it is still there. The following predictions are for weather-related hazards.

> **Being In It for the Species: The Universe Speaks**
> Reading 09 with Adriana
>
> Adriana and Marshall with live mics. William with muted mic. The following events may be anticipated on the current timeline.
>
> - Weather changes as a result of the three days of darkness and the Pole Shift.
>
>   o 30 to 50 degrees north: The area will see some nuclear winter and extreme hot weather pockets (high weather death rate).
>
>   o 10 to 30 degrees north: This region will have a mix of hot weather and nuclear winter (moderately survivable region for weather deaths).
>
>   o 10 degrees north to 10 degrees south: This equatorial region will see predominately Nuclear winter weather. (extreme weather death zone).
>
>   o 10 to 30 degrees south: This region south of the equator will see pockets of hotter weather (most extreme weather death zone).

- 30 to 50 degrees south: The area will have pockets of colder weather (moderate to high weather death rate).

- South Africa becomes the new South Pole.

After the pole shift, Earth will pass through the debris trail of the Planet X System for several years.

During this time, Earth will be settling down, and this is when we will assess the outcomes and see how old lands sank beneath the waves as new ones rose.

Monsoon-like rains will occur across the globe to cleanse the air and surface water. They will also wash the salts away from newly risen land, leaving soil that will be wonderfully fertile. There will be blue skies and sweet waters again.

Teaching Tools

Two things that have never mixed well are religion and science. On the other hand, a wise Riseling will know that spirituality and science do mix well. Very well.

Imagine you hold in your hands a fine pair of binoculars. One barrel is labeled science, and the other is called spirituality.

You see the one when you look through one and not the other. However, when you look with both eyes, what you see is three-dimensional with ample depth and detail. You see more.

When you seek truth, a holistic view is best. In essence, it is to understand, in theory, the many excellent natural systems of Creation through science while simultaneously being in spiritual awe of it.

With this in mind, the cinema teaching tool for this chapter is Interstellar (2014). Like 2001, it will be remembered as a classic, and it offers three learning lessons:

- **Cooper and his daughter Murph:** Watch their relationship ebb and flow as a great example of shawheylu, the eternal bond, which we will discuss later.

- **Cooper and Brand:** Regarding our holistic binoculars, Cooper represents science and logic. Brand, on the other hand, represents spirituality and love. What is beautiful about it is how they make it work.

- **Communication:** Cooper uses Morse Code and binary code in the movie to send messages to Murph. It works because each understands both forms of communication. As you watch this aspect of the film, imagine that Murphy did not know either. What would have been the consequence for Earth?

My survival trilogy has over 1,000 pages of knowledge; the first book was *Radio Free Earth: The Complete Beginner's Guide to Survival Communications*. Why?

If you cannot communicate, you cannot cooperate. *This is the way.*

9

Prophecy Timeline

Up to now, my dear Riselings, you've been paddling in white waters and no doubt wondering how, in all that turbulent awfulness, one can find the time to look for chutes and oxbows to bypass the worst parts of the Revelation River.

That's a valid point and entirely appropriate because, in this chapter, it will be a staccato of heavy punches by year and season. For this reason, we'll use our Indigo time pilot skills to see a more constructive vision of the future and how to get there.

My dear Riselings, you and your families are precious for the future of humanity, and sadly, I must tell you that I possess something you hold in small measure. Time.

Here is where I need to share my mission. I am in it for the species, and you, dear Rieslings, are the most precious generation to walk the Earth since Adam and Eve.

You have a mission to be a light of hope for others, and the choices you make in this life will echo throughout eternity. Remember:

> All who want to evolve must stay faithful to a life mission. This is the way.

Whatever your mission calling is, embrace it, and in times of crisis, your countenance and knowledge will inspire others.

Some may wonder if I see myself as a prophet of sorts. Oh, my no. As I said before, the hours are brutal; forget the pay, and the benefit plan is a lifetime supply of dental floss.

Instead, I'm one of God's technical writers, and many of us are out there, and we help each other when we can.

For example, two such technical writers for God are Mathew Stein and Susan Shumsky. Mathew wrote *When Technology Fails: A Manual for Self-Reliance, Sustainability, and Surviving the Long Emergency*. Everyone should have a copy on hand.

Susan spent 20 years living and studying with a world-famous Maharishi, and as an Indigo Elder, I like her books, especially *How to Hear the Voice of God*.

Mathew and Susan have in common that, like me, they are published. However, we're not the only kind of technical writers for God, and what is interesting is that one man who never published a book was God's most impressive technical writer. He was David South, the founder of Monolithic Domes in Italy, Texas.

When I explained that I was developing the Win-Win concept for underground intentional survival communities using his concrete dome technology, he asked me if I wanted to put a machine gun on the top of the dome. He added that he flatly refused the business when asked to build one.

I told him I was uninterested in machine guns because, in a Win-Win community, everyone gets a good deal and their fair share. A more legal description of a Win-Win is a church that farms and teaches farming, and the Win-Win motto is:

> Prepare for cooperation – not confrontation. *This is the way.*

Dave really liked that, and we became friends with a shared vision of helping the world's good people survive the tribulation. When I visited him in Texas, he toured me through his facilities and explained things with great care, and to my delight, he had his aquaponics engineer drive in to meet me.

I worked with Dave on three critical areas. Overcover, drainage, and how to build and operate commercial aquaponics systems with multiple aquaculture and hydroponics domes for year-round continuous harvesting.

A commercial developer would have to pay handsomely for such technical knowledge, but David gifted it to me as one technical writer for God to another. It was his gift that made the impossible possible, and this was the half of it.

Over the years, David posted hundreds of pages of information, illustrations, drawings, videos, and tools about his dome technology. It took me months to process and reverse-engineer his designs, but it was all there, and it clicked.

The point here, my dear Riselings. Generations before you have awaited your arrival and have labored with great love to help you as their calling guided them. You are not alone. You never were alone. You never will be alone, and you are loved. Know it.

Now, it's time to travel the Revelation River again and be prepared for white water.

Always be mindful of prophecy, but never live in expectation of it. *This is the way.*

NOTE: The seasons given below are for the Northern Hemisphere.

2024 – Revelation 8:7

The most fitting description for what is to come in 2024 is "The Great Awakening." Humanity is about to learn that much of what it knows is wrong, and that's not even the half of it.

The hope for this year is that the White Hat good guys can at least stop the Black Hat monsters from killing us and bleeding us dry so we can collectively catch our breath and get on with the business of survival.

If the White Hats can give us just that, it's enormous. Gargantuan. We're talking King Kong versus Godzilla big! Anything else they do for us will be gravy. Pure gravy.

It's happening, folks, and it will be over when it is over, and the final score will be God 1 – Satan 0, but we'll have to fight our way to the goalpost, yard by yard, and season by season, so let's get into it.

Midwinter

Our first prophecy for 2024 comes from the Guide Carlos from *Being In It for the Species: The Universe Speaks*.

There will be a massive volcanic eruption in the Western Pacific. The ash will disrupt regional air travel and spread across the Northern Hemisphere, with possible cooling effects.

Sadly, the eruption will be ignored by many, and most will not see the event's significance. It will be just another eruption for most, but it will not be so for you, dear Riselings, because you are in awareness.

Late Winter

The world will be shocked by an Alien False flag invasion after the violent machinations of the Monsters fail to create a third world war. Having lost the ability to control the narrative, the evil intentions of the monsters are transparent. Consequently, their final desperate act will be to create a new false flag narrative to regain control. It, too, will fail.

Like the proverbial boy who shouts wolf, the world's people will be wise to their ways, though it will be painful. It will undoubtedly include Directed Energy Weapons (DEW) attacks.

The first known DEW attack occurred on November 8, 2018, when Paradise, CA, was devastated by the Camp Fire. Trees burned from the inside out, and cars were found with holes burned through the engine blocks.

Most of the people living in this hill country region of Northern California knew it was DEW attacks despite the oppressive media coverup. It was created to force the area's residents out, and FEMA would not let the residents return to their properties and rebuild.

Another DEW attack to force a population to leave an area was on November 18, 2023, in Lahaina, Maui. Thousands were burned to death by this terrible weapon and, like Paradise, CA, another oppressive media coverup.

However, this will also be when we see an increase in genuine reports of travelers from other worlds. Some will welcome this and new friends from afar. Others will not because they want humanity to remain shackled as a slave race. There will be a lot of discussion, but what most will never suspect is that an actual alien invasion will happen in 2025.

Spring

At this time, Nemesis will be at perihelion, which will place it far enough away from the sun from our perspective to become a regular fixture in our sky.

In astronomy, the term perihelion describes the point in the orbit of Nemesis where it is closest to the sun. Conversely, aphelion represents the furthest point. When Nemesis is at perihelion, Earth will be in Capricorn, and Nemesis will appear in Taurus above the ecliptic near the Pleiades, also known as the Seven Sisters and Messier 45.

The mainstream media may dub it a comet. It is not.

Nemesis is a brown dwarf star several times the size of Jupiter. It has a fast, comet-like clockwise orbit steeply inclined to the ecliptic by roughly 30°.

The mainstream media may dub it Planet Nine. It is not.

Planet Nine is a lie! It is sick, twisted government propaganda. Who did it?

As part of a Cabal suppression of science, Michael Brown did the alleged science, and Sarah Kaplan of The Washington Post did the baseless character assassination.

What triggered the coverup was a discovery by ALMA astronomers. On December 10, 2015, they published two Planet X scientific abstracts in which they report initial observations of two substantial objects at the edge of our solar system.

They described one as a possible dead Brown Dwarf star and the other as a giant rocky planet several times the size of the Earth in the Kuiper Belt, far beyond the orbit of Neptune. Do not be fooled by the Planet Nine narrative.

There will be a lot of punditry and speculation on this. You can easily prepare yourself for this with my video, *Planet X 101: Who, What, When, Where, Why and How*.

Of more significant concern is that this is when solar sprites, or what is also called cosmic lightning, will begin and continue until 2032.

Fall

This is when the micrometeorite showers described in Revelation 8:7 begin. We will see micrometeorite showers with patches of iron dust for two to three months. The solar sprites that started in the spring will be the fundamental cause.

These micrometeorite showers will happen randomly worldwide. Their onset will be sudden, and they will dissipate quickly.

This is the warning harbinger for the deep-impact event. Riseling families, this benign harbinger is for you. Use this time to gain knowledge and build alliances.

More people will come into awareness now, but not a majority. Despite all the clear signs, we are creatures of habit. Remember:

> Never underestimate the power of human denial. *This is the way.*

This will be an excellent time to build alliances with critical and spiritual thinkers willing to take an objective view. Tell them to enjoy the 2024 holiday season, for it will have to last for many years.

2025 – Women and Gold

Late-Winter

The "Great Mountain" deep impact event will occur as prophesized in Revelation 8:8-9. It will not be an act of God. It will be a preemptive act of war by an alien race called the Anunnaki.

The Anunnaki live on Nibiru, and this "Great Mountain" attack is to soften the target for women and gold. It will be a guided asteroid with a precise military target.

It is aimed at a nexus point in the eastern Atlantic where the subsea Internet fiber cables between America and Europe pass together.

The impact will trigger eruptions and tsunamis that will lay waste on the shores of many nations bordering this great ocean. The nations of NATO will be devastated, although Russia will fare much better.

Summer

The Anunnaki invasion described in Revelation 9:1-5 occurs, and when their ships appear in the sky, they will be frighteningly real, and so will their intentions. They will come from Nibiru to take a bounty of gold and young women because they view us as their rightful property.

They'll need our gold to repair the atmosphere of their home world, for these flybys are challenging for their atmosphere. With that in hand, they will go for our women.

Speaking for myself, when that day comes, we men of the Earth rise up for our women and tell them something such as: "OK, pilgrim, there's a new sheriff in town, and you can trade for gold, but touch our women, and we'll burn you out of the sky. How many tons of gold do you need, and what have you got to trade for it?"

Dear reader, forgive my digression; I had to do that. If you wish, please think of it as an old curmudgeon tilting at a windmill.

Onward. In my 10-part video series, *Ground Zero and the Obliteration of NATO*, I describe the Anunnaki "Great Mountain" attack and subsequent disasters in detail.

Early Fall

In Revelation 9, the invaders are given five months, and their invasion ends. The science is more straightforward. The invasion fleet must return to Nibiru before Earth becomes engulfed in the Nemesis Cloud.

Preferring young women of Nordic and Ashkenazi descent, they will be used as slave mother surrogates and eventually returned, most with their memories wiped,

2026 – Revelation 8:10-11

Mid-Winter

The word "Wormwood" from Revelation 8:10-11 has long been associated with Planet X or Nibiru.

At this time, Nemesis is arcing South when Earth enters the iron dust of the Nemesis Cloud surrounding the Nemesis Constellation, much like the Oort Cloud surrounding our system.

We will smell the iron dust in the air for years, making surface waters bitter. This will be the beginning of the Great Winnowing.

Those vaccinated will suffer terribly because the iron dust from the Nemesis Cloud will combine with Earth's volcanic ash to stress their mRNA-impaired immune systems.

At this time, we will begin to see profound biosphere impacts, including widespread defoliation and the collapse of fisheries. The boils described in Exodus will revisit the world, and here is something you must remember, Riselings, for when it gets worse.

If you do not have water to wash the ash and dust from your skin, dig down one foot for fresh clay or soil and use that. Otherwise, you will develop painful and debilitating skin ulcers that will be difficult to treat.

2027 – Revelation 8:12

Mid-Winter

The ecliptic is the plane of our solar system. Imagine you have a dot in the middle of the sun, and you then expand that outward as a circle to the twelve signs of the Zodiac. This is the ecliptic, separating the Northern Skies from the Southern skies.

At this time, Nemesis will begin its transit through the ecliptic into the Southern Skies and as it gravitationally grapples with Earth, to achieve a lithosphere lock.

As the lock intensifies, it will trigger earthquakes and eruptions, and a new troubling pattern will be felt during the winter months through to the actual pole shift in 2030. It will be sporadic lurches, as though the planet seems to hesitate mid-air for a fraction of time.

Interestingly, Nemesis completed its transit from the Southern Skies across the ecliptic and into the Northern Skies on July 3, 2020, as President Trump thrilled the crowd with a Fourth of July speech and firework event at Mt. Rushmore in South Dakota.

Over the years, I've done more Planet X observation videos and image analysis than anyone else in the field, and I've seen it all. Then, while President Trump was giving his speech, a nameless White Hat in the government leaked a fantastic image of Nemesis captured by one of our solar observatories.

When I saw it, my draw dropped. It was the money shot I was always looking for, and oddly, few but myself could understand that. As one Indigo to another, does it get better? No, but it can get worse if you choose to go along to get along. Remember:

There is always room at the table for a majority of one. This is the way.

My dear Riselings, you are different; you know it, so there it is. Dare to be you, and you might surprise yourself because what comes next will be a collective gut punch for humanity.

Early Summer

This is when the days of darkness prophecy of Revelation 8:12 comes to pass with the eclipse of Nibiru as it crosses our skies between the orbits of Earth and Venus. It will be a deadly and terrifying event, and then things will mostly quiet down for nearly a year.

Consequently, the will to act for many will become diluted with conjecture as "experts" assure that danger is still years ahead, if at all—and woe to those who believe them.

2028 – Killshot Event

Late Spring

The Killshot event predicted by Ed Dames will occur. It will be a massive solar sprite, and it will cause a tremendous amount of damage wherever it hits. If you are on the daylight side of Earth and in the strike zone, your timeline ends here.

Elsewhere, this will combine with the previous disasters to create a nuclear winter environment for those surviving in place above ground.

Even though the solar sprites begin in 2024 and cause Revelation 8:7, they will primarily go unnoticed until this event. This will not be the first unforeseen event.

2029 – Final Warning

Early-Summer

The Nibiru is the third major planet from Nemesis in the Planet X System, and it has a moon, Ferrada. Note that when you hear Arboda and Helion, these are the other two major planets of that mini-constellation, as they are called in that system.

Helion is a bright gas giant with a moon, and Arboda is a rocky planet larger than Earth and inhabited. Nibiru is about five to seven times the size of Earth and has a moon named Ferrada. (Note: I named this moon to honor Carlos.)

There will be an impact between Ferrada and the Southern Polar region of Venus when Nibiru is below the ecliptic and Nemesis is on the ecliptic. The collision will send debris our way, and numerous deadly impact events will occur.

The Lithosphere lock is nearing critical mass as forces build towards the coming pole shift. Those still hoping to survive in place above ground will not.

2030 – Pole Shift

Summer

The Anunnaki will return the women abducted as surrogate slave mothers to Europe. For most, their memories will be wiped, but many of these unfortunate women will remember and suffer it. What we will learn from them is that the women underwent physical procedures to sterilize them by harvesting the eggs in their ovaries for slave breeding.

They will return childless and profoundly and spiritually broken, so great care and compassion will be necessary for those who, with the knowledge of what has been done to them.

Among these women, courage and love will compel some to speak to all the people of Earth and share the bitter memories of their experiences. The shame will be felt by all those who believe their recollections.

In this way, these women will become lights of hope and inspire humanity to unite in a universal struggle to unshackle our species from alien slavers.

This is when humanity will have to choose. Will we set our differences aside and unite, or will we let our differences lead us back into the shackles of slavery? Many races in Creation have come to such a point and failed.

We will not.

We do not need the best technology, the best plans, or the best generals to win. All we must do to break the shackles of slavery is to always reach for our freedom, no matter the cost and no matter how many incarnations. Remember:

> Make an eternal commitment to always reach for freedom, and it shall be yours.
> *This is the way.*

Regrettably, there will be precious little time to attend to these unfortunate women because the pole shift will soon happen.

Late Fall

The pole shift cannot begin until the entire Nemesis Constellation, including major planets, is below the ecliptic in Ophiuchus between the asteroid belt and the orbit of Jupiter.

This will be the deadliest of all the tribulation events. The collective gravitational forces of the major bodies in the Planet X System will be immense.

This is when the lithosphere lock achieves critical mass, and the pole shift starts; Earth's rotation upon its axis will begin to slow with a halting, gradual purpose until it stops, after which the Earth will slowly start to rotate again, but in the opposite direction.

This is when the central event of The Great Winnowing occurs. As the Earth slows to a stop, magnetic fields across the planet will run riot, which will be so disorienting it will bring all to an existential survival crisis.

At this point, what you believe or what is in your kit is irrelevant. Survival will be about what is in your heart, meaning the difference between life and death.

During this time, whatever is in your heart will be amplified a hundredfold. If you have love, it will be amplified, and all good people who survive this event will do so as flame-on, fully mature Indigos or Crystals.

Will sitting in a pew and thumbing beads be effective. Hard to say.

Instead, imagine a kindly grandmother gathering a group of orphans about her and telling them how much she loves them and holding hands; they pray with faith and love because she is a light of hope for others.

For those who love Jesus, He will be on deck for this event, so feel the love and share it every minute. You'll get through it, and so will those who sincerely pray with you. Remember this one thing about love.

Love is a desire that can transcend time, space, and adversity, but not doubt. *This is the way.*

If your love is weakened by doubt, that could inadvertently lead you to fear, and things will not end well for you, so be forewarned.

For those with fear in their hearts, that too will be amplified, and when the unnatural forces of the pole shift disrupt every sense of being, their hate and fear will be their undoing as they are multiplied one hundredfold. Then, like old light bulbs that are spent, these folk will flicker a few times, glow brightly, and then their hearts will stop.

There will be those who survive without love. They are highly disciplined or, at the outset, had themselves put into a medical coma for the event. When they emerge, they will be strangers in a strange land that will no longer be theirs to control.

2031 – New Lands

During the pole shift, Earth's shell will bulge like an egg in the direction of Nemesis, and the uplift will squeeze vast underground reservoirs, causing them to explode to the surface as sand blows and as fountains of the deep. Old lands will disappear beneath the waves as new lands rise.

To put this in perspective, were our moon to disappear suddenly, the entire surface of the Earth would collapse eighteen inches, and the ensuing disaster would be an extinction-level event for humanity.

During this tribulation, we need to keep in mind a sobering thought. The vast majority of humankind lives within fifty miles of a large body of water, and not one shoreline will escape the wrath of tsunamis passing over them like hydraulic sandpaper.

After the pole shit, we have a new Earth that is radically different because there will be changes for all three shift types:

- **Axial Shift:** inclination will decrease from 23.5° to about 18° to 19°.
- **Magnetic Shift:** The North and South Poles will flip.
- **Crustal Shift:** North America will move approximately 12° closer to the equator.

During the shift, the rotation of our planet on its axis will reverse direction, after which the sun will rise in the West and set in the East. Aftershocks from the pole shift will continue through to 2032.

Mid-Winter

With the Planet X System in the Southern Skies and speeding away from us, the post-flyby impacts will occur each winter as Earth passes through the Nemesis debris tail.

There will be residual impact events from the debris tail until 2036. The nature of these impact events year by year will initially be a mix that favors larger impactors. Over time, the mixture will prefer the smaller impactors before it ends.

These meteors will be random and difficult to observe as the skies will be heavy with particulates.

Summer

The planet will be heavily defoliated in areas, and fires will have claimed vast regions. Fortunately, this is when the cleansing rains begin.

Initially, there will be no discernible pattern or timing, but they will bless those who receive them.

2032 – Solar Calm

Mid-Winter

Post-flyby impacts will occur. There will be a lighter mix, and the impact frequency will be less than the previous year.

Summer

The good news for this year is that the sun will begin to calm, and the solar sprites will stop. Also, this solar calm has a direct benefit for Earth. The pole shift aftershocks will end.

From this point forward, survivors can work around the remaining tribulation concerns as they begin to assess their new world.

2033 – Earth Settles

Mid-Winter

The post-flyby impacts should be noticeably less this year than in previous years.

Summer

The cleansing rains will occur more often as the atmosphere and weather stabilize.

2034 – Cleansing Rains

Mid-Winter

This year will be happy because the post-flyby impacts will be very light and few this year—a harbinger of relief to come.

Early Winter

With the Earth rain-washed, the cleansing Rains stop, and weather systems complete their stabilization.

2035 – Blue Skies

Mid-Winter

The post-flyby impacts are even less this year than the year before, and everyone is almost sure it will end by next year, but there are still a few tremblers from time to time as the continents settle in with their new fault lines.

Early Spring

It is a joy to behold as the skies clear and everyone sees a magnificent blue sky that has not been seen for over a century.

As pioneer plants make way for grasses, children will find a fresh patch to lay down upon and marvel at fleecy white clouds passing overhead. Meanwhile, their parents study the snowcapped mountains surrounding their valley with relief and good cheer.

2036 – Sweet Waters

Mid-Winter

Everyone hopes to see an end to the post-flyby impacts and is rewarded with clear, undisturbed signs and no howls of sirens warning everyone to take shelter.

Summer

Hallelujah! We taste sweet waters again, thanks to the cleansing rains and snowmelt.

2037 – Our New Earth

Mid-Winter

The tribulation ends, and while there will be dead spots, it will be a clean, fresh, rain-washed New World. The post-flyby impacts are over, with no unexpected tail-end charlies to worry about.

Spring

Everyday life resumes, and the new Summer Solstice, assuming it changes, will be declared a day of celebration.

Those who attend those celebrations will be flame on mature Indigos and Crystals. As the children play in the water and the meals are prepared, the talk will be about the future and that humanity has earned the right to go to the stars as a benign and peaceful spacefaring race.

In such humble beginnings, the seeds of a Star Trek future will take root. Believe it.

Universal Constants

Three universal Planet X System constants are essential. Remember them.

- Nemesis enters and leaves the Northern sky in Ophiuchus (November 29—December 17).
- Earth is at its closest approach to Nemesis on the Winter Solstice (December 21).
- The pole shift cannot occur unless the entire Planet X System (Nemesis Constellation) is below the ecliptic and in the Southern Skies.

For you, dear Riselings, these are your chutes and oxbows, and they will help you and your families to bypass the treacherous parts of the Revelation River.

Teaching Tools

The cinema teaching tool for this chapter is The Matrix (1999). It is a helpful way to see how the characters exist in the real world and the machine world matrix.

Like the characters in The Matrix, you will be living in a world that is controlled in ways much like the Matrix, though how you process that will be with your personal construct.

The knowledge you organize with your construct will help you develop a calm countenance, which is my mission. To serve you by creating the knowledge tools you will need in time for when you need them.

To achieve this, I've spent eight years researching, traveling the country, and writing my "Survival Trilogy for The Tribulation," as I call it. It is over 1,000 pages of how-to knowledge for faith-based intentional all-hazards survival communities.

Below is a list of three books with their ISBN numbers. Please show this list to your local librarian and ask her to order copies for the library. They are:

Surviving the Planet X Tribulation
There Is Strength in Numbers
ISBN: 9781597721974

Radio Free Earth
The Complete Beginner's Guide to Survival Communications
ISBN: 9781597721950

Win-Win Survival Handbook
All-Hazards Safety and Future Space Colonization
ISBN: 9781597721738

(See Appendix C – Library List for the full list of related titles.)

When the books come in, they'll let you know. Check them out, and I suggest you read them at the library. Libraries are lovely places to cubbyhole yourself away from the world and to contemplate.

Contemplation is an essential part of being on the Indigo Path. *This is the way.*

This is essential, my dear Riselings because when the time comes, people will feel the shock of being blindsided. Then, the wise will embrace the existential need for survival knowledge, and there will be more of them.

As calmer heads prevail and survival is firmly in hand, you step forth. Here, your Indigo gift of knowing will give you a gentle countenance. You will know they are ready to take action and that you have fully prepared for this moment.

Imagine it this way. They understand they have a long and challenging journey, and the immediate need is to find a starting point. That is when you raise your hand and say, "I have a plan."

Now, dear Riselings, let's be frank. All I've done so far is buy you about ten seconds; after that, it's showtime.

Contemplation and imagination are vital to mastering the content in my 1,000-page trilogy, as they are for any other endeavor, for it is the power of your knowing.

To illustrate the point, let's imagine your family is active in a small local church, and the time has finally come for your "I have a plan" ten seconds of fame. What happens next?

Allow me to wax poetically for a moment. Just for grins, let me be your voice for a moment. Here is what we will say.

I have a plan. There are things we must gather and do, but this plan is not about what we have not; it is about what we have, and we have everything we need to survive because we have each other. The three strengths of a church are respected leadership, membership skill diversity, and emergency rapid response. No other form of organization is as well suited to survival.

This plan is based on the three pillars of survival leadership. Leaders, builders, and providers. For each of you, I bring a starting point for your respective journey.

To the leaders, the most important thing now is keeping the flock together and focused through the difficult times ahead. Understanding how to explain what is happening with a combination of faith and science is a powerful way to overcome fear and hope for the future.

For you, I offer *Surviving the Planet X Tribulation*. It will show you how to explain the bad news gently and compassionately so that everyone is not overwhelmed but inspired.

To you, the builder, it is a pro-forma business plan to build self-sustaining, all-hazards underground homes and farms using the most robust structure ever devised by man. The concrete dome. Much of what we'll need will be available locally.

Domes are strong enough to withstand direct hits by bombs, missiles, or a magnitude nine earthquake; still they are roomy and spacious inside. A proper, family-friendly solution to help us survive, thrive, and prosper.

For you, I offer the *Win-Win Survival Handbook*. It walks you through the process step-by-step. The nice thing is that it will help you educate others as to what is possible and the necessary steps to get there.

And to you, providers. All too often, the unsung heroes, you must gather and organize what a community needs, even when it does not know the necessity of such things.

What will we do when all the communication systems that have been a necessity for life as we know it, cease to operate? Will we stop talking? Or, will we want to be able to reach out to each other without depending on anyone else? Not just ourselves, but with other communities as well. There is only one sure and safe way to do this. Two-way radios for near and far communications.

For you, I offer *Radio Free Earth*. It is not written for HAM enthusiasts or engineers. It is written for moms at the baby monitor level because they will be the most significant users of these radios. It is also great for scavengers. They'll know what to pick and what to leave.

To all three of you, I have read and mastered the content of these three books and stand ready to be of service. Does anyone have a question?

10

Indigo Construct

My dear Riselings, good news. We've cleared the white-water nightmares of the Revelation River, and now we pull our time canoes up to rest on a soft sandy bank in the river for a well-deserved hot meal and some time to think about how one creates a personal construct.

Here, you must know that one size does not fit all. Like a handmade suit or dress, it is unique to you. With this in mind, I am sharing my construct solely as a reference based on three pillars: guidelines, incarnation, and the Void.

After that, you will learn how to use your Indigo powers to help your ancestors help you and your families with valuable clues for real solutions. With that, let's take a closer look at our three pillars.

Guidelines

In the Matrix movies, the Matrix is an artificial world created by artificial intelligence programs to enslave humans for power generation to benefit their machine world.

An Indigo Construct is nothing like the Matrix because it is a cosmic intelligence ability within each of us to help us break free of the shackles of slavery and to survive what is coming so humanity can achieve its rightful future as an enlightened, spacefaring species, in essence, a Star Trek future.

Again, here are the construct guidelines:

- Use imagination, observation, contemplation, and vision to build your construct.
- Your construct is always a work in progress; you alone are its artist.
- Assume everything you know is wrong and take nothing for granted.
- Trust only those truths that resonate within you because you and you alone put them there.
- Remember, hell is about being right, and Heaven is about getting it right. Keep your ego in check.
- There is no right or wrong. There is only that which is useful or useless. Keep the useful and drop the useless in your wake.
- Everything is in motion, so the only absolute is that all things can and do change.
- Do not submit to fear. It is a mind-killer that robs you of distance and clarity.
- Always be mindful of prophecy, but never live in expectation of it.
- Begin your Indigo Construct with a SPOT—a single point of truth. Like the corner piece of a puzzle, everything will connect with it.

In the next chapter, Perpetual Genesis, you will see how I followed these guidelines to create my ultimate construct. This is not an entertaining process. This is life, so we must always ask difficult questions. One such question is, is incarnation real?

Incarnation

Incarnation is about souls evolving over several incarnations to learn the Godliness of Creation and be with God in mind, body, and soul. Given that a significant minority of the population does not believe in it the natural question becomes, is incarnation optional?

In other words, you can skip it by clicking past an extended warranty offer for your purchase. No dice. Incarnation is real; your only option is to deny it at your own expense.

That works for some, but you'll be hard-pressed to find a flame-on Indigo or Crystal who does. This is because seeing oneself as an eternal being is inevitable when a soul journey follows the Indigo path. Sooner or later, one way or another, it happens.

When that happens, you understand the incarnation mission: to master our free will as Co-Creators with God. Here is the path we must walk:

Co-Creator Path

Freedom is the foundation of free will.
Free will is the energizing force of intention.
Intention is how universes come to be.

This is the way.

Intention is challenging to master, which is why most ascended masters have incarnated hundreds of times.

In the final analysis, it comes down to three things:

- **Reincarnation** is about souls evolving over several incarnations to learn the Godliness of Creation to be with God in mind, body, and soul. *This is the way.*

- **Ascension** comes through wisdom accumulated through lifetimes of encounters and actions. *This is the way.*

- **Wisdom** is a destination to which many paths of awareness lead. *This is the way.*

This gives you a high-level view of reincarnation. However, from a boots-on-the-ground perspective, it's all about awareness.

Awareness

Awareness serves an essential role in one's soul journey through multiple incarnations. One could think of it as a cosmic journal of discovery, and an odd thing is the tendency for many to believe that the path to awareness is a somewhat linear process where evidence builds, fact upon fact. Nothing could be further from the truth.

The natural path to awareness does not have all the correct elements like a Hollywood screenplay. Instead, it is more like a cosmic pinball game; you are the ball, and there is only one rule for this game.

More important than the answer is the courage to ask the question. *This is the way.*

As I explained earlier, as a lad of sixteen, God told me my life would be complex with many twists and turns, and that is how it turned out.

When you think you're going in the right direction, pal, a bumper sends you flying in another direction. Worse yet, it could be right into the path of a flipper that will send you somewhere else. Consequently, the path of awareness is more like bang, boom, flip, bang, or something along those lines.

It always begins with a question, and for me, that question was, is Creation all there is, or is there more?

There is so much more. It is called "The Void," and it helps explain why we do what we do.

The Void

There is no beginning. There is no end. Always is the Void, an endlessly eternal still darkness, and nestled within it is Creation.

Black as coal with a thin consume of dark energy and dark matter, the Void is the realm of the subatomic. It is the realm of chaos and control.

Within the Void is Creation. It is the realm of the atomic, with harmony and cooperation. We live in a multidimensional multiverse, and to imagine that there is only one universe in all of Creation is a self-imposed limitation.

God thinks big, and Creation's scale, depth, and nature tax even the most fertile imaginations beyond their limits. Yet, even as these two realms are diametric, they are intertwined and share one defining aspect.

The quest for order drives all things. *This is the way.*

This concept may be useless to a theoretical physicist, but it works beautifully for a construct as it is another single point of truth (SPOT).

That being said, scientists continually seek to create the ultimate unified Theory of Everything (TOS). One that connects all the dots to use a single theoretical framework that consistently and logically explains all aspects of the universe.

Theory of Everything

Many have tried to create the ultimate TOS, and all have failed. Evidence of this is theoretical physicist Albert Einstein. Regarded as one of the most incredible minds of the 20th century, his theory of relativity (1879–1955) changed our world.

Yet, he struggled mightily to create a TOS to unify all the forces of the universe. Alas, his years of effort were fruitless, but he soldiered on with his TOS work right up to his passing.

However, through his brilliance and that of others, we have the basic theoretical building blocks to create a helpful cosmology construct to understand the universe's history, structure, and constituent dynamics. They are:

- **Dark Energy:** A form of energy spread uniformly throughout space and time, and its anti-gravitational properties explain the current accelerating rate of expansion of the universe. It represents three-fourths of the mass energy of the universe.

- **Dark Matter:** A form of matter believed to make up 90 percent of the universe, which is why the Void is as black as coal. Dark matter does not absorb or emit light and is invisible. It does not collide with atomic particles but exerts gravitational force.

- **Atomic:** The atoms described by the periodic table. The very stuff of Creation.

- **Subatomic:** Smaller than an atom, these are the particles of an atom, such as neutrons, quarks, and electrons, which form an atom's constituent parts.

This brings us back to our two realms, chaos and harmony. The Void is chaos, whereas Creation, or Heaven if you wish, is harmony.

This brings us to the power of intention.

Physics teaches us that you cannot create something from nothing, and this is true. So then, where does God get the mass and energy to build Creation, which is an ever-expanding work in progress? From the Void, and here is the best part: it is limitless.

God uses the Void to fuel His power of intention. Remember:

The quest for order drives all things. *This is the way.*

What God does to attract and use the dark matter and dark energy of the Void is to give it order with His intentions. When God said, "Let there be light," His intention was to create a framework, and as a moth attracted to the flame, the dark energy and matter were attracted to it.

How the chaos of the subatomic responds is the variable. God will get what he intends, but the chaos Void will organize the final form. Needless to say, Creation is a work in process with ample amounts of heuristic learning. Nonetheless, this is how God created our universe.

A cosmic event we call "The Big Bang," and now I will share with you the fabulous things I learned on my path of awareness.

The Big Bang

A few years after Cable News Network (CNN) aired, I worked with them as a science feature field producer It was one of the most amazing experiences of my life, and my beat covered the colleges and universities of Texas.

At that time, the Holy Grail of science, so to speak, was big-bang theory, and this monumental task soaked up most of the available funding for astronomers, leaving crumbs for the rest.

The aim was to answer a simple question. Given that the universe is continually expanding, will it continue doing so indefinitely until Earth finds itself in a very dark and lonely part of space?

Or, will the force of gravity eventually reverse the process, thereby compressing the universe back into its original singularity, the initial point of Creation for the universe as we now know it?

After monumental sums of money, effort, and time, scientists concluded that there is a 99% chance that the universe will continue to expand indefinitely.

What is the 1% they missed? God is the Creator of all there is, and He and Creation were known to the ancient Egyptians thousands of years ago and recorded in the first book of *The Kolbrin Bible*.

Here, I must share a personal story as the publisher of this most precious ancient wisdom text. Steve, a fellow researcher, was the first to begin studying *The Kolbrin Bible* due to our Planet X work at yowusa.com.

I was going through a hard science phase of my life at the time, having retired from over 20 years in the computer and software industry. When Steve told me about it, I was cocky.

"Oh, right," I quipped. "The beautiful princess shoots an arrow into the sky, and down comes the dark lord."

"Shut up," Steve said, "just read the book."

I was shocked. "Moi, shut up! Game on, bunkie, I will give you the debunking of a lifetime."

What really happened is that I read something on the first page of *The Kolbrin Bible* I saw something that dropped me on my head.

To paraphrase that great line from Star Trek IV: The Voyage Home (1986), it was a double-dumb-ass on me, and here are the passages that did it.

The Kolbrin Bible: 21st Century Master Edition
Book of Creation

> CRT:1:4 The name which is uttered cannot be that of this Great Being who, remaining nameless, is the beginning and the end, beyond time, beyond the reach of mortals, and **we in our simplicity call it God**.

> **CRT:1:5 He who preceded all existed alone in His strange abode of uncreated light,** which remains ever unextinguishable, and no understandable eye can ever behold it. The pulsating draughts of the eternal life light in His keeping were not yet loosed. He knew Himself alone; He was uncontrasted, unable to manifest in nothingness, for all within His Being was **unexpressed potential**.
>
> **CRT:1:6** The **Great Circles of Eternity** were yet to be spun out, to be thrown forth as the endless ages of existence in substance. They were to **begin with God and return to Him completed in infinite variety and expression.**

Considering that these words were inscribed over 3,600 years ago, they are amazing. God exists alone in an "abode of uncreated light," namely, the Void.

To express his potential, God used the power of intention to create our universe, where the galaxies are "Great Circles of Eternity."

As our scientists have observed, galaxies will continue to spread apart, and gravity will not compress them back into a singularity. They spent billions to figure out what was inscribed by the ancient Egyptians millennia ago.

This brings me to my search for truth. My path of awareness. When writing my books, I do problem-solving readings with God, my ancestors, my Guides, and my Ascended Masters, and sometimes, my path of awareness gets a little bumpy.

One such bumpy stretch for me was Jesus, and I offer my story as a reference for three essential Indigo Riseling teachings. To understand "The Plan" and how to safely awaken your powers with waking dreams.

For those of you who love Jesus, as in you walk the talk, there will also be something amazing for you.

Path of Discovery

I was born to a Jewish mother and a Catholic father who insisted I be baptized, and in the middle of the ceremony, I started painting everyone, beginning with the priest. Mom said I was loaded for bear and had a pretty good lift on it.

However, my path of discovery to this point began when I was a boy of nine when I first learned that my entire maternal family in Europe had died in the Holocaust.

This black hole in my family tree gutted me, and so I chose to honor them as a Jew because both of my parents told me I had the right.

However, things changed after my mother divorced my father for adultery. That, plus my choice to be Jewish, resulted in terrible antisemitic abuse by my Catholic grandmother and father for years, and what they called me and my mother was disgusting. The only way to cope was for them to become nothing to me, and eventually, they did.

Nonetheless, the antisemitism was traumatizing for me, and for many years, Jesus was a death word. Especially when it was preceded by "My," and it stayed that way for a long time until I realized the need to find a more constructive way to deal with this.

That was when I found a way to have a relationship with Jesus, thanks to Nazi law. Under Nazi law, if you had one Jewish grandparent, you could serve in the Army as a non-commissioned officer and never hold political office. But, if you had two or more Jewish grandparents, you went to the camps.

That was when I found Jesus, in a manner of speaking.

I only have two Jewish grandparents, but he has four, which means if we both had been incarnated at that time, his ashes would be flying out of the crematoria stacks as my train would be pulling in. It was a brother of death but a step in the right direction. Or, at least, a workable one.

Then, during a major out-of-body experience in Israel at the Mount of the Beatitudes in April 2000, the Ascended Masters showed me something that made me open my mind. It also terrified me because I could imagine the sight of burning crosses on my lawn.

I turned to my Jewish friends to talk about it; they just said I was being a little crazy and not to pay attention. With no help there, I had to kick my can down the road.

That was when I began to meet what I call spiritual Christians. They're easy to find. Just ask them how many churches and study groups they have been kicked out of for asking questions not found on the "thou shalt only ask questions from this list" – list.

After we caught our breath from all the hysterical laughter, we began to have amazing conversations. It's why they are my favorite folk.

It's not about checklists or dogma. They are far past that. Instead, spiritual Christians aren't interested in go-betweens and spiritual tollbooths. They read His teachings, they love His teachings, they love Him for that, and He loves them back. It's beautiful to see, but back to cases—namely, my inability to do readings with Jesus.

I tend to get stuck on points this way, but oddly, when I started researching this with my Guides, it was the one topic I felt I had to pull teeth to get answers for because they were holding something back.

So, I pushed again, and I was told that the years of vitriolic anti-Semitic abuse by my grandmother during my childhood had deeply scarred my soul and that this was blocking my ability to read Him.

That seemed peculiar because I can and regularly read God, but not Jesus. Yet, there are a lot of Christians out there who talk with Jesus every day. It was a puzzle, so I pushed again and finally learned why the hesitation.

I was told with a certain measure of hesitancy that the concern on the other side is whether or not you can handle the truth. This is why my Guides hesitated. They explained that when people learn this, they tend to fall into deep despair with awful results, and the Guides were concerned I would do the same. Remember:

> **More important than the answer is the courage to ask the question.** *This is the way.*

Their answer made sense, so I had to think about that for a few days, and then I remember my family telling me that when my grandmother was a few weeks from passing, she moaned and cried hysterically each night, and they didn't know why.

What I learned was the scars she had inflicted upon my soul as a child had also been inflicted upon her soul as well. There are no do-overs when you scar an innocent, and you get what you give.

My grandmother came from a wealthy from a wealthy family in Italy that was closely aligned with Mussolini, so most likely, I was not the only skeleton in the closet. She knew she was dying and couldn't find Jesus. That's why she cried hysterically.

This abuse within my family was limited, and I want to point out with enduring gratitude that the rest of my paternal family gave my choice their unequivocal support.

My Uncle Pat said it best. He fought under Patton and was at the tip of the spear from Normandy to Germany and had the nightmares to prove it.

He was a mobile crane operator in a local steel mill and loved his job, family, and the Church. He said, "I can't understand why you wouldn't want to be Catholic, but this is America, and you have the right to choose."

Sadly, I lost them due to this abuse, but I will never forget them and fondly and pray that God will always watch over them.

Back to cases. So, why can't I read Jesus? At this point, it's becoming a burr under my saddle. I returned to the Guides and pressed once again, asking, what gives?

All Guides are eternally patient and helpful, but in retrospect, it wouldn't surprise me to learn the other side was thinking, "What's with this guy? Is he selling vacuum cleaners or something? We can't get him out of the house."

Oh well, like they say in sales, "close, close, close," and it was time to clear the air.

I told my Guides to relax as I cannot regret losing something I've never had nor desired, so why get upset? He's in His lane, and I'm in mine, and we're both serving the same mission: the survival and evolution of our species.

Given that we're all eternal beings, this is just a temporary failure to communicate, which can be debugged and will be after I return home.

Yes, I saw good reason for their concern. My Guides risked an answer that could drop me on my head and set me back, with a dramatic setback for the mission. Yet, they took that chance because I asked and because they love me.

Heaven is no fan of fine print, and simple works best.

Therefore, the deciding factor is the task at hand. The mission, and to date, I have achieved all of my goals without the help of Jesus. Not that I would refuse it, for scarred as I am, my thoughts about Him follow Celtic tradition, as described in *The Kolbrin Bible*.

And for those who want to know, a prayer or laying on of the hands is not how this works. I was told that while it is possible to remove these kinds of scars during an incarnation, it requires significant time and effort and can be very disruptive.

Great, we've cleared the air, and my Guides understand I can handle the truth. Still the same, I'm still working on why I can't read Jesus. The question sticks because I've asked this of my Guides a few times over the last thirty years. The answer was always, "He's incarnated elsewhere and is unavailable."

Unavailable? Say what?

Some things you let slide, but at this point, enough was enough. At this point, I feel like I've got one foot nailed to the floor, and I cannot figure out why the scenery never changes. It's time to cut to the chase.

I returned for more, determined not to take "incarnated elsewhere" for an answer. I wanted more. I pushed, and here is what I finally got.

There are many ascended masters, and each has lived hundreds and hundreds of lives, and they can do amazing things.

However, Jesus is the only ascended master, according to my Guides, who is multidimensional. (During the readings, I couldn't help but sense a little bit of "How does He do that?")

As usual, I let the answer percolate for a while and found that I was still short of the answer. Why is Jesus unavailable to me.

This time, my persistence finally yielded all the answers I needed.

Ascension Trigger

What I've observed about the other side is that they are like us in one respect. They are all a jack of all trades, so to speak, but they've all got one thing in common. They all got their "thing," which is how I connect with them.

It's like watching Curly in City Slickers wag his finger and say, "That one thing."

This may surprise you, but everyone on the other side of the veil has their own "thing." Jesus is no different, and His thing is to trigger the ascension of sentient races all throughout Creation. Here is where He is like no other.

Jesus is the only multidimensional ascended master and is the closest one to God. He alone has the unique ability to incarnate in several lifeforms throughout the Cosmos simultaneously.

Consequently, if you cannot catch him between incarnations, only those who speak to him with genuine love in their hearts for Him can. If you can, do so, and do it often.

This brings us to World War III, the White Hats, and their mantra: "Trust the Plan."

The whispered answer has always been, "What plan?"

Well, now I knew Jesus' thing and what to look for, and I found it. I think every living good soul on the planet will like this.

The Plan

I pestered my Guides like a vacuum cleaner salesman, and I know that Jesus has a thing. He triggers ascension in young species throughout the Creation. This led me straight to The Plan.

> **Youngs Literal Translation (1998)**
> John 2, Jesus Clears the Temple Courts
>
> 13 And the passover of the Jews was nigh, and Jesus went up to Jerusalem,
>
> 14 and he found in the temple those selling oxen, and sheep, and doves, and the moneychangers sitting,
>
> 15 and **having made a whip of small cords, he put all forth out of the temple, also the sheep, and the oxen; and of the money-changers he poured out the coins, and the tables he overthrew,**
>
> 16 and to those selling the doves he said, 'Take these things hence; make not the house of my Father a house of merchandise.'

Why does Jesus talk so often about our times? Because He's been here, seen it, done it, and bought all the tee-shirts. After all, He is multidimensional.

What would be fantastic for me would be to travel back in time, to be a fly on the wall, and watch Him making His whip.

He could have cleared the Temple Courts without a whip by preaching against and shaming them, which would have worked enough to make a point. After all, business is business, so when the PR is terrible, close up shop, go home for the day, and wait for it to pass.

This time, it would not be business as usual. This was the point of the whip.

A whip is like a gavel. When you hear the crack of either one, you turn to see who is wielding it. Therefore, like a gavel, a whip is also a sign of authority, so Jesus used it to deliver The Plan. What did he show us?

The whip represents the authority of law. He did not whip the evil ones. Instead, he used it to disrupt their livestock operations. Then you shame them with the truth.

With this in mind, here is my modern interpretation (with, I hope, graciously ample room for creative license) of these scriptures from John 2.

> THE PLAN: And Jesus said to the generations alive today:
>
> Children of tomorrow. Those there, the Central Bankers of your time. They are your enemies of the Truth and the Light. You will destroy them with the law, disrupt their operations, and publicly shame them with the truth of their evil deeds. Then, can you commit them to death eternal, in the Void, and forever free all of God's children from the shackles of slavery.

It was on that very day Jesus, in the name of humanity, declared war against the monsters we face today, and it has been going on ever since. It is the long march of war, dear Riselings, and winners never quit.

Jesus paid an awful price for his declaration of eternal war against the Central Bankers, and so they got the Romans to do the wet work and pinned it on the Jews. As they say, old tricks are the best tricks.

While they may have killed the man, they could not kill His Plan. See what Trump, Q, the White Hats, and the Anons are saying and doing.

- Use the law.
- Disrupt their operations.
- Shame them with the truth.

This is The Plan, pure, plain and simple. Everything else is multidimensional chess, with no exit strategy or fixed dates. Instead, this is and has always been a multi generational war for the liberation of our species.

No matter what it takes or how long, we each must put our shoulder to the wheel and lean into it. The Plan is working. Have hope and hang on because it really is working. Best of all, Heaven is working with us as well.

Waking Dreams

Since starting yowusa.com in 1999, my daily mission has been to tell people who are coming into awareness that they are not alone. While I see them all as a symphony of light, each feels isolated, like a small candle in the dark.

Sadly, the reason for their awareness is usually the same. Prophetic visions, dreams, and premonitions haunt them, with horrific scenes of impacts, floods, earthquakes, tsunamis, and volcanic eruptions.

I have observed over the years and through numerous accounts that the purpose of these experiences is to trigger the dreamers to follow the path of awareness.

The most common experience is waking dreams, which are not the same as a morning dream. Morning dreams typically happen during REM sleep, are vivid, and can be caused by many things. What you experience is within yourself.

With a waking dream, there is a brief twilight moment between REM sleep and wakefulness when those who love you on the other side can download a vision or dream before your rising consciousness blocks them out.

Therefore, these prophetic experiences are not random but rather acts of love by concerned ancestors and guides. Sometimes they work, and sometimes they do not.

Here is where everyone, especially you, Riselings, can use waking dreams as awareness triggers and tools. Then, you can begin to drive the dialogue. When you do, your ancestors will glow brightly with love, and they will happily give you powerful clues and answers to help you solve complex problems.

How do you drive the conversation? You do the following three things:

- Ask for knowledge.
- Explain your need.
- Be specific.

What kind of answers can you get? Let me use an example from this chapter: a waking dream in response to my question about the nature of the atomic and subatomic.

I received it very early in the morning, and it was so powerful I had to leap out of bed and write it down.

Here is what I received in answer to my question, word for word:

"The quest for order drives all things."

My dear Riselings, you not only have the ability to do this now. You can do so confidently, knowing you are shielded by the power of love.

What proof of this can I present? My own inability to read Jesus because of my childhood soul scars. Conversely, what about those of you who can and truly do love Jesus? This love is what shields and protects you, and this is important.

As an experienced and trained psychic, I can read God and the Guides at will, but to do so requires one to pass through a gauntlet of evil entities. These nasties are bent on creating havoc and fear in your life, and knowing how to block them requires training and discipline. It would be best if you had a mentor for this, and here is how to ask for one.

Begin with waking dreams as wisdom tools. When you need to figure out something, formulate a clear and concise question and frame it in your mind. It needs to be simple. For example, you ask a question that can be answered in ten words or less. Remember, this method is only for wisdom tools.

Before you go to bed, kneel before your bed and pray to your ancestors and loved ones on the other side for help by name.

Focus on the ones you love and respect most. When you feel that love glowing inside you like a ball of energy, release it by calling them out by name so your message is not lost in the ether.

Be sure to tell them you love them. They know you do, but it's always lovely to hear. Then, explain your situation and what you need help with in your prayers.

After that, ask a question they can answer in ten words or less with a waking dream. In this sense, less becomes more. Then, close by, lovingly telling them good night.

Will they hear you the first time, or will you get a recording? Something like, "I'm sorry, I'm taking harp lessons and cannot take your prayer now." Of course, that's nonsense. They hear you.

When you speak their name, they will hear what you say word for word and answer in any way they can because they love you and you asked.

Once you get it down to a science, you'll usually have a waking dream the following day, and they'll give you precisely what you need. However, receiving their answers may be difficult initially because your abilities need to be awakened.

There is only one way to do this. You ask the same question each night until you finally have your first dream. After that, they become mighty handy.

If you think that waking dreams are like trainer wheels on a bicycle, nothing could be further from the truth. Of all the things you can learn and do, this will always be one of the safest and most potent.

In fact, I used waking dreams to write my book, *Win-Win Survival Handbook: All-Hazards Safety and Future Space Colonization*.

When I began working on the book, I asked God to get me started, and he gave me only three things. First, there were the rules of species for colonization; second, my mission was to change people's minds; and third, I needed to work with my ancestors to solve problems.

Rules and ancestors were one thing, but changing people's minds; don't you just love the easy ones? Here, I chose to use waking dreams instead of readings because my questions were very technical.

I was literally giving my ancestors questions they could research in the Akashic Record, and they could then fashion this into a concise waking dream.

I often tell folks that writing the book for me was a candle-to-candle experience, and a good example was below-ground aquaponic farming. It is vital for survival when the planet is going bonkers.

This presented me with a series of challenges, and while I'm a retired Silicon Valley geek, I barely know enough to grow weeds. But that didn't matter because my ancestors have the library card of Creation and are most happy to help me with research and did.

In a manner of speaking, I was in a long pitch-black tunnel, and on the other end, was not an oncoming train.

But it was pitch black, so when I asked for a waking dream, the following day it would come. Not like a beam of light, but rather, a candle in the darkness, beckoning me ahead. I would go to it, and on the tunnel wall, the candle lit the message.

When I had that answer, I could go forward to the following technical challenge, and the process repeated again, so this is how I wrote the book from candle to candle.

Now, dear Riselings, imagine that you dial in your ancestors and get it working. When things are going sideways, they can help you each day to make effective life-saving decisions to help you and your families in ways others could not imagine.

Teaching Tools

Waking dreams can become a light of hope for solving survival problems. To both parents, when your Riseling is open to this, discuss it with them and advise them on who to ask, by who they were in life. Your Riseling will make the ultimate choice, so help them to make it a good one. Now for the moms.

In the next chapter, I will use the concepts and tools presented to build a complete model of my construct, which I've named Perpetual Genesis, a construct for species survival and ascension.

The foundation for that construct was cast when I was a young man in my late twenties when I experienced a profound out-of-body experience during my vision quest, during which I was shown Heaven.

I saw a web of tunnels of light connecting every sun, planet, and moon in Creation, and souls used it to travel anywhere they wanted in Creation. It is a web of light, and when we cross over, we do so at the threshold of a tunnel of light.

I experienced my vision quest in 1979 and later learned I was not unique. What I beheld has been reported by many others as well, across the world. Then, four years later came a big surprise, which also happens to be the cinema teaching tool for this chapter.

It is the movie *Brainstorm (1983)*. A sci-fi thriller far ahead of its time, it follows a team of researchers as they develop a system that allows them to jump into people's minds. For example, someone could record themselves skiing down a mountain trail. Then, a wheelchair user could replay that recording, seeing and feeling everything the skier experiences.

The director was Douglas Trumbull, a legendary special effects ace; his credits include *2001: A Space Odyssey, Silent Running,* and *Close Encounters of the Third Kind.* He is meticulous and obviously did his research for the final scenes in the film. You will see an outstanding representation of the tunnels of light I saw during my vision quest.

11

We Are a Hunted Species

In my mind's eye, I see the year 2024 as the year of The Great Awakening. Humanity will learn that it is not the apex predator on the planet.

This will no doubt come as unwelcome news to all those who believe we cannot be preyed upon by inhuman monsters because such things can only exist in the fearful mind of a child hiding under a blanket. Wrong!

The monsters are real; they have been here long, plundering us, and they have no intention of quitting.

In effect, we have been like cattle basking in the sun of a comfortable feedlot with ample feed and water. When the music ends, it ends badly, and we're processed into commodities.

Waking to this reality will be difficult for everyone, and there has been a steady stream of bad news in this book thus far. Therefore, let's take a moment to reflect on your feelings.

Are you now, or have been feeling:

- Alone
- Defenseless

- Helpless
- Isolated
- Vulnerable

Of all the questions awakening souls will ask, this one overarches the rest, but once you understand how things work on the cosmic level, these negative feelings will vanish like tears in the rain, and you will possess a powerful tool for survival.

The goal of this chapter is to help show you how lateral thinking can give you a decisive edge in defending your life and those of your loved ones.

A simple way to think about it is that if you need to figure out which options are the least problematic, you have a shortage of options, and it's time to find more. An excellent example of lateral thinking is the Bible story of David versus Goliath.

In this chapter, you'll learn how to make your own leather sling and to pick a suitable stone for the job, so let's get into it, my dear Rieslings.

A Few Good Seeds

The point of this book is to give you knowledge tools that you can use to help you and your loved ones survive, thrive, and prosper. As you begin reading this chapter, I expect you to ask the same question religion endeavors to answer. "Who am I, and where do I fit in with all this?" Or, in other words, "What is the meaning of all this to me?"

Here is the short answer.

Evil manifests itself in many ways but has only one real power over us. The power of deception. It is why the monsters have been using Indigo Elder profiles to identify and nullify, with psychotropic drugs, entire generations of Latchkey Indigos.

An old friend and mentor, Robert Reiland, once told me, "When God destroys a world, he always saves a few good seeds for the next."

You, my dear Rieslings, are those very seeds, and here is where you need to give your parents a big hug and thanks because they have protected you as a healthy, heterosexual, unvaccinated child of Alpha Generation age.

After reading this chapter, you will understand the meaning of everything at a basic functional level and possess the knowledge needed to navigate those troubled times. If I have done it right by you, you will confidently know you can say, "I can do this."

First things first, my dear Riselings. Sadly, we're a hunted species, and we're easy game. Therefore, the first and most important thing is understanding why it is this way.

We are a Hunted Species

The first thing these inhuman monsters are happy to tell you and show you is where you are weak and where they are strong. They have hunted us for thousands of years, much like we hunt deer and other game.

For example, the strategy is simple, even for deer hunters. Camouflage yourself, lie in wait for your game, and follow these guidelines:

- Hunt the inexperienced young or injured, diseased or old, and weak.
- The older ones can be wise, but most are not intelligent enough and can be deceived.
- Generally, hunt any animal that cannot escape you or lacks the experience to recognize danger.

Now comes a natural question. If this is the strategy for hunting deer, can you use these guidelines to hunt two-legged animals, such as humans?

Yes, because humans are now easier to kill than deer. That may sound strange given that most falsely view humanity as the apex predator of this world, but it is true.

Society has been dumbed down, and as a result of mass media, automation, and technology, we've mostly lost our animal instincts and intuitive sixth sense of danger, particularly in the cities and suburbs as opposed to rural areas.

However, even country folk are still relatively easy pickings for the monsters, and here is how "They" hunt us.

They tell us that "They" are:

- Trusted authorities

- Good people
- Doing this for the good of all
- Doing this because it is necessary

How did it work out? According to the United Nations, at least 65% of people in high-income countries such as France, Japan, and the United States are partially vaccinated.

It is like two out of three deer walking up to the muzzle of your rifle and saying, "Take your time. I'm not going anywhere." It was just too easy.

Only one in three people in these countries are unvaccinated, and even if you only had one low-dose COVID mRNA vaccine, you need to begin working on a detox strategy to neutralize the spike proteins in your body, or you will not survive The Great Winnowing.

Please do not give up hope, for although it is difficult to expect a complete reversal of the damage being done by these vaccines, there will eventually be a way to permanently disable the graphene, spike protein, and cancer components of these depopulation bioweapons and to stop their spread.

This will be a blessing for families with a mix of vaccinated and unvaccinated, but in the meantime, common sense and compassion are the rule.

This is how we are being hunted, and now that you know that the monsters are on the back foot and that good will prevail. No government feared by its people will survive what is to come, and when the time comes, the hunters will become the hunted.

What these inhuman monsters know is that unless they can deceive us into their shackles of slavery, all that awaits them terrifies them.

What is coming is not justice per se because that is about punishment. This will be a reckoning, the aim of which will be to ensure that this never happens again and that They never happen again.

Consequently, we see a global freedom movement taking down corrupt governments, corporations, and institutions.

Nonetheless, whatever form of remaining governance we have, it must earn the trust of the people, and I believe we will see that, though the path to getting there will be awfully rocky.

May the last words those with a taste for innocence hear be something like this: "For crimes against humanity and other offenses, we now commit your soul to death eternal in the Void."

Nonetheless, new governance will not prevent the prophecies mentioned in this book from happening, though it offers a unique potential to save hundreds of millions, if not billions, of lives. Such change will also provide ground-level support for Win-Win all-hazards communities.

All these are good reasons to never give up hope and to engage with the future constructively, and doing that begins with tools.

Indigo Freedom Tools

When you unmask the deception, it and the underlying intentions of the monsters become transparent. This is when you see them coming in time to outmaneuver them.

Now that you know where "They" are strong, here is where they are not.

> Overreach, overcontrol, and overbearance are the weaknesses of evil. Exploit them without mercy. *This is the way.*

Now you know their weaknesses, but you also know they have massive, vast networks of assets that run deep. Is it practical to think a little guy can go up against this kind of power and win?

Good question and King David in the Bible answered the question with a smooth stone, a leather sling, and some rather creative form of thought called lateral thinking. The strategy is to find more options if you do not like the ones you already have. Remember:

> Good creates and is unpredictable, whereas Evil calculates and fears well-aimed sabots. *This is the way.*

In the early days of automation in France, workers would throw their sabot, a wooden shoe, into the machine works, jamming them up. Frequently, with considerable damage.

The point is: Earlier, I said that governments are psychopath magnets and that once the psychopaths gain power, they hire all the vegetables.

Yes, they also get some clever folk, but most of their front-line minions are self-interested nobodies who will do anything they're told, and their personalities are about as bright as petty retail clerks. What makes these cruel dullards effective is that they follow a playbook.

Using lateral thinking to bypass their techniques helps you target their vulnerable points and massively disrupt their operations. This begins with language.

Language is a Weapon

Sophistry is "Their" most effective language weapon against us. It is systematic and subtly deceptive reasoning or argumentation designed to deceive or mislead.

"You'll Own Nothing, and You'll Be Happy" is a catchphrase from a 2016 essay published by Danish MP Ida Auken as part of a 2030 prediction video series for the World Economic Forum—classic communist sophistry.

Beware of the poetry of evil. It begins with the poets, such as our celebrities, who seduce the masses with their poetry. Then, once the people embrace the poetry, the monsters push the poets out of the way, seize control, and the music ends.

Subliminal Programming

We hear a lot about MK ultra and CIA mind programming techniques, and people who believe those conspiracy theories are proof the programming works because they reflexively say things like, "I am clever, in control of my faculties, and beyond this."

Really? Imagine:

- You hear an attorney say, "Isn't it true that you told the police you were never there?"

- You hear an automobile salesman say, "Wouldn't you love for your neighbors to see you driving this beauty?"

- You hear a land salesman say, "You can't go wrong with this investment."

A negative contraction is a simple construction of two parts in all three examples. For example:

- Can't translates to: can not.

- Wouldn't translates to: would not

- Isn't translates to: is not.

Negative contractions will appear in a dictionary as colloquial contractions. What professionals know about negative contractions gives them a decisive advantage.

This is because these innocuous terms always give a false message because, subconsciously, listeners never hear the second part of the contraction.

This is subliminal programming, and what the listener actually hears subconsciously is as follows:

- "**Is true** you told the police **you were never there**."

- "**Would love** for your **neighbors** to **see you** driving this beauty."

- "You **can go wrong** with this investment."

Now that you know negative contractions are used as the poetry of evil, you'll think differently about them and who uses them.

Here is where your third eye gives you a real advantage. When you instinctively suspect the poetry of evil, be aware of it and its source. Call it your Spidey sense, gut instinct, whatever, but always trust your instincts when they happen, not your fears.

Paralinguistics

Evil is the master of disguise, and it knows the words we like to hear and when. They also use manipulative language to provoke negative emotions and behaviors. You're being played if you only listen to the words and infer the message's intent from them alone.

Instead, you must pay attention to "Their" paralinguistics, which is how a thing is said. It will more accurately reflect their actual intentions.

How a thing is said matters more than words. *This is the way.*

What you are looking for are paralinguistic signs, much like a professional poker play looks for "tells" the subconscious signals of the other players. Emotion is an obvious paralinguistic sign, but equally valid are signs of discomfort, such as hesitation and irregular breathing.

If you can observe them as they speak, study their Kinesics: body movements, facial expressions, posture, and eye contact. When people are honest, they look you straight in the eyes. Otherwise, they avert your gaze to whatever degree of deception they are performing. Beware of psychopaths. They can sell snow in Siberia.

However, your best communication tool is your ears and what is between them.

Effective Listening

Now that we've examined language as a weapon let's combine it with your best communication tool. Your listening skills.

- **No Emotions:** Emotions telegraph weaknesses. When you listen, do so with an impassive facial expression. In other words, develop a good poker face.

- **No Anticipation:** If you begin thinking of your answer before the other party finishes, you will usually insult them by talking past them. Instead, pay attention to them and what they are saying to the exclusion of your thoughts.

- **No Clipping:** Interrupting with your answer before the other party finishes speaking is highly insulting and paints you as being crude and uneducated.

- **Pause for Effect:** After the other party finishes speaking, pause as you consider your answer. This will enhance the acceptance of your reply by showing respect. Furthermore, a well-placed pause will build anticipation and interest in your answer.

- **Confirming Questions:** A confirming question is a simple request for verification. You say something like, "I want to understand you correctly. Is this what you are saying..." A confirming question demonstrates deference and genuine interest in understanding the other party. hey are also an excellent tool for buying time while contemplating the answer to a thorny question.

These are all excellent tools to help you win the language war. Keep them in mind and always remember that the hallmark of an Indigo is observation and contemplation.

Less is More

People often like to hear themselves speak and can become tediously blabby or, worse, then can be cryptic and unyielding.

In contrast, when you answer in a laconic style using as few concise words as possible, you will be better understood, and this is always important because there will always be two truths—the one that is spoken and the one that is heard.

As the communicator, it is your responsibility to be understood, and the more you listen and the less you speak, the wiser you will appear. Remember:

> **Hell is about being right, and Heaven is about getting it right.** *This is the way.*

Another useful way to keep your answers short is with similes, metaphors, and analogies.

We often use analogies that compare the seasons of the year with the stages of life—two entirely different things with similar patterns. The use of analogies offers a practical approach to understanding problems and affairs.

In the Native American tradition, the Medicine Wheel presents the stages of life as metaphors. A metaphor is used in place of something to describe it. For example, lizards are the metaphor for toddlers because they behave similarly.

Visualize a lizard moving about. It runs to a spot, stops, looks around, and then bolts off in a different direction, much like a human toddler exploring the world.

Then there are similes, a type of metaphor. It typically contains the words as or like for comparing two unlike things, such as, "her cheeks were like roses."

With that, you have several helpful communication tools to help you see what "They" are actually doing and saying. You could say these are your Earthly tools, and as impressive as they are, you have even more remarkable tools.

They are called observation and contemplation. What are you looking for? A weakness, and here is your strategy affirmation:

> Good creates and is unpredictable, whereas Evil calculates and fears well-aimed sabots. *This is the way.*

There is a valuable history behind the word sabot. They were the wooden shoes worn by French workers. To protest automation and working conditions, they threw their shoes into the factory machine works, resulting in expensive repairs for the employers. From all this, we have the word sabotage. Final tip. It is more fun and profitable to hunt in packs, so remember:

> Pragmatism, common sense, and cooperation are the whetstones of teamwork.
> *This is the way.*

Network with your brothers and sisters in awareness. Share your passion for freedom and the Godliness of a good life and resolve to never walk in darkness again because more friends are watching over you from the light above than most could ever imagine.

Channeling

Channeling is how light beings send and receive messages across the veil, that thin perimeter between us in our physical form and Creation. When practiced by those in the light of God's love, it is spiritual networking across the veil. In simple terms, you use your third eye, the sixth chakra, to open communication channels with the other side.

One thing I've come to cherish after a lifetime of experiences is that we have friends on the other side, ever-ready to do what they can for us. Over the years, I've made outstanding and lasting friendships with Guides because we're all on the same team.

In the tribulation years ahead, you will begin building similar friendships, especially during The Great Winnowing, which will save you immense grief. But in the meantime, to the present.

Networking with like-minded others will become a cherished part of your life, and with channeling, you can cast a much larger net and go far further.

Our ability to see is limited to the far horizon in everyday life. With channeling, you use your third eye to see far beyond the horizon, and there are two basic categories, each with its own kinds of channels:

- **Secure Channel:** You are safe from the predations of harmful imposters through a restricted, love-based connection. Two examples are waking dreams and the ability of those who sincerely love Jesus to speak with him as much as they can.

- **Open Channel:** Everyone can do this, but only trained and disciplined psychics will know how to block harmful imposters and conduct unrestricted, love-based readings. This book is an example of a mix of secure and open-channel readings.

The distinction between secure and open channeling is vital, so let's compare the two using the Hypertext Transfer Protocol.

In the early days of the Internet, most websites used the basic address that began with "http://" plus the website domain name. These communications were secure but could be spoofed, so financial websites started using https:// with the extra "s" standing for secure. So here is what that looks like:

- Secure Channel = https://
- Open Channel   = http://

Waking dreams and the ability of those who sincerely love Jesus to speak with him as much as possible are love-based connections. However, a third kind of Secure Channel called Remote Viewing is available, and it works more like a library card.

Remote Viewing

During the Cold War, the American CIA and the Russian KGB both conducted psychic and remote viewer operations. The CIA favored remote viewing, whereas the KGB favored psychics. Here are the principal differences:

- **Psychics:** Sophisticated open channel operations, limited only by the psychic's abilities. For example, there was an attempt to turn psychics into remote assassins for psychic hits. While it is possible, no psychic would do it.

- Remote Viewers: Remote viewing is a technical form of secure channeling where you use your third eye to access the Akashic Records. One could think of them as Heaven's library. It is an ever-expanding repository of all universal events, thoughts, words, emotions, and intentions that have occurred and been recorded.

I began following the work of Technical Remote Viewing Instructor Major Edward A. Dames after he released his first *Kill Shot* video in 2004. This is when he explains the Killshot event, which the Guides have predicted for late spring of 2028.

The ability to use Remote Viewing (RV) as a survival tool has always intrigued me, and in April 2015, I was gifted tuition for a two-day RV class taught by Ed. I never pass up a good thing, so I jumped on it.

After the opening session on the first day, I visited Ed while the students were getting refreshments. I introduced myself and handed him a signed copy of my book, *Being In It for the Species: The Universe Speaks*. He said, "I've often heard about you."

I told him that my work corroborated his work and that we kept coming up with similar results through entirely different means. I said, "You're right. The kill shot will happen."

Ed answered solemnly. "I take no joy in hearing that."

Some people attack him with monikers such as "Dr. Death" and other disparaging terms, but I know him.

I will tell you, whatever his past was, he is a lightworker, and ninety percent of the people who take his course want to know only one thing. A location where they can be safe when the guacamole hits the fan.

When Ed teaches the course, he gives you a code for whatever you are supposed to view during the exercises, and it usually sounds like a dyslexic password. It could be anything. A building in Reno, a piece of paper in his briefcase, and so forth.

On the last exercise on the second day, Ed gave us another cryptic viewing code, and afterward, he surprised the whole class by telling us that we had each viewed where we would be during the Kill Shot event and whether we survived it.

He asked who viewed an ocean liner sailing away from them or surgery with tiled walls and blood. A good portion of the class raised their hands, and he told them they wouldn't make it. They were crestfallen to hear it.

I was among the rest who had a very different experience. I saw where I would be, and it was inspiring.

I learned during the class that I have an uncommon viewing ability. Where others see what is before them from a fixed position, I can fly above what I observe for a revealing look-down view.

During this exercise, I viewed myself in an underground Win-Win survival community—built on a mountainside with a slope of approximately 30°. The community was constructed using concrete domes, of which several were spread across the mountainside.

With remote viewing, you can see, hear, feel, taste, and smell with the same clarity as prophetic dreams, and we're talking 4K here.

What I experienced in the viewing mortified me. I began the viewing by hovering above the mountainside and looking at a ridgeline in the distance. The planet was rumbling and howling like a tormented beast. The skies were dark red and troubled with terrible electrical storms.

Then, I descended into the mountainside into one of the domes at the other end of the community. The people inside were huddled together, and as I looked down upon them, I could see their gratitude for being in a safe place.

Then, I flew through several other domes along the mountainside and viewed more people gathered here and there and domes used for practical purposes such as workshops and aquaponics.

In the last part of the viewing, I was hovering over myself, sitting in what appeared to be an underground horse livery beside someone who, according to the technique, would be a significant other or spouse. Also, I distinctly remember smelling axle grease and wet leather during that viewing.

When Ed Dames told the class that we all had just viewed where we would be and what we would be doing during the Kill Shot, according to the Akashic Record.

There is a quaint saying. Life is that funny thing that gets in the way of all your plans. As a result of this viewing, my Indigo sense of knowing was on fire, and my life suddenly went from zig to zag, lasting over eight years and three books.

When I wrote my third book in my survival trilogy, *Win-Win Survival Handbook: All-Hazards Safety and Future Space Colonization,* I recreated what I viewed in sufficient technical depth a faith leader can hand the book to a builder, point at an illustration, and say, "Make it so."

You have a lot on your plate, so tuck this one aside for the right moment, but when you're ready, begin exploring your online and local RV training options. Just know that RV is safe and yields useful and revealing results, and every survival community should have at least one Remote Viewer in the membership.

With that, my dear Riselings, you have three safe and effective ways to get Heaven working with you:

- Waking Dreams
- Speaking with Jesus
- Remote Viewing

For those of you who are interested in exploring your psychic abilities with open channeling, you need to do two things. First, learn and practice RV. It will help you discipline your mind, which is essential because both RV and psychic dialogs occur in the brain's right hemisphere, requiring the third eye connection.

By becoming proficient in RV, you will master your mind, and this will help you to become a more effective psychic.

The second thing you must do is pray for a mentor as you would a waking dream. Then, wait for a divine appointment to happen. There is an old saying that the teacher will appear when the student is ready, which is how it works: Provided you register for class. In other words, ask your Guides and be patient.

Here, I must share with you that, in terms of survival, the three kinds of secure channeling techniques discussed in this book are essentially a complete tool kit, and you can skip ahead if you like.

On the other hand, do you want to see how deep this rabbit hole goes?   Really?

OK, Riseling, you have heart, so let's dive into it.

Out-of-Body

Please fasten your seat belts and return your tray table to its full upright and locked position because there is a fourth kind of secure channel communication you need to understand. They are called profound out-of-body experiences, of which there are three experience types:

- **Near Death:** The most common experience is when people medically die, and their souls pass out of their bodies. They report going into the light and seeing themselves as eternal beings.

- **Shared Death:** Sometimes, a departing one can share the ascension experience with a willing loved one. These are very useful for passing along vital survival information.

- **Profound:** An intentional or unintentional out-of-body experience. The soul travels out of the body into space and is sheltered by loving Guides, and life lessons are shared.

I've had a powerful shared death experience with my mother when she passed and several profound experiences on my own. The operative word is "profound." A profound experience changes you in three specific ways:

- You see yourself as an eternal being.
- You completely lose your fear of death.
- You understand that reincarnation is how things work.

When you have a profound experience, it is life-changing and will bring you closer to God.

The Great Winnowing

During the tribulation, most will have near-death or share death experience, and here is an essential part for Riselings. Each time you have a profound experience, your third eye will open more.

Before the pole shift occurs, every mature Riseling, Indigo, and Crystal will have multiple out-of-body experiences, and this will help them to prepare others who survive and are in the light of God's love to cope with the effects of the pole shift.

The concept tends to remain at arm's length when discussing a pole shift because we believe we have no frame of reference for what will happen. Not so.

We have a real-life pole shift simulator in The Mystery Spot in Santa Cruz, CA. When I lived in the area, it was always on the tour itinerary for visiting family and friends.

It is nestled deep in the redwood forests outside Santa Cruz and features a unique gravitational anomaly. Some believe a buried alien beacon causes it, and others offer the usual swamp gas explanations, but in the final analysis, nobody knows.

What is known is that the anomaly is found on a steep slope and is a circular area of effect around 150 feet or 46 meters in diameter. The site is a popular tourist destination, but the queue moves faster than in a theme park. The experience is why.

When you enter the anomaly, your perceptions of the laws of physics and gravity cease to exist. At first, it feels novel, like those wavy, fun house mirrors that make us look like odd blobs. That turns into puzzling as you realize a loss of physical reference.

Then, it becomes disorientating, uncomfortable, and overwhelming, so you do what everyone else in the queue does. You step away from it, visit the snack bar area for a treat, and sit on a bench to sort everything out.

If you are so fortunate to visit this place, my dear Riselings, before you enter the queue, spot a quiet place to gather after the experience and then get in the queue.

After you experience the spot, go directly to your quiet place, take a knee, and perform the clarity mantra affirmation.

Clarity Mantra

Who am I?
I am a Good Person.

Where am I?
I am in the moment.

What am I prepared to do?
To be a light of hope.

This is the way.

With the sensations of this experience fresh in your mind and your thoughts cleared, focus on this knowing.

During the pole shift, this unsettling Mystery Spot effect is what everyone alive and conscious at that time will experience. Not for a few minutes, but continuously and without relief, for several days.

A few with closed third eyes will survive the pole shift, but those with love in their hearts and who survive the pole shift will emerge as mature Riselings. When they ask you how, here is what you tell them.

To walk out of the tribulation alive, you must walk through it with the Creator. This is the way.

A practical understanding of out-of-body experiences as a form of secure channeling is essential to being a light of hope so you can help others gracefully embrace their experiences without fear so they can survive.

Riselings, you now possess many tactical skills, such as effective listening to defend yourself and those you love. Master them, and they will serve you well. They are your edge in defending your life against the monsters who have skillfully hunted us for thousands of years, much like we hunt deer.

What makes us different from deer?

If you disregard these skills, there is no difference. Like a deer, you cannot see beyond the far horizon.

Use these skills as a Riesling, and you will see much further, and your knowing will reliably pierce the fog of deception.

In addition to these tactical skills, are there other kinds of psychic experiences? Yes, and they can be life-changing. So, it was during my vision quest in my late twenties, as you shall learn next.

Teaching Tools

As explained above, there are two general types of channeling: Open and secure. We covered the secure types, but as stated above, this book is an example of a mix of secure and unrestricted open-channel readings.

Again, anyone can do this if they set their mind to it; however, open channeling is only for trained and disciplined psychics. Never attempt this alone. You need to seek a mentor before exploring this natural talent.

One important thing is to invoke protection before you begin anything, which is simple. Here is how I always start:

> "Dear God, shine your radiant white light of love and protection upon me so I may feel your energetic presence passing through me, shielding me, and enfolding me."

Feel free to use it as a reference to create your own, but always ask because God's love and protection are always there for the asking.

With that in mind, you may wonder what it is like to develop the natural psychic skills that have always been yours.

For me, it has been a lifetime of seeking balance because, as one of God's technical writers, I work on both sides of the veil, so to speak, and over the years, I've made numerous beautiful friendships with the Creator and many loving Guides.

For me, Heaven is like Creator, Inc., and the business of Heaven, in a word, is survival. Everything else is details, and theoretically speaking, if I could register a trade name for Heaven without question. It must be Survival "R" Us.

What I routinely experience across the veil reminds me of when I was consulting in Silicon Valley. Some of my most enlightening moments were in the lunchrooms, where we could freely discuss how things work and where things seemed to be going.

Oh, excuse me. I forgot to mention where I am.

I'm beavering away down the cubicles and working with other wonderful souls, and there is no ranking system. You do what you can, and everyone is on the same team, and oh my, what a glorious team it is.

There is no competition, only cooperation, and those more capable than you across the veil will all tell you the same thing. What you are now, we once were. What we are now, you will become.

With this in mind, the cinema teaching tool for this chapter is *Astral City: A Spiritual Journey (2010),* a Brazilian film with English subtitles. The story follows a self-centered doctor dies on the operating table and finds himself in Astral City. A heavenly place of healing that hovers in the upper layers of the Earth's atmosphere.

As you watch the film, focus on the soup, unconditional love, forgiveness, and cooperation on the other side of the veil. The soup will help you appreciate my lunchroom view of Heaven, God's Plan, and how it works.

12

Perpetual Genesis

The previous chapter gave you the tools you need to defend your life and the lives of those you love. The knowledge presented in this chapter serves another mission. It is about being in it for the species.

> **If we cannot love our own species, who in the universe will?** *This is the way.*

What is this other mission I mentioned? It is the Creator's mission. Yes, God has a mission, as do we all. The reason is apparent.

> **The quest for order drives all things.** *This is the way.*

Therefore, precisely, what quest for order is driving God's mission?

It is answered by a construct I created, which I call "Perpetual Genesis." It explains God's mission as the perpetual Creation of life from the lifelessness of the Void.

When you embrace God's mission as I have, your life is never the same, and there is only one immediate benefit in taking the high road. There is no traffic congestion, as the grades can sometimes be steep.

The key to making this uphill journey easier and quicker is not only to know how things work, which is obvious, which brings us to the mission of this chapter.

It is helpful to tell you how things work, but that is not enough. More useful is a simple, functional construct that explains why it all works the way it does so that you can work more effectively within it. We, therefore, must ask, to what purpose and what, ultimately, does the Creator want to hear from each of us?

"Father, you can take the trainer wheels off. I've got this now."

For this reason, I named this construct Perpetual Genesis because of my eternal commitment to serve His mission. Likewise, the mission of this chapter is precisely that, and to do that, we will track the mysterious voyages of a little photon.

Follow the Photon

Explaining how and why Heaven works is a tall order, but we have tools to help us, namely similes, metaphors, and analogies. In this case, we will use a photon of light as our metaphor to understand how things work at an operation level.

Theologians and philosophers struggle to explain it all in the context of their faith but not in terms of survival. To illustrate the difference, let's imagine a fish tank in a classroom. It is a rectangular tank with several species of fish inside. It has two sides and two ends; consequently, if we want to study the fish within it, we have four views to work with. This is what you could call a lunchroom view of it all for us working stiffs.

With theologians and philosophers, their passion to understand more commands a different view. For them, the fish tank is circular with 360 different views, and while they labor with great vigor, the truth is, if you glued a hundred human brains together, it's still not enough to take it all in at once.

As for me, I understand the need to go beyond four views, and after the better part of a lifetime, I've made progress. However, I'm still in single digits, so we'll have to go the working stiff route.

My most engaging contract during my Silicon Valley consulting days was with Lockheed Martin. I was a senior technical writer/systems analyst. What does that mean? People get an idea and spend a boatload of cash to build it.

Publicly, they hire someone like me to explain it to everyone else. Privately, they want to see what they've done through a fresh pair of eyes because their Creation will always be a work in progress.

My assignments focused on the ground control systems for a civilian adaptation of a KH-11 spy satellite. We were told that all sorts of secret stuff were removed or changed to make this downscale version. That and a dollar will buy you a cup of coffee... maybe.

The first assignment was to write a deployment plan for moving all the equipment from Sunnyvale to three ground control stations. They liked that, and my next was a plum.

It focused on helping the future controllers working in those stations to identify communication problems quickly by explaining how the satellite communication system relays their commands. It's not an easy trick because there are a lot of twists, turns, gizmos, and gadgets both ways to consider.

I began by sitting in front of various video monitors and control panels as I mulled the need to sort this out. As I clawed through a bevy of ideas, I focused on the blinking underline of the cursor on the command monitor to the right of a question mark.

Nothing came to mind, and after a while, I got a cup of coffee and decided to step outside for a breath of fresh air. It was a delightful day, and I looked off in the distance at the massive satellite dishes and studied them until I had an epiphany about that flashing cursor.

Imagine a single photon of light representing the blinking cursor. When I type a command and press the enter key, where will that photon go, and what will happen to it?

I had my knowledge and woohoo, the game was afoot. There were all kinds of cabling and black boxes to consider, and I started with the enter key itself.

With that, I followed the photon everywhere, and the engineers were concerned to see me crawling behind equipment racks and pulling up floor plates to track every cable, every connection, and every piece of equipment that the photon passed through.

I wrote it all up, and when I was finished, something unique happened. In my entire consulting career, I never had engineers come to me to ask them how their part of the system worked.

Those familiar with consulting in the technical arena understand that such behavior borders on heresy. We're talking about getting out the pitchforks and torches heresy. Yet, what happened was that I had a steady stream of engineers unashamedly beating a path to my cubicle to commit collective heresy. Honestly, don't you live for days like that?

What I learned is all of the engineers were compartmentalized. Each was instructed to make one part of the system without understanding their role in the overall scheme of the system.

The point is that when you cannot see the complete picture, you depend on those who claim they can. Here is where you can run afoul of deception.

Poetry of Evil

The poetry of evil seduces us to abandon critical and spiritual thinking by appealing to our appetites, impulses, and desires to be a part of something big and powerful.

It usually begins with sophistry, which inevitably leads to gaslighting, a form of psychological abuse, and other such depraved, manipulative, and dissociative techniques.

Sophistry uses plausible-sounding reasoning that makes the case within itself on a superficial level for those willing to accept it without challenge. Sadly, many do and suffer from it. Those who will peel back the reasoning to examine it invariably reveal it is unsound or, in some cases, used to deceive.

This is nothing new for critical thinkers, and a quick way to parse through the manipulations of sophistry is by using tried-and-true tools such as Occam's razor. It is a principle that when you have two or more competing theories, the simplest explanation of the entity is preferred. To that, I add:

> The only truth that matters is the truth that resonates within you because you and you alone put it there. *This is the way.*

Remember, sophistry only resonates with the seduced, so be particular about the thoughts and musings you encounter, and always consider the source.

Source

Before I place a basic four-sided aquarium with four views before you, with which to study our Perpetual Genesis construct photon, I must present myself. This book is an accumulation of a lifetime of psychic experiences and observations but is principally driven by two keystone events in my life, which I call "downloads."

As most Indigos and Crystals do, I began exploring my psychic powers early in life, and when I was in my twenties, I asked the Creator to send me a mentor, and he did. A Native American medicine man who, for months, kindly and patiently taught me the wisdom of the Medicine Wheel and many other soulful beliefs.

Were I to compare the religions of the West with Native American spirituality, only two words are needed. For the West, that one word is entitlement. For Native Americans, it is appreciation. In a more enlightened world, I believe we will see a harmonious blending of the two, but for now, the matter at hand is my vision quest.

One day, my mentor casually asked, "Have you decided where?" I told him I had, and he answered, "You're ready."

A few weeks later, I was halfway across the country in the beautiful hills of Prescott, Arizona, at a small family cabin in the Prescott National Forest. Behind it was a mountain with a soft sandy saddle between twin peaks.

The vision quest is a sacred coming-of-age ritual when a young brave finds the greater meaning of life and his place in it. It was a transformative and purposeful experience. After fasting and preparation for a day and a half, I arose at the break of dawn and made for the saddle with nothing more than a canteen and pistol.

It was a pleasant hike, and I found that my sandy saddle was a very old arroyo, which folks often call a "dry gulch" because they are intermittent streams. The sand was soft and cool to the touch. I found where I wanted to be: undressed, folded my clothing, and set everything aside.

Sitting cross-legged in the sand, I began to still my mind, and I had been taught to focus on my senses to the exclusion of all thought. Sitting with my back to the breeze, I felt its cool April air, sweet with the scent of desert flowers.

The sand beneath me was comfortably cool and surprisingly soft, as though worn by time. I heard quail rustling about in search of sustenance as the morning sun warmed my back. It was perfect.

With each breath, I became more grounded and less conscious of myself until suddenly, I was floating in space in a profound out-of-body experience, my Vision Quest.

Ascended masters had brought me to a place facing the sun's Northern hemisphere, well above the ecliptic—the plane of our solar system. Floating in a relaxed fetal position, I could not see most of the sun below me.

When I saw myself this way, as an eternal being, I immediately knew that reincarnation works, and in that instant, I lost all fear of death, and then something magical happened.

I felt loved and connected in a way I've never known. It is so complete and beautiful you do not want to return, but return you must. This is when the first download began. I beheld beams of light coming at me from the sun.

As they raced towards me, I could read them like the title printed on the spine of a book. As they came to me, I reached out to grasp a few, and one that caught my eye was "The Difference between Men and Women." Gals, we'll discuss it later, and I think you'll like it.

When the download was complete, I knew it would take me decades to unpack it all, or at least enough of it to make sense, and the Ascended Masters instructed me to turn around, so I lowered my head to look down and rotated around effortlessly.

When I stopped, I was floating with my knees apart, and between them, I could see Earth well below me, about the size of a tetherball. Then, I was instructed to look up and saw Heaven from there.

What was arrayed before me was a vast web of light tunnels connecting every significant object in space, and within it, souls passing back and forth throughout like in much like gentle butterflies of light.

The Ascended Masters allowed me to take it all in with the time remaining and told me I could always return for more. With that, I was back in the arroyo, and such experiences leave you depleted.

By the time the sun was overhead and I could feel its warmth on my shoulders, I had risen up, dressed, and made my way back down the mountain, a changed man.

My second download happened half a life later. It was in early 2015, a few months after publishing *Being In It for the Species: The Universe Speaks*.

In writing that book, I worked with an ascended master named Rowena of the Elohim. I met here through Rebecca during our channeling research years earlier, and this was our second book together.

Then, one day, I was talking about Rowena with William, who had been my research and archive partner for the project, and he had a suggestion. He said, "Have you thought about channeling God because you could?"

It had never occurred to me, so I asked Rowena, and she was happy that I asked. She told me I was ready to do it and urged me to do so, and I agreed. The next day, I reached out to God, and the connection came fast and was powerful.

The first thing God said to me was, "Questions come later. Now, you must listen."

I listened for over two hours daily for three days before completing it. It was like trying to sip water out of a fire hose, so I let it wash through me as I did during my vision quest in Prescott.

These two download experiences were like the two main tent poles in a circus tent. Everything else is shaped by my many conversations with my Guides throughout my life in preparation for this book.

What about all that downloaded information and what happened with it? Worth question.

When I started this book, I swore by everything holy that it would not be over one hundred pages long. Well, life is the funny little thing that tends to get in the way of all our plans, and as you can see by the size of the book, that was not to be.

What happened is that as I began writing, I started unpacking the downloads, which is why whatever you have to say about this book, one thing for sure: it is not one hundred pages long, and that, my dear Riselings, is as good as it gets when considering this source.

Go with your gut and call it because what comes next is the whole enchilada.

Goals

My Perpetual Genesis construct, which I present in this chapter, is essentially a four-sided lunchroom view of how it works and why, and here, I must admit, it gets personal.

What disgusts me is watching wonderful, good people being repeatedly blindsided by the monsters. Enough is enough, and while this will not sound terribly elevated, it's time to open a can of whup-ass and get some.

You see them coming, so you can bypass their machinations and prevail. Yes, the monsters do awful things, but we need to stay frosty and focused to overcome it effectively. Or like they say in Texas, "Don't get mad and don't get even. Just get your way."

That's the goal in a nutshell, my dear Riselings. I'm sick and tired of seeing wonderful folk like you and your families being blindsided, and all that can come to a screeching halt once you understand how things work the way they do.

To succeed in helping you this way, what I share with you must be practical, and while there is a bit of wonder in all this, this will not be a celebratory fireworks show where you gather your stuff and boogie home after the oohs and aahs.

Instead, I will use the approach I developed with co-author Duane W Brayton for our book *Radio Free Earth: The Complete Beginner's Guide to Survival Communications.*

Duane was my brother from another mother, and I could not have done it without him. The foundational concept for our book is found in the affirmation:

If you cannot communicate, you cannot cooperate. This is the way.

While countless other books about two-way radio communications exist, they are all written for enthusiasts, hobbyists, engineers, and HAMs. For survivalists, these books are loaded with time-stealing technobabble, rabbit holes, and gotchas.

When things start going sideways, and folks realize the need to get on the air, an esoteric technical dialog will not do.

This is why Duane and I had to write a book for the rest of us. Something that breaks it all down in practical terms. That is what we did. If you know how to make a baby monitor work, this book will work for you–fast!

Using the same approach here, you will learn. Who and where, why things work the way they do, and then you will be ready for God's plan, and trust me, you'll love this. Duane and I dedicated our book to Nikola Tesla, the inventor of wireless radio communications. It was not Marconi who invented it, which was decided shortly after Tesla's death by a Supreme Court ruling.

In this book, Nikola once again shows us the way.

"If you want to know the secrets of the Universe, think in terms of energy, frequency and vibration."– Nikola Tesla.

Nikola Tesla was a highly evolved soul if not an ascended master, and later, we will add energy, frequency, and vibration to this construct. For now, we need to focus on terminology for a brief moment.

Lexicon

Over the years, one thing that astonishes me time and again is the language skills of God and the Guides. Hardly a reading goes by when I do not have to look up a word in the dictionary.

I would be familiar with these words but not clear on their meaning. Each time I looked up a word, it was, by definition, the most perfect word and was always used most correctly.

Likewise, we use terms here on Earth that are recognized and respected but not used on the other side. For this construct, I will use their terminology. Below is a simple lexicon.

- **Creator:** There are many gods, but there is only one Creator. God is used interchangeably for our benefit, but as long as you intend to speak to the Creator, you can address Him as Great Pumpkin, if need be, with no worries about losing brownie points. However, I must hasten not to expect you will gain any either.

- **Yeshua:** On Earth, Jesus, also called Jesus Christ, Jesus of Nazareth, was born Yeshua Bar Yosef. Yeshua was the name given to him by his mother, and it is taken from the Hebrew verb yasha, which means "to deliver, save, or rescue." No matter how many names you have on Earth, in Heaven, you are as your mother named you, and it is done without exception to honor motherhood. Imagine this like a zip code. If you want to address Him as Jesus, it's a five-digit code. If you address Him as Yeshua, it's a nine-digit code. Either way, it gets there. No worries.

- **Creation:** Creation is everything we can see with our two eyes and so much more. Even if we glued a hundred brains together, we still wouldn't have a chance to take in the big show.

- **Heaven:** With your third eye, you can begin to see Heaven because we incarnated souls are a part of it. This notion that we're down here and God and everyone else is up there, waiting to scold us, "That's it, kiddo. No milk and cookies for you tonight. Go straight to your room." Nothing could be further from the truth because we are continuously surrounded by love in multiple dimensions.

- **Gaia:** In the Avatar films, the moon of Pandora is ruled by a benign spirit named Eywa. Thematically, the characterization draws from Gaia of Greek mythology. An Earth Mother worshiped as a fertility and Earth goddess. Gaia is the governing soul of the planet. Her mission is to provide sentient lifeforms with a habitable biosphere, nothing more.

Imagine a baby in a crib. Gaia never interacts with the child in any way. Instead, you could say her mission is to decorate the nursery, and she's brilliant. Also,

Earth is Gaia's eightieth incarnation. After this flyby, the next will be the end for Earth, and may our descendants come to our Earth Mother and say, "We've got a sweet planet for you, so let's get the band back together."

- **Vehicle:** We are always taught the body is a container for the soul. If there is a possible pet peeve for the other side, this is it. You pay someone to store a container on a shelf and periodically dust it. For a modest fee or donation, of course. A vehicle is a container with wheels made to place. God didn't make Creation for you to sit on your backside; He wants you to kick the tires, light the fire, and make your incarnation go places. Oorah.

- **Return to God:** The concept of death, as most understand it today, is the most extraordinary con job ever perpetrated on humankind because it defies the sacred duality of reincarnation and redemption. Refuse to participate by never saying the word "death." Instead, always say, "Return to God" or "Return to Creator."

On a personal note, while doing my readings for this book, the Creator tasked me to explain the sacred duality of reincarnation and redemption because it is the path to evolution and liberation of our species.

As this construct unfolds, bear in mind the following three affirmations:

The quest for order drives all things. *This is the way.*

The greatest truths are by and of necessity–simple. *This is the way.*

Wisdom is a destination to which many paths of awareness lead. *This is the way.*

The Void

It is the time before the Creator. There was never a beginning, nor will there be an end. Always, the Void, always.

The Void is a lightless, featureless, unexpressed emptiness as black as coal and everywhere. This is consistent with what Astronomers have learned, in the better part of a century, that the space between the stars in our galaxy is not entirely empty.

Most will tell us space is filled with gas wisps and small dust grains; some will say to us that and much more.

During the mid-1980s, I was a science feature field producer for the Cable News Network. At the time, the network was making its bones and doing brilliant reporting compared to today's harmful propaganda and lies. My beat was the colleges and universities of Texas, and Big Bang Theory was the number one story I was always on the hunt for.

At that time, the holy grail of science was the need to understand if our universe would keep expanding until it recombined with something else or if gravity would eventually take hold and squeeze everything back into another singularity.

There was a Big Bang theme song to go along with it all, well, sort of. Peggy Lee singing "Is That All There Is" on a virtual loop.

Nonetheless, it was such an essential question that this research became a vacuum cleaner sucking up the budgets of many worthy astronomy projects.

After spending a king's ransom, they determined with 99% certainty that there would be no big squeeze. The funny thing is, the ancient Egyptians told us that same thing some 3,600 lunar years ago. OK, it's a push.

However, what science learned about space was invaluable, especially regarding dark energy and matter.

There is a fascinating tug-of-war between dark energy and dark matter, much like Doctor Dolittle's fictional pushmi-pullyu (pronounced "push-me-pull-you").

Dark energy is about 68 percent of the universe's total mass and energy. It speeds up the universe's expansion. It is a sort of anti-gravity due to it being a repulsive force.

Dark matter, on the other hand, is 27 percent of the universe's total mass and energy. Like a sea anchor towed behind a ship to slow it down, it works to slow the universe's expansion.

The remaining five percent of everything we see and interact with today is Creation, and it did not exist in the time before Creation.

Absent conclusive data, what existed before the Creator is difficult to say. After all, how can we know dark energy and matter are real beyond any hypothetical argument?

Here it is. The Void is an endless black expanse permeated by a thin consommé of dark energy and dark matter. No awareness, no sentience, no life whatsoever, just a lot of sub-atomic particles going helter-skelter one way and another because, as we know:

The quest for order drives all things. *This is the way.*

The Void is pure chaos, a subatomic realm that gives us an unlimited supply of mass and energy. All you need is a conscious entity capable of tapping into its potential, and endless possibilities exist.

Enter the first and only sentient entity produced by the chaos of Void to suddenly appear.

I Am

To help visualize the moment Creator became self-aware, imagine a 25-watt crystal clear incandescent light bulb with a dimmer switch. You set the power low, turn it on, and see the filament suspended mid-air, glowing brightly.

Let's study it for a moment. The crystal-clear bulb reveals a filament that is bright with light, like the sparks from a roaring fire, and you see the shape of the bulb encircling it. Remember this visualization, as we will refer back to it often.

Now, it is time to follow the photon.

Imagine the endless pitch-black stillness of the Void, and suddenly, in a fraction of an instant, a light appears, much like the filament in our light bulb. It is our proverbial photon.

Suspended in time and space was something never before seen, an eternal sentient light being, and its first thought was, "I Am."

With I Am, there was now a new realm. The realm of the atomic and the relationship between the atomic realm of I Am and the subatomic realm of the Void is complementary.

The Void does not know that it needs anything but is driven by an eternal need for order. On the other hand, I Am required much and could satisfy the Void's boundless quest for order. It was the classic win-win deal and the beginning of big things.

The subatomic realm of the Void can provide an unlimited supply of mass and energy. All that is needed is a way to tap into the reserve. For I Am that was simple, because I Am is of the Void, and It will forever sustain Him in all He does and creates.

The first order of business for I Am was to find another of His kind, which presented challenges because the Void is undistinguished. Without a sound navigational strategy, I Am could waste one eternity after another going in circles.

Driven to find another of his kind, I Am devised a navigational strategy that would indirectly lead to the Creation we know today.

The strategy was simple. Create navigation beacons of different types that would all be unique and identifiable. As there is never a shortage of space, He had ample canvas to master His techniques.

Each beacon was unique enough to be identifiable at a distance, and then, I Am connected all these celestial navigation bodies with tunnels of light. To record His journey, I Am created an eternal soul upon which He could imprint a complete multidimensional map that would follow him everywhere he went.

With that, the strategy was complete, and His journey to search for another began. It always seemed to go on and on for I Am, always knowing where he had been. As to the future, His hopes dimmed a bit more with each passing eternity.

Finally, one day, I Am's hopes for finding another flickered like a spent light bulb near its end. And then, they were spent, and I Am was alone with Himself.

It pains me to think of how isolated I Am must have felt then. To be the first and only one of a kind in existence is a dreadfully lonely place.

I Am is not like us, nor are we like him. We are one, and at some point, we must stop, look around, and choose another path. At that moment, I Am made the choice never to be lonely again and was reborn as Creator, with a handsome cosmic dowry no less.

Creator and Creation

Driven by the loneliness and despair of his failed search, the Creator created the framework of Creation, a multidimensional multiverse replete with all celestial phenomena—a veritable treasure trove.

On a personal note, I learned much of this part of the story in direct readings with the Creator plus more with Ascended Masters over several years, and every question I asked was answered with love.

Yet, there was one question I held back on for many years, and it was until I began work on this book that I knew the time had come to ask, and I did.

I asked the Creator if He was holding onto any hope that Creation would someday help another to find Him. He told me he was alone, and there was no other, but what got my attention was how He said it.

When you communicate with anyone over time, you learn their mannerisms and subtleties. For example, Rowena of the Elohim was mellow, pleasant, and had a great sense of humor.

With Creator, two words say it all for me. "Pleasant persistence." Over the years, I've noted the subtleties in our readings, which are precious to me because they add dimension. However, there was something new in this reading—nothing I had ever encountered.

As the Creator answered my question, His sadness was unmistakable. There is no other. It was a gut punch for me, and my love for the Creator grew.

To you, my dear Riselings, as well as those who anger at the Creator, know this:

There is only one Creator;
There is only one Creation;
There is only one Heaven;
and all we have is ourselves.

This is the way.

Creation is hundreds of billions of years old, and it no doubt took a few to get Creation working and to bring on extra hands, so to speak.

Now, let's follow the photon to Heaven and use it to build a basic four-sided aquarium with four views. Call it our lunchroom solution for working stiffs, and the first step in any such journey of wisdom is to consider the source.

Heaven

Many of our notions about Heaven are unidimensional in that they exist within a single dimension of existence and consciousness. Hence, we often consider ourselves here on Earth separate from Heaven above. However, there is a broader view.

Heaven is a multidimensional multiverse with many levels of existence or consciousness; we are an integral part of it. There is no physical boundary because Creation and Heaven exist within the Void, and the Void exists within them.

In other words, you, dear Riseling, are of Heaven in this dimension. Granted, it's the lowest run on the ascension ladder, but it's wherever everyone starts.

During my vision quest, I was shown a vast web of light tunnels connecting every significant object in space, and within it, souls traveling through it. These are the thresholds of Heaven, and when we are told to "go to the light," it is the divine light of the Creator's love shining out of the threshold to a tunnel of light we see.

This prompts a necessary question, given that the cinema teaching tool for the previous chapter is *Astral City: A Spiritual Journey (2010)*. I did not observe such things as Astral City during my vision quest, so why is this, as in, do we need to find fault? No.

In the film, Astral City is one of several such cities floating above Earth, where souls return to God. What they find are beautiful modern cities of spiritual healing.

During my vision quest, I saw the tunnels of light and souls moving within them. That was the dimension the Ascended Masters showed me. Astral City, which I have no reason to doubt exists, does so in another dimension.

What proof can I offer to support this multidimensional claim? Yeshua. He is the only multidimensional Ascended Master who can securely communicate and incarnate simultaneously in multiple lives and dimensions—ipso facto. With that thought in mind, let's follow our photon to you, me, and everyone else.

co-Creators

In Genesis, we're told that the Creator created man from dust from the ground, and in the Qur'an, we're told the Creator created man from clay. All this is true, given that we are made of the star stuff that makes up the Earth, a habitable world thanks to the watchful eye of Gaia.

Of importance here is that for the Creator to create us as co-Creators, He gives us a soul and a spirit, both of which are cleaved of Him. The word "cleaved" is off-putting, but that is what the Creator calls it, as it perfectly describes what happens.

Some believe that all the souls ever created have been created. Not so.

The Creator is continuously making new ones because it serves His mission. The perpetual Creation of life from the lifelessness of the Void. Consequently, He does not need sycophants and mindless minions as creative as leadless pencils.

He needs co-Creators for companionship and to form them to lean into the wheel of Creation in new and inventive ways, and here is how He does it.

He cleaves from himself a clean soul and, within it, places a spirit. The soul is ours eternally, and it defines who we are. Upon it, we imprint the experiences of our lifetimes, determining who we are, where we have been, and where we are now.

To power your vehicle, the Creator places your spirit, the light of His love, within your soul.

And so, we are made as unexpressed co-Creators, on an as-needed basis as livable space becomes available.

Here is where Gaia plays a vital role in providing a suitable environment for life. Something the many lifeless planets of Creation show us is far more complicated than most would imagine.

When your vehicle, your physical body, is created of star stuff of Creation on Earth, this planet becomes your point of origin as an undefined co-Creator.

Hence, the lineage of those of us who first incarnated on Earth will forever be as children of the Earth. This, plus the name our mothers give us, forever defines us.

What is important to remember? Your soul is you, and it is yours for eternity. Your spirit is not of you. It is of the Creator and always will be; a helpful word exists to describe it.

It is namaste; in the Hindu tradition, it is expressed with folded hands and a slight bow as a respectful greeting or farewell. This wonderful word has countless definitions and rolls off the tongue with elegant alliteration.

Here is my favorite. "That little bit of God in me greets the little bit of God in you."

Now, let's raise the photon analogy to the next level. Up till now, the photon first represented I Am and then Creator. Beginning now, it is your turn, dear Riselings, to be the photon. Tag, you're it, and you're in Heaven.

Life Force Energy

Previously, you learned the difference between a container and a vehicle. A vehicle is a container with wheels and is designed to go places. OK, that works, but how do you power it to make it go? For that answer, we find a fabulous clue in Genesis 2.

> **Young's Literal Translation 1898**
> Genesis 2
>
> 7 And Jehovah God formeth the man — dust from the ground, **and breatheth into his nostrils breath of life**, and the man becometh a living creature.

For the Creator, accessing the energy and mass of the Void to build Creation is intuitive and seamless. However, because we must exist in a physical dimension, we need life force energy to animate our Vehicles.

We need our metaphor with a 25-watt crystal clear incandescent light bulb with a dimmer switch to help explain that.

Imagine yourself sitting and quietly observing your dim, incandescent bulb. The crystal-clear glass bulb represents your soul. It is yours and always will be. The lit filament is your spirit, which is of the Creator and always will be.

In another dimension, a soul and a spirit are all that are necessary, and this is how we return to the Creator.

However, with incarnation, it is like going into space. The soul and spirit need a spacesuit. Namely, a body made of star stuff that depends on a continuous source of life force energy to operate in a physical dimension.

Therein lies the question. How do you feed the beast?

The answer to this will give you a vital clue to unraveling the meaning of all this so that you can use it to your advantage in service to your family and loved ones.

The power source needed to fuel our bodies with the life force energy, also known as prana, is the dark energy in the Void. While this dark energy is limitless, our bodies cannot draw on it in the physical realm.

Therefore, what the Creator uses to create a power channel between us and the Void is called energy transformation, or energy conversion. It is changing energy from one form to another.

Each time you use an AC wall adapter to charge your smartphone with DC power, you celebrate the process, which tends to work well, as the following analogy explains.

After your charger is plugged in and ready, you only need two things to charge your phone: a connection point for the USB connector and a battery to store the energy.

The other side of the analogy is your body. The connector is your spirit. It is the key to the Kingdom; through it, the life force energy you need can be drawn into your physical body and stored there in a usable form.

Here, we return to the chakra system. The soul and spirit reside in the seventh chakra, the Crown Chakra. The process of fueling your body with prana is the pumping process of breathing.

When you breathe in, your spirit draws fresh prana in, and as you exhale, it pushes exhausted prana out of your body.

As prana enters the Crown Chakra, the pumping action of your breathing pushes it down through the other chakras to a repository in the first chakra, called the Root

Chakra, where it is stored in what Koreans call the "Danjeon." A region of the human body known to women as the womb. With that in mind, let's re-read Genesis 2.7.

> **Young's Literal Translation 1898**
> Genesis 2
>
> 7 And Jehovah God formeth the man — dust from the ground, and breatheth into his nostrils **breath of life**, and the man becometh a living creature.

"Breath of life" perfectly describes the energy transformation and delivery process that makes our bodies work. I cannot overstate the importance of this concept because it is essential to understanding how to do defeat the monsters.

Likewise, you need to understand that you are not alone, and you've never been.

Our Home

Heaven is multidimensional, and we cannot see another because we are in one dimension. It does not mean we are not part of Heaven, as in being in Heaven. Quite the contrary. To explain why, let's return to our smartphone metaphor.

Imagine that this is all about hardware and software. The hardware is Creation, and Heaven is the software. Hardware exists where we put it. Software can be anywhere, on the phone, in the Eternal Cloud, wherever.

Heaven is not a place you go to as a reward. This is because with your first incarnation, you become part of Heaven, and what distinguishes you from the other members of Heaven is your ascension path, or soul journey, as I call it.

Here is the path.

Unless you are a Star Seed, you first incarnated as a Child of Earth and, as such, are designated a soul to learn life lessons.

Unfortunately, regretful things happen, and consequently, through reincarnation and redemption over several lifetimes, we finally return to the Creator as clean and pure as we were in our first incarnation.

Then, we evolve to our next mission level as ascended souls. As such, we take on more responsibilities and explore Creation in an apprenticeship to become ascended masters. We do not incarnate during this level but work intensively as messengers.

While souls that have returned to the Creator use the tunnels of light to move about through Creation, ascended masters do not require the tunnels. They can travel to any place, time, or dimension in Creation at the speed of thought.

Above the ascended masters is Yeshua, the only multidimensional ascended master in Heaven. He's been with the Creator since the beginning and does fantastic things.

For those who want the numbers, here you go:

- Creation is many billions of years old
- There is 1 Creator.
- There is 1 Yeshua.
- There are thousands of Ascended Masters
- There are millions of Ascended Souls (Apprentices)
- The number of incarnated souls is beyond counting.

If you are running the numbers in your mind, let's compare.

Creation is many billions of years old, and the goal of all these souls beyond counting is to ascend. Conversely, there are only millions of Ascended Souls and only thousands of Ascended Masters. What's missing here?

What is missing is the lack of planets with evolved sentient species. In other words, it's nice that there is no limit to the number of students seeking advanced degrees, but there are not enough institutions of higher learning to accommodate them.

That's right. Heaven needs executive staffing and training facilities; sadly, the human species is not even at the junior college level. We're more like an inner-city junior high school with bloody food fights, though we have promise.

In fact, my dear Riselings, we're nearing breakout as a species, thanks to reincarnation.

Reincarnation

The vast majority of people alive today believe in reincarnation, and a vast wealth of information is available. In Indian religions, karma describes a principle of cause and effect, called the principle of karma.

The cause is the individual's intent when free will is used to act on that intent, and karma is the consequence. Here, there is one immutable law of reincarnation you need to impress upon your memory.

> The journey is more decisive than the destination. *This is the way.*

There are three types of karma, and for the purpose of this construct, they are defined as:

- **Past Life (Sanchitta karma):** Free-will actions in past lives. Your soul is a repository of every action from every lifetime you have lived, for good and evil.

- **Present Life (Parabda karma):** These are your current free will actions, and here is where you have immense power to be a light of hope through redemption.

- **Future Life (Agami karma):** Your choices of today will echo throughout eternity and set agendas for future lifetime actions.

At an individual level, all three types of karma are equally important. This is important for you.

For the Creator, the collective past and present of all souls on Earth will determine the future karma of the species level. Hence, here is the crux of it from the Creator's perspective:

> The essence of reincarnation is the cumulative experiences in one species. *This is the way.*

On a species level, this is why we are at a breakout point as a species. We've paid our dues through countless generations and can forever unshackle ourselves from these monsters.

Right now, we've got enough good karma and physical numbers as a species to make it happen, and the monsters are desperately trying to steal our rightful destiny from us.

This brings us back to you, my dear little photon, and your collective karma quotient (CKQ), as I call it.

One of the first things you learn when doing past-life psychic work is that everybody has killed somebody, somewhere, and sometime during a previous lifetime, if not more, and the closet could be stuffed with more.

Eh, whaddya gonna do? But don't beat yourself up. Human beings are the apex predators on this planet, or so we're told, but even if we're running in the back of the pack, nobody comes home from school with a reincarnation report card with an "A" for "Works well with others."

For those of you worried about your collective karma quotient, no worries. The Creator gave us redemption to build it up. It's like improving your credit score but without the blood-sucking interest.

Redemption

There is a magnificent symbiotic relationship between redemption and present karma, and when you understand how to work with it, your soul journey will improve.

What you first need to understand about reincarnation and redemption is:

> The cumulative quality of incarnations drives soul growth, not quantity. *This is the way.*

In other words, redemption brings harmony and enlightenment, but for now, it's the good old two-step from one incarnation to the other. You know the drill: two steps forward, one step back, two steps forward, three steps back, and so forth.

However, despite the ups and downs, the ultimate goal of your ascension is to return to the Creator as an ascended soul. Your soul returns as pure as it was when you first incarnated. That's it, the big enchilada.

Likewise, another term is used by Guides.

Soul Scaring

The term "soul-scaring" serves as the linchpin principle of redemption, and it is simple.

You get what you give. *This is the way.*

In past lives, when we, through intention, exercised our free will to harm innocent people, the scars we made upon their souls become scars upon our souls as well. That, plus secondary scaring, such as the mourning of loved ones.

When our victims return to the Creator, the scars you gave them are purged. However, the scars you reciprocally incurred are bound by your intention, and unless you resolve them through redemption, they'll stay with your soul forever.

If you are feeling depressed because now, you'll have to do something to deal with your past life karma, like laying a dead chicken on your smartphone and moonwalking backward around it, repeating, "I'm not worthy." Oh please. Only in Hollywood.

The way to redeem your past karma is simple.

Good lives make for good souls. *This is the way.*

That's it. Lead a good life, and you'll eventually remove the scars. Simple in concept until you become a lazy student and aim for a C+ average.

Here is the bottom line. This is like paying off your karma debt with high-interest-rate credit cards. It's a slow and expensive way to get debt-free.

To speed things up, service to others is the way for those seeking to improve their collective karma quotient, and here is the affirmation–again.

You get what you give. *This is the way.*

For example, the house of faith you attend offers you the opportunity to go on a two-year mission to help poor folks in the third world by digging wells, giving care, and the like.

From a reincarnation and redemption standpoint, what have you to gain? This is a worthy question; we'll fly in a gas balloon named Heavenly Ascension to answer it.

You scramble into the gondola, and there you see a pile of small bags of various sizes filled with sand, and no matter what you try to do, you cannot touch them.

And so, the balloon ride begins as soon as you draw your first breath. However, due to the ballast of your past lives, it rises slowly but steadily.

From that point forward, each time you scar an innocent soul in the present, a new sandbag will appear on the pile, and thanks to secondary scaring, several more bags can also appear. After, you're still ascending but just a bit little slower.

This brings us back to the two-year mission. You give up fame and fortune and go to where life holds on by a thread to help other children of the Earth. Each time you are a light of hope for them, such as curing a wound or bringing in a new water well, you get what you give, and it comes back at you with secondary results.

That is when you'll see some of those old bags of sand starting to disappear out of the gondola and begin to feel things moving upwards at a more pleasing rate.

On the other hand, do these karma balloons ever crash and burn? Oh, yes, and this brings us to the sad duty of understanding lost souls, for they are the monsters, and this is the knowledge they fear and suppress.

Lost Souls

So far, the conversation has been on the positive side of things, and you understand how things work in terms of this construct and what you need to do to survive and to help humanity achieve its rightful destiny with a Star Trek future. To you, I say, may your balloons of redemption rise so quickly that you need fewer incarnations to finish the job.

Now, let's talk about the balloons that crash and burn. During an incarnation, a soul can become sick for many reasons. For example, A small percentage of pedophilia victims will go on to become offenders, while the vast majority do not. The victims become pedophiles and, in turn, scar the souls of innocent children.

In Heaven, allowing such sickness into one's soul is seen as a self-inflicted evil that, unless resolved, can eventually lead to death eternal in the Void.

Hence, we often hear Q and Anons calling the monsters "sick people." That is what they are called in Heaven, "sick souls."

When past and present life scars are so great, they act as overwhelming ballast; the soul goes into descension, that is, a descending path away from the Creator if you will.

There are rules with reincarnation.

- **First negative incarnation.** If the balance of all your incarnations is positive, then you receive the benefit of the doubt and will reincarnate.

- **Second negative incarnation.** If the balance of all your incarnations is negative, but you are actively in redemption, the Creator will give you the benefit of the doubt, and you will reincarnate.

- **Third negative incarnation.** Now you're a three-time loser and a loose cannon on deck. The Creator will hear you if you reach out to Him. However, this time, you will not receive the benefit of the doubt. If the Creator looks away, as is often the case, the sick soul can immediately accept death eternal in the Void or become a demon. Either way, it ends in the Void.

Interestingly, more than one psychic has told me that the few three-time losers who get a last chance repeatedly reincarnate as victims with short, tortured lives, not as punishment but as a way to spare good souls.

My feeling on this is that it is practical, and if there is one thing I've learned, it is that Heaven is always practical.

There are libraries of books explaining forgiveness, and from the viewpoint of Heaven, it only takes six words to describe.

Forgiveness is the cessation of judgment. *This is the way.*

Forgetting is hard, and something can never be forgotten, nor should it be. As for the rest, the calendar fixes everything. However, once you stop judging whoever hurt you, you free yourself from the ownership of the scar.

Why? Because it's the practical thing to do. It's like sticking the schmuck who hurt you with the check.

Another oddity is the rhetorical concept of the veil between us and Heaven.

We often imagine the veil as an imaginary boundary between Earth's physical dimension and Heaven's. That fits easily into a three-dimensional model, but not here. It is not what happens.

Death Eternal

Years ago, I was curious as to what it would be like for a soul who has ended life with a third negative incarnation. I asked my Guides for protection and asked them to help me experience what that is like. That moment of choice is when sick souls either earn one last chance or waste it and what becomes of them.

Here is what I experienced. When a soul leaves the body after the third negative incarnation, it enters a transition zone between the lifelessness of the Void. The soul floats like in a pool, and the Void is comfortably cool and absolutely quiet.

At that moment, the sick soul is free of all the woes and anger that perverted its incarnations. It is a comfortable and quiet place, above which the soul can see the threshold to the tunnel of light and is growing steadily more distant.

This is when the sick soul has three choices. Beg the Creator for forgiveness and a second chance, knowing there will be no benefit of the doubt, remain there to see what the Void has to offer. The vast majority of sick souls choose the latter to their regret, no doubt reasoning that since the Creator is of the Void, they can also be.

Those who choose poorly keep sinking into the lifelessness of the Void, and then when they lose sight of God's light of love shining through the threshold, they float in the coolness which, due to the radiance of Heaven, retains a shade of gray.

They float there calmly and peacefully for some time until it begins. The hunger. A hunger they've never felt, and because the soul has repressed its spirit for so long, it will not notice its return to the Creator.

Absent the key to the Kingdom, the soul still requires life force energy, and now a great punchline from the comedian George Carlin describes the situation of the lost soul for Heaven. "It's a big club, and you ain't in it."

Heaven uses the term lost soul because, at that point, even the Creator cannot find it. It is death eternal in the Void. At that point, the lost soul realizes that absent a spirit, it will continue its descent into the Void, and there are uncertainties as to what happens to a lost soul there.

Will the hunger persist? Will they continue? Frankly, even the Creator does not know the answer because never in the history of Heaven has a lost soul returned from death eternal in the Void to tell the tale.

Then there is the other choice: to feed the hunger, and it is an ugly business. The only way demons can hope to satisfy their hunger is by stealing life force energy from the incarnated, and there is only one way to do that. Create fear and terror.

When an incarnated soul is overwhelmed by fear and terror, it hemorrhages life-force energy, letting it pass out of the body like water through a colander. Then, the demons can feed on it, like starving cats lapping up a windfall of spilled cream.

They favor no political, religious, or social beliefs, only to use them to provoke emotions that reward them with what they seek. But then, it's not pure gain either because there is always a bigger fish, and you've got to pay the vigorish when you're a little fish.

The big fish is inevitably a false god whose only way to hold power and feed is with deception and violence. The false god Satan was an angel who fell to Earth and eventually became a lost soul and a demon. During the process, he was gifted an artificial intelligence symbiont named Lucifer by a soulless extraterrestrial race.

Unfortunately, we're about to learn what has been painfully and repeatedly learned throughout the history of Creation. It never ends well with c

At present, Satan and his minions understand their end is drawing near, and for over a century, they have done everything imaginable to keep humanity enslaved because if we can free ourselves from the shackles of their deceptions and if our species persists in reaching for its freedom, we shall have it.

What will they have? Absent a food source, all they will have left is each other to cannibalize until they all are committed to death eternal in the Void. They all know that, so they are blundering about in such panic. Their food source is rebelling, and if they cannot maintain control, they will starve, so here is the mission statement, my dear Riselings:

> Stay frosty and let the monsters eat vacuum. *This is the way.*

Never let them manipulate you ever again. Rise above their realm of chaos and into the Harmony of Heaven for a magnificent future ahead.

For those who cling to the notion we're unique in the whole universe, get over it. We're not. Over time, there have been countless species at this point in their history where they either win or lose and what is happening now has happened numerous times before.

Well, are you beginning to feel a sense of destiny mojo? If so, in the words of my generation, "groovy baby," because you're ready for the Creator's Plan and your role in it, and I think you'll love this.

Reach for Freedom

The Creator has a plan for us, and it is working and on track, although to look at the headlines, one wonders if that claim is Pollyannish. For that, let me return to the channeling research we began in 2007 and finished in late 2008.

This was depressing because I could see evil winning, and good seemed clueless, if not indifferent. After a few months of being depressed, I turned to my best psychic for help. She was remarkable in that she could channel almost anyone, and when I shared my feelings with her, she said, let's put it out there and see what we see.

She took three deep breaths to clear herself as usual. A few moments later, she announced, "I have Serapis Bey, a former high priest of Atlantis and Ascended Master, with me, and he would be most helpful for this question as this is the question he always seeks to answer for seekers of truth such as yourself."

I welcomed Serapis and explained my dilemma and sadness, which he answered with an explanation that soothed my soul. Here is what he said:

Serapis Bey, 2009
Reading by Marshall Masters

"Marshall, the story of humanity is a very large book of many chapters, most of which have yet to be written. This present chapter you are in is the domain of those you called the Elites. They own it, and there is nothing you can do or say to take it from them. Therefore, do not waste your time attempting to do so."

"But what they know and what you may not know is that this chapter, like all chapters and all books, will come to an end, and the end of this chapter is a few pages away. The Elites know that the next chapter is yours, not theirs, and if they are to take it from you, they must bluff you to do so."

"To win your freedom, you must do two things. Ignore their bluff and always reach for freedom. Reach for your freedom, and it shall be yours."

After that, we discussed it further and closed the session.

As I mentioned earlier, the Guides are always specific in their choice of words, and the one that caught my attention in this reading was "reach." After years of pondering on this reading, I came to four specific findings:

Serapis Bey:

- Did not say that we need to fight for our freedom.
- Did not say that we need to hope for our freedom.
- Did not say that we need to purchase our freedom.
- What he said is to "Always reach for freedom."

In other words, humanity can win without artificial intelligence and other technologies and methodologies. We win by repeatedly reaching for our freedom; no matter the sacrifice or the number of incarnations, we must always reach for our freedom.

When I did that, reading some fourteen years ago, aside from a few on the fringe, mainstream humanity was reaching for the television remote. Those were dark days for me, but things have changed.

Humanity is reaching. Parents are being arrested for speaking out against grooming, successful people losing careers because they refuse to submit to medical tyranny, and more.

As a species, we are coming into awareness, and we are taking action to break free from the shackles of slavery that bind us. Whether you live to see this happen in your lifetime or not, it will happen because this is a critical part of the Creator's Plan.

Creator's Plan

During our readings in 2007 and 2008, we met ascended masters, those who have never incarnated on Earth and those who had, plus several extraterrestrial races from the far-flung corners of our galaxy.

The extraterrestrials all focused on the same issue. They always told us that humanity is reaching a critical evolutionary point. If we choose wisely, we will have a bright future, but if you are weak and choose unwisely for expediency or ease, you will condemn yourselves and countless generations to slavery.

They all gave the exact reason for this. Each of their species had chosen badly and long suffered for it. In other words, they failed to reach for their freedom and do not want the same for us.

Another thing that was a steady message throughout our various extraterrestrial readings was a warning. With artificial intelligence, it never ends well. A theme often replayed in the fiction of our day, such as in the Battlestar Galactica television series.

However, the most exciting revelation occurred during our study's last interview with an extraterrestrial entity from the far side of the galaxy.

We had a delightful and informative conversation, and I decided for the first time to ask a question I long had in mind.

I told the entity, "I really appreciate the information you are giving me today, but you are on the other side of the galaxy, and we shall never meet, so I must ask. Why are you doing this? What's in it for you?"

The answer left me stunned. The extraterrestrial said, "Marshall, you have over 7 billion souls currently incarnated on your planet, yet Earth only has over 2 billion native souls. The rest have incarnated on Earth at this time to help humankind prevail and evolve. This is why we are interested, Marshall, because you have our ancestors."

Remember that this reading happened fifteen years and a billion or so babies ago.

This was my first introduction to the Star Seed concept of souls from other worlds traveling through the tunnels of light to Earth and incarnating here in service to the Creator.

Star Seeds are more commonly known as Angels on Earth, but the questions remain the same even for them. Why are you doing this, and what's your angle?"

Let's put this in perspective. It's nice that some six billion souls from all across Creation have incarnated here at this time to help humanity break the shackles of slavery once and for all. This is not a small task when you consider how it plays out.

They leave their soul families on other planets, slog halfway across Creation in the tunnels of light, and incarnate in a species about to hit the wall at a thousand miles an hour, and here is the corker. At the moment, the best Earth can offer is a quick end to your misery. Think about it. We're talking slim pickings at best here, so what's the angle?

Humanity has proved itself to all of Heaven. Parasites and predators in multiple dimensions infest us, most of our own making. Sadly, they feed from us and seek to suppress our species from ascending less they starve.

Yet, no matter how much they poison our food, our bodies, and the environment and plague us with divisive wars and endless misery, we are irrepressible. We have shown Heaven that we, as a species, reach for our freedom in the most noble and compassionate ways.

- Heaven sees us reaching. Rejoice.
- Heaven sees us reaching. We have old enemies and new friends.
- Heaven sees us reaching. The help of new friends is good, but this remains our fight in the eyes of the Creator.

Here is the reason six billion or so souls became Star Seeds. When you incarnate in a species' home world, you likewise become a child of Earth, and what they see is a winner.

You, my dear Riselings, will survive, live long lives, thrive, and raise our species out of the chaos to become an enlightened spacefaring species. Your descendants will span the galaxy in the hundreds of billions, and every soul wanting to ascend more quickly will be on the standby boarding list.

Here is the deal for the Earth and Star Seeds children. Keep the faith, obey the rules of reincarnation, and you get to the head of the line for humanity's Star Trek future. No standby for you.

This is why billions of souls from across Creation have incarnated for all the pain and misery to unfold. They want to earn their prepaid boarding pass to a magnificent incarnation. That works for me, but we have also paid a terrible price for countless generations.

Doctors will tell us our bodies can theoretically live 130 years or more. Yet, we never live long enough to get a good bead on things. The result is that humanity has been doing pulse reincarnations. Consequently, we must incarnate in shorter lives far more often; this is just how it is.

My dear Riselings, this is why you were not born a flame-on, fully mature Indigo or Crystal. By 2030, you will be, so do not let this get you down.

In the meantime, here is a tip to lift a down thought.

During WWII, there was a popular aphorism, "Illegitimi non carborundum." A Latin-like phrase meaning "Don't let the bastards grind you down." Say what you will, but it helped the men and women who carried the torch for freedom in a two-theater war, and we won it. Old tricks are the best tricks, and this one is a keeper.

But here is the more significant point. What we are going through as a species is a process that has been repeated countless times throughout the history of Heaven, and there is a time-proven playbook.

The Great Winnowing

The term "Great Winnowing" is first mentioned in *The Kolbrin Bible*. It's the plan, and as it implies, the process separates the wheat from the chaff. It is how the Creator frees a species from slavery. To help explain why, Nikola Tesla gives us the necessary clues.

> "If you want to know the secrets of the Universe, think in terms of energy, frequency and vibration."– *Nikola Tesla.*

In the Great Winnowing, the Creator purges all souls who cannot sustain ascension. In other words, what we know as the Great Winnowing here on Earth is called "The Purge," in Heaven.

With that in mind, here are the basic concepts.

- **Energy:** The Creator transforms the dark energy of the Void into the life force energy we need to exist in the physical realm. Lost souls and demons need it to survive and create mayhem and misery to get it.

- **Frequency:** Creation is a multidimensional multiverse; what we see with our two eyes is the dimension of Creation. With our third eye, we begin to see the higher dimension of Heaven.

- **Vibration:** When a species collectively ascends, its vibration rate for incarnation rises substantially from previous generations, making the species desirable for those within a few incarnations of becoming ascended souls.

The critical point to remember with the Creator Plan is that it has been refined over time, and here is the mission, so buckle up, Riselings.

For Heaven, the plan goal is to help a deserving species break free from the shackles of slavery. Then, millions and billions of new incarnation opportunities for souls across Creation on the standby list for their ascension journeys will have a new destination.

Unfortunately, given its present state, humanity cannot hope to serve that purpose.

However, after the Great Winnowing, our species will evolve to a higher state of enlightenment, and survivors and their descendants will lead joyous and fulfilling lives as free beings.

To make that happen, Heaven needs to gather all the sick souls, lost souls, demons, and false gods in one place because now they are scattered and difficult to locate.

As to the sick souls, the pole shift event will be the end of them, save for a few. The focus here is on the nasties.

With the coming tribulation, billions will perish, and, in their terror and fear, they will serve up an irresistible life force energy banquet such as not been seen in eons of time for lost souls and demons to feast upon.

They will know it is a trap, but their hunger for life force energy will delude them into believing they can outmaneuver the Creator because they have found ways to travel through Creation without the tunnels of light.

I call it the delusion of hunger, and after they all arrive and grow fat on the bounty of a tortured world, the Creator springs the frequency trap. Remember, the term frequency explains the difference between us in a physical dimension and our Guides in the dimension of Heaven.

Here is the gotcha for the nasties. Only the Creator and Yeshua can operate simultaneously in multiple dimensions and will do with a tag team takedown of the nasties.

As the nasties are feeding and distracted, Creator and Yeshua will close off all their egress routes, imprisoning them here. Then, after the Great Winnowing, the survivors, except a few, will become enlightened and fully mature Indigos and Crystals.

In essence, to survive the pole shift will be as tricky as passing through the eye of a needle. Those who thread it will rise out of the chaos so far that the nasties can never come close to them again.

For the Creator, this is not about justice. This will be a reckoning; if you cannot thread the needle, there will be no second chances. No benefit of the doubt. No unwritten rules. Weakened by hunger, their souls will be committed to death eternal in the Void in a massive purge we could not imagine.

Yet, when it is done, Earth and humanity will be pristine and welcoming for future generations. In that future, I am told two or possibly three Ascended Masters will incarnate to help us achieve our rightful future.

I hope that humanity will reach for its freedom, and with the help of wise and compassionate leadership, because more of us can survive than otherwise would not. I see the efforts of these Patriot souls, and they are magnificent light workers, but no matter what they achieve, nothing can stop what is coming—namely, the Creator's Plan.

With all that in mind, what about you? What is your role in all this?

Your Role

My dear Riselings, what is your role in all this? You give it meaning. You give it hope and must do so with gentle words and thoughts and with the courage to be a light worker. Remember:

> Man moves mountains, and Heaven moves minds. *This is the way.*

If you exhibit signs of fear or doubt, the confidence of others in you will part like quicksand.

Nor should you present yourself as a definitive source because time never reverses course, and everything in Heaven and Creation is a work in progress. The aim is survival, and what all the Guides want you to know is this:

> Survival is about learning enough about what works before what hurts kills you.
> *This is the way.*

This, you do for others. For yourself, the personal path is different. You must master the symbiotic relationship between incarnation and redemption, for redemption is not something you promise Creator you'll do if you get just one more freebie.

Given that you are very young, does not mean you can ignore your karma from past incarnations or schedule a token redemption ceremony.

When we return to the Creator, we arrive with past life warts and all, and this time, you will not get a pass if you haven't kept the faith. But if you are in a state of redemption, you will get that pass when you return.

Therefore, incarnation is about souls evolving over several incarnations to learn the Godliness of Creation, and ascension comes through wisdom accumulated through lifetimes of encounters and actions. The godliness of Creation is to be with God, the Creator of all there is, in mind, body, and soul.

Begin your path of redemption today with this affirmation.

To all sick souls, lost souls, and demons, I command you:

- Never defile my mind with deception.
- Never feed off my body for life-force energy.
- Never infect my soul with your sickness.

This is the way.

Remember the power of redemption and use it to confront evil whenever and wherever it appears, or evil will come to own you.

Teaching Tools

At this point, my dear Riselings, you're undoubtedly overwhelmed by all this information. If so, welcome to the party. This has been your download, and it will take time to unpack it all, but everything you need will be waiting for you where you know to find it.

In the meantime, once hormones start to flow, your thoughts will be more immediate, as in, after I grow a bit, where will I find my special somebody, and what if we do not run in circles?

Different circles will be critical in finding a mate because we are entering a time when humanity faces the existential threat of genetic extinction, and to make marriages work, we'll have to work with others in ways we normally would not.

With this in mind, the cinema teaching tool for this chapter is *My Big Fat Greek Wedding (2002)*. I put myself through college as a wedding photographer, and of the over one hundred and fifty weddings I photographed, my hands down favorite nationality was the Greeks. You'll see why in the film. Opa!

What to look here for is how this man and woman brought two completely different worlds together with love, respect, and honor.

We must return to tradition. One man. One woman. One God. I have a question for those whose sensibilities may be offended by this.

According to one study, scientists tell us that during an ancient catastrophe, our ancestors were whittled down to a population of less than a thousand and with as few as 40 breeding pairs, according to one study.

The question is if those 40 breeding pairs had been comprised of Lesbian feminists and feckless snowflakes, where would humanity be today? Take your time. No rush.

As to you, my dear Riselings, and your families, I hope you will survive and become a new hope for a new world. In the years to come, you will find each other and be worthy of your calling. Remember:

> All who want to evolve must stay faithful to a life mission. *This is the way.*

Your mission, my dear Riselings, is to grow strong, wise, and free. The families you build together will be a consequence of your calling.

What will that calling be?

When my vision quest mentor asked if I had found the place, I said yes, and that was all that was necessary because this is something only you and you alone will know. Remember:

Marshall's Motto

Destiny comes to those who listen,
and fate finds the rest.

So, learn what you can learn,
do what you can do,
and never give up hope.

This is the way.

Here are a few quick tips on boosting your psychic ability naturally through diet and exercise.

The monsters attack all the glands in our bodies, and the one they go for with zeal is the pineal gland. Their principal line of attack is to calcify the gland with fluoride. For this reason, drinking fluoridated water or using fluoridated dental products should be avoided.

While this should not be an immediate concern for Riselings, due to your age, older family members are likely to have some calcification, which can be reversed by supplementing with Lugol's iodine.

Many people report experiencing improved mental functioning, memory, and mental endurance. I use it, and it does precisely that. I suggest they use the following search string to learn more, "decalcify your pineal gland."

Another thing I strongly recommend to the whole family is to explore the energy arts for healing. There are many excellent choices, and when you speak with a healing master, inquire about energizing the root chakra.

I personally do Danjeon Breathing. In 2013, I worked with Master Roar Sheppard on creating a home study system for this non-invasive self-healing energy art. I learned a lot about life force energy by producing this system I call Feel Better on Your Own, and the knowledge I gained was instrumental in completing this construct.

The point is if you want to turbocharge your psychic abilities to a whole new level, ditch the fluoride and decalcify your pineal gland if need be, and then begin exploring the compassionate, healing world of energy arts in search of root chakra prana boosters.

13

Shawheylu

At the outset, I asked you, dear Riselings, to save yourself for marriage, or at least until you've finished reading this book, because I had something to tell you that would make it all worth the effort, and here it is.

Previously, we learned that during the Great Winnowing, the Creator will purge all souls who cannot sustain ascension. In other words, the unresolved weight of their soul scars from several lifetimes will become an existential issue for them, and I will discuss it in great depth in the next chapter.

For now, my dear Riselings, put this concern out of mind because it does not apply to you in any way possible because you are the light of hope for a species on the threshold of ascension. It is why you and your families will play a pivotal role in the Creator's plan for humankind.

On a soul level, the goal is the same for every healthy, sentient soul. To be in ascension and eventually return to Creator, as clean and pure as our first incarnation. When that happens, we go from being sentient souls to ascended souls in apprenticeship to the Creator's perpetual mission to create life from the lifelessness of the Void.

In this regard, dear Riselings, you were born to rise above the chaos and to ascend in harmony and love closer to the Creator. Keep faith in your destiny, and it will be yours. This is another reason I call you Riselings because it will be that, but more. Much more, for you will be the ones to write the next chapter in the history of our species.

Ascended Species

As souls use the power of redemption to speed their ascension, so do species. Throughout, I've intertwined many spiritual experiences to build my construct, and this one time, just for you, I will share a direct quote from the Creator when I began authoring this book.

I asked the Creator what He felt was the most important thing to explain, and He told me it was the symbiotic and healing relationship between incarnation and redemption.

My response was to ask for a SPOT—a single point of truth. Like the corner of a picture puzzle, everything connects back to it. And now I will share the SPOT the Creator gave me, word for word. Here it is:

> "The essence of reincarnation is the cumulative experiences in one species." *This is the way.*

In other words, my dear Riselings, our species, homo sapiens, is going through the Great Winnowing. After the pole shift, we shall see a new age of enlightenment as an ascended species, and this broad, unblemished canvas will be yours to paint in bold, joyful colors.

The Earth will be different but in a good way. We'll still have four seasons, but winter and summer will be shorter and less severe, and fall and spring will be more prolonged and gentle.

Across the planet, old lands will have sunk as new ones rose. The cleansing rains will wash the salts off the new lands, leaving incredibly fertile new lands to sustain us. The blue skies and sweet waters will be a magnificent call to begin again.

As we rebuild, the observation data from the flyby will eventually be released, and the world will learn that the Nemesis orbit has been shortened, perhaps by half and that eighteen hundred or so years into the future, the flyby will be the end of all life on Earth.

Once humanity wraps its head around that reality, the race will on to find new worlds to inhabit, and what we've learned so far is that there is no low-hanging fruit to be found, so we'll need courageous souls to terraform new home worlds for pioneering families.

One day in a distant future, our descendants will return home with a message for Gaia. "We just created a beautiful new world you might be interested in, and sure would love to have you."

It is delicious to contemplate our future as an ascended species, but before the sweetness comes the bitterness. It is time to be in the moment with two essential questions.

How will we know we have become an ascended species? Acquisition will no longer be the driving force of our lives. Humankind will have risen above the chaos of the Void, expressing itself with brutal, controlling behaviors.

Your future children will live in harmony, seeking harmony within themselves and with everything about them. Yes, even enlightened species are driven by the quest for order.

In the future, what will be the most precious form of harmony? It is and will always be Shawheylu, as I call it, the eternal bond of trust, and here is terrific news.

While it is difficult to be enlightened during tribulation, there is a way to feel and live the future today and through all the trials to come.

Imagine our species as a great sailing ship, as its skilled sailors throw mooring lines to the hands on the pier so the vessel can be made fast.

Shawheylu is the Creator's way of throwing you a line, and now I will show you how to catch it. The first time I caught a line, so to speak, was in an orphanage.

John and Sally

When I was fifteen, my mother became seriously ill during a family vacation to San Diego, CA, and needed months for recovery. I remained near my mother and found myself in an orphanage called Hillcrest. A compassionate place for good kids in bad situations; it was my great fortune to be sheltered there in the storm of a family crisis.

Early on, I became good friends with another fellow my age, John. He had come to Hillcrest a different way. One night, he heard a shotgun being fired downstairs and raced down to see his mother's brains painted all over a wall as his father stuck the barrel in his mouth and blew his brains out.

After that, John had no other family and spent years bouncing from one foster home and institution to another and finally was allowed to stay at Hillcrest until coming of age. He knew what was out there and was grateful for this good fortune.

About a month after I arrived, a social worker brought two new children into the community playroom and introduced them to us. A fourteen-year-old girl and her ten-year-old brother. The kids all gathered to greet them.

Both were as white as snow, emaciated bags of bones with huge, terrified eyes. When the social worker left, they raced to a corner and huddled together like we would do something awful to them. This was not without merit.

Typically, children can be cruel bullies in such situations, but each of us there was them. We knew the pain and collectively what to do. We melted away, giving them space, and in the following weeks, we witnessed a magnificent transformation.

We later learned that their parents had chained them both to posts in the basement for over a year. They lived on scraps and were never allowed out. It was their good fortune that a meter reader for the power company noticed them and reported it to the police. Their parents were arrested and given very stiff sentences. This is how they made their way to Hillcrest.

Then, John and the girl, whom I shall name Sally, found each other. After that, I began seeing less of John and knew they were getting close.

When the good news came that my mother would be discharged and that we could drive home, I was happy to move on, though I would never forget those months at Hillcrest as a gift of God to me in a hard time.

Our family car was brought to Hillcrest, and I set about to clean and prepare it for the journey home and discovered half a pack of cigarettes. Eureka, a fortune, I thought to myself as I slid it into a front pants pocket. I would give it to John as a going away present and went looking for him.

I didn't have to look far because he was on hall monitor duty that afternoon, and Sally was sitting next to him at the table. I walked up to the table, pulled out the package, and slid it across to him, palm down with a grin.

With gratitude, John looked under my hand, hesitated momentarily, and then pushed my hand back with the package. I pocketed it as he looked at Sally, then turned back to me and said, "I really thank you, but if they find me, I'll be thrown out." He turned to face Sally and continued, "That means I'll lose her, and I can't risk that."

As the two looked into each other's eyes, my focus shifted unexpectedly as though someone or something wanted to show me something. This was when I saw Shawheylu, the eternal bond of trust, for the first time.

Spirits and Souls

Previously, we used a crystal clear incandescent light bulb as a metaphor for the soul and spirit. The soul is represented by the bulb and the spirit by the filament. Now, let's take that to the next level.

Let's imagine not one but two incandescent light bulbs that are in phase with each other and so share the same time and space. The two glowing filaments are entwined in a manner reminiscent of the yin and yang symbol.

Then, the bulbs surrounding them offer a gold tone, and when you come close, you can feel the warmth of the love shared.

What I saw before me was stunning—two unfortunates with no families, poor, young, set adrift by misfortune with meager prospects for the future. Yet, what I saw in that moment was glorious.

In all this foulness of life, John and Sally found each other, a great love and new hope for the future. There is no ceremony to tell you that you have achieved Shawheylu with another soul because both who share it will know it. That together, neither soul will ever be unloved or alone again.

This bonding is eternal, and once two souls are bound this way, they will intertwine time and again in some fashion or another during future incarnations. To break this eternal bond of trust is the most grievous of scars and unthinkable to a healthy soul.

Right then and there, I knew John and Sally would be inseparable and that they would share a promising future together. Sadly, I wondered if I would ever find Shawheylu as they did.

I'll never know how it all worked out for them, as that was the last time I saw them. Yet, when I close my eyes, I can see it clearly.

They were enveloped in the golden light of their two souls in phase with each other, how their spirits were joined between them, and how I felt the radiant warmth of their love.

Looking back on it, I needed to know if it was a fluke or if there could be others. Could other young men and women find each other this way and make the eternal bond of Shawheylu?

Leaving San Diego, my mind turned to other things, and I set this memory aside, but my soul did not.

Weddings

In my first year of college, I landed a weekend job as a wedding photographer for the largest studio in Phoenix, Arizona. Over three and a half years, I photographed over one hundred and fifty weddings; my favorite were the Greeks. Opa!

While photographing my eighth wedding, something odd happened. The couple I photographed was clearly not going to make it because of the crazy times for American culture.

In 1969, California Governor Ronald Reagan legalized no-fault divorce, and it spread across the county like wildfire; a few years later, Roe v. Wade legalized abortion. Like the two blades of a pair of scissors, they quickly cut through the fabric of society with disastrous results for the future.

Today, couples wait to marry because it is hard to get a start, but back then, it was still customary to marry young, and what I saw was a perfect storm of irresponsibility.

This will sound blunt, but two-thirds of all the weddings I ever photographed, some one hundred or more, failed within the first three years, and I could see it coming a mile away.

Weddings are big business, and what I saw as a photographer was a lot of inexperienced kids playing king and queen for a day and one or both walking down the aisle with their fingers crossed and thinking, if it gets bad, I can bail without having to take responsibility for my deeds. It was a social carnage, and many things I witnessed saddened me.

Back to my eighth wedding and the couple that would not make it. After finishing up, I wrote on the work order, "Sell fast because they are not going to make it."

The next day, I got a call from the studio's head, and he laughed at me. He teased me about being a psychic trying to read spoons and said I did not have to do this again and that he would process the wedding albums, which took about ten days.

A week later, he called me back to inform me that after they finished everything, they contacted the couple to schedule an appointment and learned that they had filed for an annulment three days after the wedding.

He then told me that I would be most welcome to make similar helpful suggestions in the future.

I said I would, and after I hung up, I leaned back as my memories of John and Sally flooded my mind. This was when I started my secret mission to find couples bonded by Shawheylu.

My first was to test for psychic connection because bonded couples can sense each other's needs. When I photographed a couple, I had a good test. If I began to sense the bond. I would wait for the reception, and after cutting the cake, the brides and grooms tended to work the room, and I waited for them to separate.

When they were at two different ends of the hall, I would go to the nearest one and pump myself up to seem important and worried, and I would say, "I need to take a picture of you and your spouse right now. This instant. This is urgent! Granted, I laid it on with a lot of schmaltz, but it always worked.

A few minutes later, the other suddenly appeared, and I always asked the same question. "Why are you here?"

Each answered, "Because I felt the need to be here." Then I knew it was real, and I would take them to the side room and explain this to them. After that, I would dip into my back of tricks and create for them the most memorable wedding photos possible in those days.

However, Shawheylu comes in many forms and in many ways, and the one wedding that proved it to me was a Chicago pimp and his high-class call-girl wife. Apparently, they have been quite successful, and they had just purchased two new McDonald's franchises in Phoenix, AZ.

After cutting the cake, I approached the groom and asked, "Can I ask a personal question if you don't mind," I queried. He nodded with a smile. "Given your backgrounds, I'm curious how the two of you actually fell in love?"

He chuckled a bit, and here was his answer. "We've both been selling for so long; neither of us knows what it is anymore, but I do know this, she is my best friend in the whole world, and I want to do this with her."

That, my dear Riselings, is another example of flame-on Shawheylu, which proves it comes in many ways.

It was towards the end of my career as a wedding photographer that I finally saw Shawheylu for the second time. This has always been my most cherished memory from the over one-hundred and fifty weddings I photographed.

The groom was in his mid-twenties, and the bride was in her early twenties. They lived in a small rural farming community outside Mesa, AZ. The groom ran a maintenance center for a large corporate farm with several men twice his age under his command.

He was very well-liked, and the corporation allowed them to use the facilities for the reception. A wash house for the field hands and a large tin Quonset hut large enough to hold a multi-engine bomber or transport airplane. Also, they let him use equipment and vehicles and topped it off with a whole steer for the reception.

The two fathers and their friends took a couple of large trucks and loaders off to a field in Prescott where the forest service was cutting down juniper and mesquite, burning them, and giving them away. They loaded up, headed back, and dug a large pit for the BBQ.

That night, all the men tossed wood into the pit to build up a bed of embers, and in the morning, they covered it with dirt and then a layer of straw. On top of that, the dry rub steer in canvas, another layer of straw over that, and finally, a dirt cap.

As they did that, others volunteered to clean the facilities, and the wash house was so clean the next day you could eat off the floor. They were all sleepy but in good cheer as the wedding day unfolded.

The bride was delicate and gentle. She and the groom had grown up knowing each other, and their families respected and liked each other. It was a traditional wedding in a huge Catholic church, and the gathering felt blessed.

After the wedding, we took the usual photos in the church, and after that, I would usually go directly to the reception, but the bride asked me to follow them to take pictures, and I happily agreed.

Their limo drove to a tiny house on a dusty road, and there, that mailbox next to the picket fence, the bride's great-grandmother waited for them in her wheelchair and made her caregiver stand back on the porch.

Getting out, they both walked up to her, and I followed with my camera. The magic happened. They both kneeled before the bride's grandmother and bowed heads to receive her blessing. I can never forget how that woman looked upon them with so much love and delight.

It was the one and only time I ever witnessed something like that, and as their marriage was being blessed, I took several pictures, and then, as I lowered my Leica M2-R and looked over the viewfinder, I saw it again. Two souls intertwined. I could see it. I could feel it.

They said their goodbyes, and we left for the reception at the field house and hut, which was another wonderful surprise. The couple told everyone not to bring a present but a large tray of the house's specialty. Oh, my Lord, what a feast.

First, there was the BBQ. After they dug up that steer, the meat was so tender you could not eat it with a fork. You needed a spoon, and yours truly consumed mass quantities of BBQ that night. That was awesome, but then there were the enchiladas. Woohoo.

Everyone brought lots of yummy Mexican dishes, and what caught my attention was two eight-foot-long takes loaded with pan after pan of homemade enchiladas, and no two were the same.

Mind you; I never cared much for enchiladas because what they serve in the restaurants is a tube of whatever is smothered under an oozing pile of melted processed cheese.

But these looked interesting, so I tried one. It was like a three-year-old tasting chocolate ice cream for the first time, and your hair stood straight up. I was now a believer in enchiladas, and spread out before me was what I believe was to have been the most extensive selection in the history of all enchiladadom.

That night, I set another all-time record. We always carried twice as many rolls of film as we expected to need for a wedding, which was usually about 10 to 12 36-exposure rolls for most weddings. For a large wedding like this, I carried 20 and always returned with handfuls of unused cassettes.

Well then, to keep eating BBQ and enchiladas, I worked my fanny off all night, and it was a good thing my studio liked my dance photos as I was very good at it. Folks love to dance at Mexican weddings, and the pictures sell nicely.

Everyone knows it is time for the dancing to begin when the band plays the traditional Mexican wedding entertainment song, "Testing, Testing, Uno Dos Tres."

After that, the floor fills quickly, and the crowd slowly spins like a galaxy in space. Easy pickings for me, and by the end of the evening, I couldn't eat another scrap, and low and behold, I used all twenty rolls.

There are other forms of Shawheylu as well. For example, men who have been in combat do not miss the horrors of war, but they do miss the camaraderie. The guy in the bunk next to yours could snore like a pig and tell the stupidest jokes, but he's your brother, and it's about one for all and all for one.

A Win-Win survival community needs a core leadership group of combat veterans and first responders. If the community is to be successful, it must come together similarly with camaraderie and commitment.

Now, let's talk about how to make it work for you.

Making the Bond

Perhaps you are wondering, of one-third of the weddings that did not fail, how many were marriages with spouses bonded in Shawheylu? Of the over one hundred and fifty weddings I photographed, I can count the number on both hands.

With this group, I break it down into two categories: good marriages and bonded marriages.

What makes a good marriage? Any such couple will tell you that if you want your marriage to work, you must work at it daily. This is a good marriage.

Couples with a marriage bonded in Shawheylu do not work at their marriages. This is because their marriages work for them, making them inseparable.

It is hard for people to achieve Shawheylu because as we age, we tend to hold back that last ten percent of trust. The whole trust but verify thing is a problem for us as we suffer the slings and arrows of life.

For example, the expression "giving it to God" begs the question, give what? You stop holding back. You trust the Creator 100%, and getting to this point usually entails a lot of hard knocks for most of us. The same holds true with any relationship, including marriage.

When the day comes, trust your Indigo knowing, my dear Riselings. You'll know she's your gal and he's your guy because you will know each other. This is a personal process, so here are a few wedding photographer tips for the tribulation.

- Save yourself for marriage.
- Look first within your community.
- Know your partner and marry young.
- Gain the support of your families.
- Share a vision of a long and purposeful life together.
- Make each other laugh, and dance together often.
- Commit yourselves to the community.

Above all else, you must give each other courage to face the difficult times ahead and those who come to take a spoil of you. Share strength and remember:

Humility leads to courage, which is about doing good and opposing evil. *This is the way.*

When will you know that you share a bond with Shawheylu? Sometimes, it happens quickly and soon, or it can take years, but when it does, you will both know. If you need to test it, here is how.

You face each other, and first, the man and then the woman say, "My life for yours," without hesitation, and with complete love, the bond has been made. To cherish and grow it, always look for ways to make your spouse feel good about him or herself, and above all, listen to each other using your Indigo skills.

For now, you have what you need to know. You have what it takes to thread the needle of this tribulation and create many bonds of eternal trust, and these will be extraordinary times for you.

Beyond that, in a time I call the backside, you will inherit a new world to build a future for our ascended species and the hope of an enlightened Star Trek future. It is all yours, my dear Riselings, and when you are ready to stand tall, open your arms to heaven and proclaim, "Creator, I am with you. I can do this."

The journey is more decisive than the destination. *This is the way.*

Teaching Tools

The cinema teaching tool for this chapter is Arrival (2016). In this superb science fiction film, extraterrestrials land ships across the planet and are peaceful, but the ability to communicate is challenging.

What you see in the film is that the governments of the world become paranoid and lash out because they cannot determine the intention of this alien race.

Here is where your natural abilities as a mature Indigo will serve you well. With your third eye fully open, you'll easily spot the nasties, and they, in turn, will avoid you. As you watch this film, note the behavior of the character Louise Banks. A classic crystal, if there ever was one.

Now, here is the final assignment for Riselings and their families.

Take time to begin enjoying the beauty of our world, for within its subtleties are the brushstrokes of the Creator.

Sit together on a porch to watch a sunset and imprint the memories in your soul, for it may be a very long time before you see such things again, and these memories will help get you through the dark patches ahead. Remember:

> Survival is less about holding onto things and more about holding on to each other.
> *This is the way.*

May the winds always be at your back and the sun upon your face. Your journey begins.

14

Call to the Nation

Dear Riselings, you and your family are welcome to read this last chapter, but it is not written for you. Instead, it is written for those capable individuals reading this book and asking a rightful and necessary question. "I'm not a Riesling, so what is this to me?"

The spirit is of the Creator and always returns to Him. This is why we should never say that we die. The spirit always returns to the Creator, with or without the soul.

In the Great Winnowing, the Creator will purge all souls not in ascension and commit their souls to death eternal in the Void. Let's do the numbers.

At this time, every incarnation imprint on your soul will be tallied in a grand count of every unresolved scar from your incarnations since you were first cleaved of the Creator and born a child of Earth. Please note that counsel may not represent you: no plea deals, no golden parachutes.

What you have will be your collective karma quotient (CKQ), and the bottom line will be in the black or the red. What does it take to be in the red? A CKQ of -0.000001. If this is your final score or worse, you'll be supping on the vacuum of the Void.

What does it take to be in the black? A CKQ of +0.000001. Yes, the margin is thin, and there is a simple way to see your bottom line today.

When you turn out the lights for the night and close your eyes, what do you see? Remember what Shakespeare said, "To thine own self be true."

If you walk humbly with the Creator, close your eyes, and imagine a beautiful, loving universe of possibilities, then your third eye is open. Even if your CKQ is in the black by the tiniest crack, you will know it when you are close enough to the Creator to feel His presence.

Rieslings will make the cut when the Great Winnowing occurs, and so will you. Is this a family plan? No. Members of your family and those within a Riseling family are subject to the same rules. This is the big leagues now, and you make the cut or you don't.

Good News – Bad News

OK, let's assume you've made the cut. What's at the end of this rainbow? Let me put it this way. The opportunities to reincarnate in an ascended species can be as scarce as hen's teeth.

Here is the good news. Every child of Earth who makes the cut will get a prepaid, first-class ticket to a Star Trek future incarnation.

For those who say, well, that's all fine and good, but I'm not into science fiction, here is what I have to say.

Get out of my way because I've got twenty rolls of film and a mighty hunger for BBQ and enchiladas. Smile please.

That was the good news. Now, the bad news.

If you close your eyes and all you see is the back of your eyelids, your third eye is closed tight, and your CKQ is in the red, it could go one of two ways during the Great Winnowing.

Your CKQ is so metastatic you're on the reincarnation "Do Not Travel" advisory list and are immediately imprisoned in a drop-ship bound for the Void. Nobody will miss you.

Then again, you might be within range of a solution that puts you in the black because you're not that bad. Granted, you're not the brightest bulb on the tree, spiritually speaking, but with the right effort during your present incarnation, you can make the cut.

You could think of it as flight and trip interruption insurance for the ascension-challenged souls.

What does the policy cover? The whole enchilada. Assuming you are interested, it's time to look at that ledger. In terms of risks, what are the purge percentages?

Can You Handle the Truth?

When looking at purge percentages, there are two basic categories, each with its own level of risk. Lost souls and incarnated souls.

Lost Souls is often used by the other side to define Satan, his minions, and all the other spiritless nasties afflicting the children of the Earth. Here is what will happen.

During the Great Winnowing, the Creator and Yeshua will work together to sweep them up as quickly as a whale scoops up krill, after which they will eat vacuum in the Void. The percentage for this category is 100%, and good riddance.

Those in the other category are called sick souls on the other side. However, in the context of this discussion, I will identify this category as salvageable souls. Look at it this way: even if you hold a salvage title, you're on the road if your tags and insurance are current. I say never pass up a good thing, so go burn gas!

So, what is the percentage for this category? This is an impossible call because the incarnation stories of each life are imprinted on the soul and no place else. So, the only practical thing to do is what lawyers call "A Solomon." You split the difference at 50-50.

Here is the part where they say, can you handle the truth?

I never thought much about this until I began writing this book, and then I realized I needed to ask because you need to know.

Souls committed to the Void will carry the histories of their lives with them. Everything they were, are, and ever could have been will vanish like tears in the rain, and it will be as though they never existed. You do not want to go there.

Knowing this, I initially guesstimated a conservative loss ratio of 5% to 10% for incarnated sick souls. When I did my reading on this with Creator, it baked my noodles.

One in three sick souls incarnated on Earth will fail the cut and be purged into the Void.

Let that sink in for a moment.

One in Three

I do not know about you, but learning one in three will be purged stunned me. Mind you, this does not include the nasties, and thankfully, they will be put down like the rabid beasts they are.

Yet. The inescapable fact is that of all the souls presently incarnated on Earth, approximately 2.7 billion of those currently walking the Earth will fail the cut, and their end shall be death eternal in the Void. Shocking to hear, but begs the question. Were they warned?

The phrase "fear God" is mentioned over 300 times in the Bible, depending on the version. Ask yourself. Who is the Creator speaking to?

Is He speaking to those in ascension? No, because it makes no sense to fear God when you love and serve Him.

In fact, it compels a query. Does the phrase "fear God" suggest that one must first accommodate Satan's fear of God as a way of expressing our love for the Creator?

It reminds me of that old saying in the travel business. Even after you die, you still have to connect through O'Hare. Let's leave it at that because, from the start, the Creator has warned everyone about the coming purge. Full disclosure. Case closed.

So enough already with the hills and valleys. Let's turn this lemon into lemonade.

Flight Insurance

The term flight insurance is a metaphor for redemption, and it is a most useful one because if you feel the light within calling you, all you have to work with is a fraction of an incarnation, as opposed to multiple incarnations with the luxury of time.

Now, a quick disclaimer. I'm not a priest, rabbi, shaman, or minister, but I can photograph your wedding. The point is that terrestrial religions are, for a better lack of words, a bit too terrestrial for more cosmic thinkers like me.

I'm a technical writer for Creator, Inc., and this book's construct represents my lunchroom view of Heaven. You can call me a Geek for God if it makes you feel better.

In other words, I live on Earth and occasionally commute for work assignments. I do love my job.

But let's assume this is Earth, and you find me in the lunchroom eating homemade enchiladas; you pull up a chair.

We do the chit-chat until you finally ask, "I'm not feeling strong about my CKQ. Is there something I can do for a bit of insurance?

"Sure, it's easy to put your shoulder to the wheel. All you have to do is to write somebody deserving a generous check," I answer half-heartedly.

You ask quietly, "And what does it buy me?"

Now, I finally put my fork down. "A minimum monthly payment on a maxed-out credit card with a 29% interest rate."

You nod, showing that you've begun to sort things out, and ask, "And what if I want a flight insurance policy with double indemnity?"

Now you have my undivided attention, and I push my enchiladas aside and lean across the table. "Winners never quit, and quitters never win. What are you prepared to do?"

Without hesitation, you answer, "Whatever it takes."

"OK," I answer with a smile. "I'll go downriver with you, but first, you need to know the rules, what is desired of you."

What Creator Wants

After this awful tribulation will come the backside, as I call it, and what the Creator wants to see there is an ascended species, and what the Creator wants, the Creator gets. Works for me.

With what is coming, humanity must face a near-extinction-level time of suffering and emerge authentic and durable.

For this to happen, humanity will need lightworkers—men and women who walk humbly with their God. This is the commitment if you want double indemnity.

Do it, and your life will change after committing to becoming a lightworker and to being a light of hope for others. It will start getting a little better each day, and here is why.

As an Alpha-age child, I grew up watching our heroes rocket into space because we were Americans, and we could do anything we set our minds to.

Conversely, today's Alphas watch reruns of victims leaping to their deaths from the Twin Towers and live in a society that inspires the worst in us and not our best.

As a lightworker for the Creator, privacy remains yours. There is a scar-healing purity in that, and so here is the first rule when forming a survival community in service to the Creator.

If you cannot produce healthy babies, you must produce extraordinary results.
This is the way.

That's it, and in the spirit of full disclosure, Heaven is non-negotiable on this one as well as should be because we are in deep kimchee, and enough is enough.

If you seek double indemnity, what the Creator wants is commitment. Not only do you put your shoulder to the wheel, but you must lean into it with everything you've got and serve His will for our species to ascend as an enlightened species and populate the galaxy. Remember:

> It is not enough to put your shoulder to the wheel. You must lean into it. *This is the way.*

In the days ahead, you will often reflect upon your karmic past. While past life regression can help you understand yourself better, another practice called past life reconciliation is not helpful. Nonetheless, please do not spend time with them because there are more productive things to do. This is a matter of discretion.

> Time is a river. It never flows backward, and neither should you. Forward, always, forward. *This is the way.*

Each time you look back, you will not be looking forward, and that's when distracted people have sudden and unfortunate encounters.

This is why labeling acts and things as right or wrong, good or bad, and other subjective measures only mask the survival criteria you need as a lightworker. Remember:

> If a thing is useful to your construct, take it. If not, drop it in your wake. *This is the way.*

Now, I want to share an important message of hope you must carry to the world as a committed lightworker.

> Enlightenment will come when harmony within ourselves and everything about us becomes the driving force of our lives. *This is the way.*

If humanity is to reach for its freedom, it must know what it will feel like once it is hand. Always tell people, especially when life is pressing:

On the backside, we will see blue skies and taste sweet waters once again. Believe it. *This is the way.*

To get there, we need families, and they need places to be safe. You'll do the same for your loved ones, but here is where I can share a new construct just for you. I call it "turbo redemption."

Turbo Redemption

The easiest thing to do is to write and check for a CKQ minimum payment and hope for the best, and if that is good enough for you, good luck with that.

Or are you asking yourself, "What's with this turbo redemption thing?" If so, remember:

Winners never quit, and quitters never win. *This is the way.*

If you are to win at this, your immediate goal is to get the Creator's attention in just the right way. A ukulele and a snappy tune will not get it. You must be sincere and pure in your intentions.

As a technical writer for Creator, Inc., this book has been flashing a neon sign in front of Heaven that continually flashes, "Survival "R" Us Help Wanted – Anyone Good."

Let's dispense with the formalities, and let me say welcome to Creator, Inc. We are an equal redemption, Heaven, and the Creator has an eye for talent.

Ergo, your immediate task is to make the employee of the month.

At a minimum, you'll need a worthy performance record, but what the Creator likes to see is the same thing every manager wants to see—engaged employees with high emotional intelligence, a sense of initiative, and a positive attitude. Remember:

Pragmatism, common sense, and cooperation are the whetstones of wisdom. *This is the way.*

With this in mind, let's be pragmatic. Every success coach tells us that to be an effective negotiator, you need to see the deal from the other side of the table, so let's do that.

What is the Creator's mission statement? To perpetually create life from the lifelessness of the Void.

What is the goal of His mission for our species? To purge all that is holding humanity back so we can emerge from the tribulation as an ascended species.

Leave the purge thing to the Creator and Yeshua. They've got this, and nothing can stop what is coming. Your focus is on the one area that is certain to be a hot-button issue: Healthy babies from healthy, unvaccinated, heterosexual parents.

I must share that I've toyed with this turbo redemption construct for some time, looking for an enabling tool as a reliable way to achieve it. It was a mystery in search of a clue, and with such things, I stuck them in a glass jar, sealed them, and put them on the shelf. Eventually, Heaven will fax you a label; sure enough, it came in.

With that, I knew what to do, but I needed to confirm one thing based on this affirmation:

> When you scar a soul, you get what you give. *This is the way.*

This affirmation describes the primary scaring you caused, which is bound in equal measure to your soul by your intention. In addition to that, there will be collateral damage with secondary scaring, such as children losing a parent.

The karmic debt we incur due to our actions can be collectively massive. Hence, I wanted to know whether this primary and secondary debt-scaring process could be reversed and whether I could proceed. I ran it past management, so to speak, and my elevator pitch got the thumbs up, so here it is.

The Old You

When you scar a soul, you get what you give. *This is the way.*

The New You

When you heal a soul, you get what you give. *This is the way.*

This is the enabling mechanism, if you will, for turbo redemption. How you use it will determine the results, and here is where you get noticed just the right way.

When the Creator joined your new, unblemished soul with His spirit gift, you were designed to become a co-Creator, should you choose to be on the team.

This will be your moment of truth, as in what are you prepared to do? Remember:

> There are always a thousand reasons for failure and only one for success.
> Choose wisely. *This is the way.*

The first step in making a wise choice is to do your due diligence; Heaven likes that. Since we're on the cutting edge of redemption here, how about we ask about the previous employee of the month and how they got there?

Lucky you, the cinema teaching tool for this chapter is *Lilies of the Field (1963)*. This one is my all-time feel-good movie, and the lead character, Homer Smith, is played by Sidney Poiter.

Poitier portrays handyman Homer Smith, an ex-GI driving through a remote area of Arizona and stopping for water to cool his car engine. He builds a chapel for a small order of nuns, barely scratching out a living.

In addition to building the chapel, he also takes a part-time road construction job to buy groceries for the nuns. In the end, the chapel is finished, and Homer has become a respected man in the community with good prospects and the promise of a good life there.

Yet, at the movie's end, he seeks nothing for himself except a unique opportunity to speak to the Creator, and then, as the film ends, we see him driving away.

I hope you watch that film because it is a spiritual classic with many powerful messages, and intention is at the top. Let us review that affirmation.

co-Creator Path

Freedom is the foundation of free will.
Free will is the energizing force of intention.
Intention is how universes come to be.

This is the way.

We incarnate time and again to master our free will for good, and when we begin to see ourselves as co-Creators so that we can become employees of the month. Here, the purity of the intention makes all the difference.

If you provide for your loved ones, this is good and ordinary. But remember, you must produce extraordinary results.

Therefore, you become a Homer Smith. He didn't do it for the nuns or to feather his nest, for they were strangers to him. He did it for the Creator and then just moved on.

What did Homer do in this movie? He touched the souls of a whole community lovingly and harmoniously by building the nuns a chapel and then moved on. In that act of selflessness, his intention was as pure as Heaven itself, and that is how you get noticed in just the right way.

We have awful times coming. There are a lot of Riseling families we need to circle the wagons around because when the Creator destroys a world, he always keeps a few good seeds for the next. They will be these seeds, and they will need help.

The Win-Win plan for survival communities is simple.

Find a safe niche in the world where history can mostly pass you by and go to ground. *This is the way.*

The Win-Win plan for you is also simple. Find worthy strangers and serve the Creator's mission by being in service to them with selfless dedication. Help them to help humanity without thought of self. Your reward is that every soul you heal this way, plus all the secondary healing.

When you save a child's life so they can save humanity, you heal every child born to them. Think about what happens in the movie and everyone and their children.

Will this be a difficult mission?

At first, it won't be easy because you'll likely be thinking about your opportunity costs. That plus folks telling you that you're not the brightest bulb on the tree and that you are one can short of a six-pack. Before you're tempted to cut your losses short, consider this.

For starters, if they are abusing you, maybe it is because they could be that 1 in 3 who don't make the cut and ends up sucking vacuum in the Void. Forget them. Besides, you know what they say: misery loves company.

Remember how I said you can call the Creator the Great Pumpkin without losing brownie points? That stands, but here is the flip side, and I think you'll like it.

When you're true to your mission and refuse to flag despite terrible difficulty, Heaven takes notice, which can pay off like a stuck slot machine. Or, on a more conservative note, at the very least, you'll get an "A" for effort, so take it.

When naysayers get thick and slimy, grin, soldier on, and think about all those lovely brownie points you're racking up. So, lean into it–hard! Turbo–style!

That, my friend, is how turbo redemption works.

How will you know if it works? It is when you begin to feel the harmony of Heaven. That's when you know you've made the cut and that boarding pass in your hand has your name on it. It is unlike anything else you could spiritually feel.

There are no ceremonies and such. It is like Shawheylu. One day, you'll know, and you'll also know you'll keep doing it. Build a chapel here and there, and then on to the next, because your life has changed in ways you possibly could not imagine. This is how you keep the faith.

Staying the course can be difficult, and when a difficult decision is to be made, here is the one criterion I always use.

One day, I will return to the Creator, and when that day comes, we'll both know that while I am not a perfect man by any measure, I kept the faith. Remember:

> If we cannot love our own species, who in the universe will? *This is the way.*

Destiny comes to those who listen, and fate finds the rest.

What are you prepared to do?

Epilogue

It has been several years since the end of it all, and the Earth is well settled into the pole shift changes. There are new lands. Cleansed by the rains, they replace those lost beneath the waves.

We still have four seasons, but the changes are longer and gentler. Like Earth, the moon's surface has shifted, but our relative orbits remain unchanged.

Interestingly, south-facing and east-facing dwellings received the most sunlight before the pole shift. Now, the south-facing as before and west-facing for now, as the sun rises in the west. Also, the magnetic poles have shifted, so we must be mindful when using pre-shift compasses.

After years of filthy skies, Gaia has washed our atmosphere, and we see blue skies again. Not the blue of our times, which is dimmed by hazy particulates. Now, I see the same blue sky I saw as a young boy, and I took it for granted, believing it would always be this way.

It's so good to see a patient old friend at work. First came the pioneer plants, we call weeds, and they broke up the hard baked soils of a ravaged world so that grasses could take root, and then came the shrubs. We're picking berries for the first time since the tribulation began, and they are luscious beyond belief. They make yummy pies without the need for added sugar.

Most delightful for me and the children are the grassy meadows we see popping up everywhere with wildflowers as far as the eye can see because this is a glorious spring, and to our surprise, we see honey bees again. Honey bees. With all that insanity of the tribulation, how did these precious creatures survive?

Einstein is undoubtedly doing back flips in Heaven because he warned us, "No more bees, no more pollination … no more men!" Well, Albert, the bees are back, and so are we. What's not to love? Especially on a day like today.

Share Day

Today is Share Day, and our Win-Win survival community has agreed to host a gathering of visitors from other communities to meet to share news, parts, tools, and, above all else, seeds. An American-style celebration to celebrate our pioneering spirit.

I'm sitting in a rocking chair atop a tall knoll overlooking the raised gardens of our Win-Win community. As I sun myself in the light of a kinder sun, the warmth sinks deep into my old bones as I take it all in.

It is an inspiring view that could not have been possible without the selfless help of a wonderful Homer Smith or two. The first round will be on me when I meet them on the other side, and I know I will because this is their Share Day, too. After all, they kept the faith.

Throughout the tribulation, our Win-Win community continued producing food underground. We worked with local elected officials ten times more than our needs and continuously supplied their churches and charities with fresh food. I see the county sheriff there, and he's come to enjoy himself as a welcome and honored guest. He has our backs, and we have his.

The things we value in life have changed, and the naughty word is any imaginable form of centralization. Now, dependency upon others is scorned, and the most popular affirmation of the day is:

> **It is better to eat beans from your own bowl than steak from another man's hand.**
> *This is the way.*

After the meteorite showers eased up, communities began growing above ground in raised bed gardens to experiment with new seed varieties, and we've found that there is a secret to excellent yields. Let a ten-year-old do it. They are out in force today, and it is a hoot to see a handful of adults following these kids around, glued to their every word.

East of me, on the modest slope of a large mountain, I see our new tree nursery, sporting long rows of trees of every kind, but mostly those species native to these soils. Like toy soldiers standing at attention, they'll march to their new home this summer as we begin planting them.

West of me, I see young Riselings on horseback driving a small herd of cattle to a paddock rich with sweet water and verdant grasses, and before me is the big show.

Our men worked hard and built a spectacular outdoor dance floor; square and contra dancing are the rage.

Today, a small group of young men from another community sing old romantic rock-and-roll sounds from the sixties. What do you know, they are surrounded by swooning girls, carrying on as though these strikingly handsome fellows are rock stars.

It makes me think.

We've just gone through a brutal tribulation and learned that we are a slave species and that most of everything we knew was wrong. In the process, we dropped tons of old stuff in our wake and paddled on. Yet, some things endure, and to my amazement, here we are in an ascended species, and we still have groupies. Who knew? Works for me. I like it.

Another thing I like is the HAM shack over by the picnic tables. They are doing radio relays today.

Amelia

The operator is Jerry, and his apprentice is Amelia, his granddaughter. There is some interesting backstory here.

After the tribulation, terrestrial Internet communications were smashed and useless, and our transit through the Nemesis cloud tore massive gaps in our global communication satellite coverage. However, in every dark cloud, there is a silver lining.

Over a hundred years ago, amateur radio operators (HAM) organized message relay systems to pass messages along from one station operator to another until they reached their destinations. The most common messages were health and status, such as marriages, births, deaths, etc.

It works beautifully because HAM radio is what we geeks call peer-to-peer. What I transmit is received by your radio without any middleman technology and vice versa. Our communication is clear. Anyone can hear and join in. However, nobody can push a cancel button on you because there is no third-party service provider.

The children in the community must be proficient in Morse code with a speed of twenty words per minute, and most local traffic is with handheld and mobile radios.

For long-distance, a popular way for community leaders, engineers, and healers to communicate using two-way shortwave radios with connected laptops for real time, keyboard-to-keyboard chats. Once the radio operator establishes a link with another station, people can type messages back and forth, as their characters sputter across the screen.

This brings us back to Jerry, whose apprentice is Amelia, his granddaughter. They are part of the magic because attendees give them health and status messages to relay. Plus, Amelia organizes chats for them with their communities with Share Day information.

I've been watching Amelia with great interest because she reminds me of what I learned about the difference between men and women during my vision quest in the beautiful Arizona hills of the Prescott National Forest.

During the download, I saw how this was explained. The difference is the perception of time. It was a mystery to me, and I tucked it aside for the longest time, attributing it to reproduction cycles, though it was always a square peg in a round hole.

It wasn't until a few years ago that it clicked. Folks who teach land navigation, such as in the military, know this skill comes more naturally to men than women. In other words, it takes an extraordinary woman to navigate on land, as well as a common man.

Here comes the flip. As an ascended species, the potential power of the feminine will no longer be suppressed, and then it will take an extraordinary man to navigate time and space as well as any common woman. This is the true power of the feminine, not anger and mockery.

The power of the feminine was suppressed by American feminists who favored fortune over family. In contrast, the feminists of more family-oriented cultures see feminism as the liberation of their families, and we salute them.

A new sensibility emerged after the pole shift between men and women, defining their survival and pioneering family roles as bringers and binders. The men are the bringers. They bring wisdom, sustenance, and security.

The women are the binders of souls; the source of the power of their femininity is in their connections.

A woman is always a loving and supportive maypole for her circle of family and friends. Her husband cherishes and watches over her and all those tethered to her in an array of brightly colored ribbons. It is a joyful dance of life together in a new age of enlightenment.

This is not far-fetched!!! Once we no longer have monster boot heels pressing down on our necks and are free, truly free, there will be a magnificent renaissance. Yes, the Great Awakening is about learning what "They" are doing to us, but so much more.

We'll learn our true history as a species, who our true enemies were and are no more. That will be eye-opening, but we will also realize we have old galactic friends and the promise of new ones. What is the draw? A whole new kind of Indigo.

Pathfinders

Our Indigo ability comes through our third eye and inherent telepathic powers. Indigos, Crystals, and Riselings, it's all the same. We're all some variation of Indigo 1.0. So, what happens with Pathfinder Indigos, as I call them, or Indigo 2.0 if you will? It's all about progression.

I am an Indigo Elder of the Boomer generation, followed by Latchkey Indigos, Crystals, and Riselings. All those who survive the pole shift will become mature Indigos, save for a few.

With the emergence of Pathfinder Indigos, we will begin exploring our psychic and telepathic powers as groups of people and perhaps communities. This will be possible on the backside because we will no longer be hunted as a species. This will provide fertile soil for new seeds to take root. It will be the awakening of our telepathic powers, which will vary by individual.

This is why I'm interested in Amelia. She is sitting alongside her doting grandfather with a kind and cheerful smile, taking relay messages, and as they say, she's the brightest bulb on the tree with a natural knack for organization.

It was a special project of theirs. After the pole shift, many things changed, and so did the behaviors of the shortwave frequencies used by HAM operators. Each has its characteristics, best purposes, good seasons, and off-seasons.

After the shift, it all changed, and after Jerry told Amelia that new antennas would be needed to evaluate the bands and that this would entail a lot of work.

Jerry is a seasoned HAM operator, but arm wrestling an antenna mast is a job for young fellows with strong backs. Amelia stepped up to the plate and put out the word. She needed pickers for parts and materials, someone to recycle old scrap forge, new parts, etc. That was easy for her.

The challenging part was finding a suitable antenna engineer because the talented ones have a sixth sense of what works and are often uninterested in using a two-way radio.

Amelia pondered this for a while and set her sights on Russell, a local boy her age; he is an apprentice in this community machine shop.

Citing a backlog of projects, he feigned off Amelia's first request because all he wanted to know about two-way radios was what buttons to push. Other boys and some men offered to help, but Amelia thanked them for their offers but kept her focus on Russell. She could sense antenna greatness in him.

Who knew Russell had strong antenna kung fu? Only Amelia, and once she set her sights on him, he never had a chance. To explain why, here is my generic wedding photographer advice to all newlyweds.

> To the groom, I say, "If you want your marriage to be successful, listen patiently to everything she has to say and then do as you please."

> To the bride, I say, "If you want your marriage to be successful, you have to let him think he's getting away with it."

Amelia won him over, and to his credit, he was not half-hearted about it and pulled his friends in when needed. She was right about Russell. He had a sixth sense of things and did everything she asked of him because he came to understand the need for it. He also saw something else.

In my Vision Quest download, I learned that a woman's brain is wired for time travel. This is the difference and why the Indigo trait almost always follows the mother's bloodline.

Here is an important thing to consider. When I worked with psychics in my channeling study, the most effective and consistent were typically in their late thirties with a happy family.

Critical to her ability was always a loving husband who honored and supported her psychic abilities. In essence, these women were fully tethered and free to experience the true power of the feminine, and they were often my mentors.

In a simple difference between man and woman, only one word each is necessary as to their roles as indented by the Creator.

For men, wisdom represents the power of the masculine. For women, connection is the power of the feminine. To ensure the future of our species, good men and good women must join with love and be daring enough to succeed. I see this new view of life breaking out everywhere, and I'm loving it.

Then, one day, a little bird brought me a message. Well, wouldn't you know it? Russell and Amelia have begun the walking-and-talking. This is more than interesting. It's suspenseful because Amelia is a very capable Crystal, and the genetic trait for twins runs deep in her family.

Here, we see something extraordinary happening, and I'm picking it up on the nets more frequently now. Our initial incarnations of Pathfinder Indigos are with twins conceived after the pole shift. Initially, they are born completely telepathic, but only with each other. They can converse and share feelings, images, and so forth purely through thought. It works whether they are standing next to each other or apart on opposite sides of the world.

I wholeheartedly believe that when this generation of Indigos fully emerges, they will serve a brilliant role as pathfinders as humanity collectively grows to understand ourselves as an ascended species and what we can do. It is happening, it's inevitable, and the future of this coming generation of Pathfinder Indigos is theirs to write, and it will be a wonder to behold.

However, I know today is my day to go home, and my focus turns to something I have long planned for this moment.

I've been thinking about future karma (Agami), and maybe it works both ways, like turbo redemption. In other words, instead of sending karmic debt notices to my future self, I want to see if I can create an imprint to guide my next incarnation.

Here is what I want—the old-school American family plan. I want to fall in love with the girl next door in an enlightened age, bond in Shawheylu, marry, and make a big happy family together.

Of course, even in an enlightened age, you still have to pay the plumber. So, to underwrite all this, I formulated a plan based on my interests and skills. I've decided to be an author and a historian, and here is where I'm banking on past life regression.

If I'm going to support a big family, I need a big topic to own, so I will be a Trump historian because when it comes to content, he is an eternal well of history and ideas. Need a new book, drop the bucket in the well. If you need a television series, drop the bucket. What's not to like? He'll be the gift that keeps on giving.

That settled, the next thing is to create a soul imprint, and instead of words, I've chosen an image. The cover of the first book I'll write. It will simply be titled Trump, and I'll use a hologram of his arrest photo.

His defiance in that photo is penetrating and iconic, like the image of an unknown protester in Beijing on June 5, 1989, who defiantly stood before a column of tanks leaving Tiananmen Square and stopped them, never to be seen again.

That was a good start, but I wondered how to make it unique and finally came up with an idea. For the background, behind the floating arrest photo, there will be four horizontal stripes, with a single color each, just like a flag.

So, I imagine the cover with a background made of four stripes, and the colors from the top to bottom are red, white, blue, and magnificent orange. Yes, yes. Magnificent orange. I think that will do just fine.

Well, I finally got that one off the bucket list; time has flown, and dusk has come. My eyes soften. In the distance, I could see the twin peaks and sandy saddle in Prescott, where I had my vision quest.

I close my eyes and can smell the same sweet puffs of April air as I did that day, and I can feel the soft, cool sands of the arroyo beneath me. I begin to hear the quail and know this is my boarding call.

I open my eyes for one last gaze, and before me is love and Heaven's harmony. We reached for our freedom, and by golly, we did it. We actually did it. We're a free species now; in time, other ascended races will embrace us and say, "Where humans go, life grows."

It's begun.

One last breath is possible, and I whisper...

Perfect.

Appendix A – Affirmations

The Indigo Affirmations in this book describe something declared to be true. Each affirmation ends with, "*This is the way.*" These affirmations offer a combination of axioms and the author's sayings, sometimes called "Marshallisms."

Dedication

We always honor our heroes, creators, thinkers, and those who inspire us. *This is the way.*

Chapter 1 - Look Up

The one law of survival for sentient species: if you are stupid, you deserve to die. *This is the way.*

When your friends are watching, win by a nose. When the world is watching, win by a length. *This is the way.*

Never underestimate the power of human denial. *This is the way.*

Survival is less about holding onto things and more about holding on to each other. *This is the way.*

Survival is about learning enough about what works before what hurts kills you. *This is the way.*

If we cannot love our own species, who in the universe will? *This is the way.*

Indigo Mentor Maxim

To teach is an honor.
To mentor is a greater honor.
To learn is the greatest honor.

This is the way.

Chapter 2 – Planet X System

Hell is about being right. Heaven is about getting it right. *This is the way.*

Winners never quit, and quitters never win. *This is the way.*

I always protect myself. *This is the way.*

Chapter 3 - Previous Planet X System Flybys

Find a safe niche in the world where history can mostly pass you by and go to ground. *This is the way.*

Chapter 4 - Indigo Riselings

Indigo is the color of awareness that connects us to God's love and wisdom so we may serve the greater good. *This is the way.*

When you are ready for the answer, ask the question. *This is the way.*

The cumulative quality of incarnations drives soul growth, not quantity. *This is the way.*

Good lives make for good souls. *This is the way.*

Be young in your heart and old in your thoughts. *This is the way.*

To open your third eye, be humble, compassionate, and merciful. *This is the way.*

Chapter 5 - Revelation River

Wars are created by evil for evil and do only evil. *This is the way.*

There is strength in numbers. *This is the way.*

Clarity Mantra

Who am I?
I am a Good Person.

Where am I?
I am in the moment.

What am I prepared to do?
To be a light of hope.

This is the way.

Chapter 6 - Revelation 8:7 – The Blood

Survival is about learning enough about what works before what hurts kills you. *This is the way.*

Never underestimate the power of human denial. *This is the way.*

Chapter 7 - Revelation 8:8-9 – The Mountain

Always be mindful of prophecy, but never live in expectation of it. *This is the way.*

Chapter 8 - Revelation 8:10-11 – Wormwood

If you are doing it wrong, do it consistently wrong. *This is the way.*

The stouthearted will not go down to destruction. *This is the way.*

Life is what you make of it. *This is the way.*

Chapter 9 - Pole Shift

If you cannot communicate, you cannot cooperate. *This is the way.*

Chapter 10 – Prophecy Timeline

All who want to evolve must stay faithful to a life mission. *This is the way.*

Prepare for cooperation – not confrontation. *This is the way.*

Make an eternal commitment to always reach for freedom, and it shall be yours. *This is the way.*

There is always room at the table for a majority of one. *This is the way.*

Love is a desire that can transcend time, space, and adversity, but not doubt. *This is the way.*

Contemplation is an essential part of being on the Indigo Path. *This is the way.*

All who want to evolve must stay faithful to a life mission. *This is the way.*

Chapter 11 - Construct

Reincarnation is about souls evolving over several incarnations to learn the Godliness of Creation to be with God in mind, body, and soul. *This is the way.*

Ascension comes through wisdom accumulated through lifetimes of encounters and actions. *This is the way.*

Wisdom is a destination to which many paths of awareness lead. *This is the way.*

More important than the answer is the courage to ask the question. *This is the way.*

Co-Creator Path

Freedom is the foundation of free will.
Free will is the energizing force of intention.
Intention is how universes come to be.

This is the way.

The quest for order drives all things. *This is the way.*

Chapter 12 – We Are a Hunted Species

Overreach, overcontrol, and overbearance are the weaknesses of evil. Exploit them without mercy. *This is the way.*

Good creates and is unpredictable, whereas Evil calculates and fears well-aimed sabots. This is the way.

How a thing is said matters more than words. This is the way.

Pragmatism, common sense, and cooperation are the whetstones of teamwork. This is the way.

To walk out of the tribulation alive, you must walk through it with the Creator. This is the way.

Chapter 13 – Perpetual Genesis

If we cannot love our own species, who in the universe will? This is the way.

The only truth that matters is the truth that resonates within you because you and you alone put it there. This is the way.

The greatest truths are by and of necessity–simple. This is the way.

There is only one Creator;
There is only one Creation;
There is only one Heaven;
and all we have is ourselves.

This is the way.

The journey is more decisive than the destination. *This is the way.*

The essence of reincarnation is the cumulative experiences in one species. *This is the way.*

The cumulative quality of incarnations drives soul growth, not quantity. *This is the way.*

You get what you give. *This is the way.*

Good lives make for good souls. *This is the way.*

Forgiveness is the cessation of judgment. *This is the way.*

Stay frosty and let the *monsters* eat vacuum. *This is the way.*

Man moves mountains, and Heaven moves minds. *This is the way.*

Survival is about learning enough about what works before what hurts kills you. *This is the way.*

To all sick souls, lost souls, and demons, I command you:

- Never defile my mind with deception.
- Never feed off my body for life force energy.
- Never infect my soul with your sickness.

This is the way.

Marshall's Motto

Destiny comes to those who listen,
and fate finds the rest.

So, learn what you can learn,
do what you can do,
and never give up hope.

This is the way.

The journey is more decisive than the destination. *This is the way.*

Chapter 14 - Shawheylu

Humility leads to courage, which is about doing good and opposing evil. *This is the way.*

Chapter 15 – Call to the Nation

If you cannot produce healthy babies, you must produce extraordinary results. *This is the way.*

It is not enough to put your shoulder to the wheel. You must lean into it. *This is the way.*

Time is a river. It never flows backward, and neither should you. Forward, always, forward. *This is the way.*

If a thing is useful to your construct, take it. If not, drop it in your wake. *This is the way.*

Enlightenment will come when harmony within ourselves and everything about us becomes the driving force of our lives. *This is the way.*

On the backside, we will see blue skies and taste sweet waters once again. Believe it. *This is the way.*

Pragmatism, common sense, and cooperation are the whetstones of wisdom. *This is the way.*

When you scar a soul, you get what you give. *This is the way.*

When you heal a soul, you get what you give. *This is the way.*

There are always a thousand reasons for failure and only one for success. Choose wisely. *This is the way.*

Epilogue

It is better to eat beans from your own bowl than steak from another man's hand. *This is the way.*

Appendix B – Cinema List

Chapter 1 - Look Up

ROCKY (1976)

Chapter 2 – Planet X System

Million Dollar Baby (2004)

Chapter 3 - Previous Planet X System Flybys
Avatar (2009)

Chapter 4 - Indigo Riselings
Avatar: The Way of Water (2022)

Chapter 5 - Revelation River
Titanic (1997)

Chapter 6 - Revelation 8:7 – The Blood
Don't Look Up (2021)

Chapter 7 - Revelation 8:8-9 – The Mountain
Deep Impact (1998)

Chapter 8 - Revelation 8:10-11 – Wormwood
The Martian (2015)

Chapter 9 - Pole Shift
Interstellar (2014)

Chapter 10 – Prophecy Timeline
The Matrix (1999)

Chapter 11 - Construct
Brainstorm (1983)

Chapter 12 – We Are a Hunted Species
Astral City: A Spiritual Journey (2010)

Chapter 13 – Perpetual Genesis
My Big Fat Greek Wedding (2002)

Chapter 14 - Shawheylu
Arrival (2016)

Chapter 15 – Call to the Nation
Lilies of the Field (1963)

Appendix C – Library List

Dear Public Librarians, the list below contains this title and others by the same author referenced in this work—all case laminate editions.

Revelation and Planet X: The Kolbrin Bible Indigo Connection

- ISBN: 978-1-59772-201-8
- Case Laminate
- Published: 01/2024
- 8.50" x 11.00" x 1.313"
- 620 Pages, 3.769 lbs
- Marshall Masters, Author

Millennia ago, Egyptian and Celtic authors recorded prophetic warnings for the future, and their harbinger signs are now converging on these times.

The Kolbrin Bible: 21st Century Master Edition

- ISBN: 978-1-59772-110-3
- Case Laminate
- Published: 08/2013
- 8.50" x 11.00" x 1.313"
- 620 Pages, 3.769 lbs
- Janice Manning, Editor
- Marshall Masters, Contributor

Millennia ago, Egyptian and Celtic authors recorded prophetic warnings for the future, and their harbinger signs are now converging on these times.

Planet X and the Kolbrin Bible Connection: Why the Kolbrin Bible Is the Rosetta Stone of Planet X

- ISBN: 9781597721165
- Case Laminate
- Published: 05/2008
- 6.000" x 9.000" x 0.191"
- 92 Pages, 0.648 lbs
- Greg Jenner, Author

According to Jenner, "The Kolbrin Bible is the Rosetta Stone of Planet X!" This is because the historical accounts in this ancient secular anthology have enabled him to correlate a broad range of wisdom texts, folklore, and prophecy.

Win-Win Survival Handbook: All-Hazards Safety and Future Space Colonization

- ISBN: 9781597721738
- Case Laminate
- Published: 01/2021
- 8.000" x 10.000" x 0.938"
- 438 Pages, 2.448 lbs
- Marshall Masters, Author

This book guides you through the development process with detailed instructions for designing, building, and shielding communities for self-sufficiency, survival, and colonization.

Radio Free Earth: The Complete Beginner's Guide to Survival Communications

- ISBN: 9781597721950
- Case Laminate
- Published: 07/2021
- 8.500" x 11.000" x 0.875"
- 378 Pages, 2.561 lbs
- Marshall Masters, Author
- Duane W. Brayton, Co-Author

Radio Free Earth shows you how to select and use a wide range of affordable consumer and amateur two-way radios for long-range and short-range communications.

Surviving the Planet X Tribulation: There Is Strength in Numbers

- ISBN: 9781597721974
- Case Laminate
- Published: 07/2021
- 8.500" x 11.000" x 0.75"
- 336 Pages, 2.34 lbs
- Marshall Masters, Author

Imagine that you live to see Planet X with your eyes. What would you do, with whom, and more importantly, how will you work together to survive?

Being In It for the Species: The Universe Speaks

- ISBN: 9781597721219
- Case Laminate
- Published 09/2014
- 7.500" x 9.250" x 0.750"
- 320 Pages, 1.687 lbs
- Marshall Masters, Author

To help humanity seize this opportunity in a loving and decisive way, the

, those who reside in the presence of the Creator as enlightened beings, share the signs and events of what is to come so we may survive.

Alphabetical Index

9/11 .... 82, 99
Adam and Eve 19, 24, 129
Adrenochrome 25
Adriana .... 104, 122 ff.
Affirmations 28, 199, 265
AI 99
Alien invasion 38, 96, 98, 104, 133
ALMA astronomers 133
Alpha generation 19, 21, 23, 57, 59, 170
Amelia .... 257 f., 260 f.
Anunnaki .... 95, 97 f., 100, 105 f., 121, 134 f., 138
Anunnaki Invasion + Ground Zero and the Obliteration of NATO .... 95 ff., 100, 105
Aphelion 133
Aquaponic farming 166
Arboda .... 34 f., 138
Arizona State University 38, 54
Armageddon 99
Arroyo 193, 195, 263
Artificial intelligence 80, 149, 216, 218
Ascended Master 204, 217
Ascended Masters .... 156 f., 194 f., 203 f., 209, 223
Ascended species .... 230 f., 240, 244, 248, 251, 257 f., 262
Ascension .... 65, 151, 160 f., 167, 183, 204, 208, 211 f., 222, 224, 229 f., 243, 245 f., 268
Ashkenazi 98, 135
Aspirin 57
Asteroid belt 38, 53, 139
Astronomers 34, 46, 133, 154, 199
Atlantis 217
Aura .... 61 ff., 70, 73
Avatar Color Scheme 55
Awareness .... 21, 28, 57, 62 ff., 74, 132, 134, 151 f., 154, 156, 163 f., 178, 199, 201, 219, 266, 268
Baby Boomers 66, 71, 74
Backside 18, 81, 112, 199, 240, 248, 250, 259, 271
Basalt rock 114
Battlestar Galactica 219
BBQ .... 237 f., 244
Being In It for the Species .... xiii, 52, 95, 97, 99 f., 104, 121 ff., 132, 180, 195

Big Bang Theory 200
Bioweapons 172
BitChute ....24 f.
Black Star 34
Blue Kachina ....35 f., 111
Bluebonnet ....35 f., 48
Blueshift ....36 f., 112
Bouncing Betty 39, 54
Brown dwarf star ....33 f., 51 f., 94, 107, 133
Buddhism 62
Cable News Network 154, 200
Camelot 68
Capricorn 133
Carlos ....xiii, 35, 52, 95, 97, 120 ff., 132, 138
Carlos Muñoz Ferrada ....xiii, 35, 95
Catastrophism ....26 f.
Celtic ....45 f., 160
Celts 35, 45
CERN 38, 97
Chakras ....62 f., 207
Charka ....62 f.
Chinese 35
Chutes ....85, 101 f., 129, 144
CIA 174, 180
Cinnamon 17
CKQ ....211, 243 f., 247, 250
Clint Eastwood 40
CNN 154
Co-Creators 205, 253
Comet Hale-Bopp 53
Construct ....80, 82 f., 86, 95, 145, 149 f., 167, 190, 198, 213, 247, 249 ff., 268, 271
Costa Concordia 89
Costa Rica ....xiii, 36, 47 f.
Council of Nicea 45
COVID 172
CQD 89
Creation ....26, 61, 65 f., 82 f., 126, 139, 150 ff., 161, 166 f., 178, 189, 191, 198 ff., 202 ff., 208 f., 216, 220 ff., 268 f.
Creationism 26
Creator ....87 f., 151, 155, 185, 187, 189 f., 193, 198 f., 201 ff., 214 ff., 219 ff., 229 ff., 239 ff., 243 ff., 261, 268 f., 277
Crystal ....23, 28, 58, 67, 69, 71 ff., 140, 144, 151, 184, 193, 223, 259
Crystal Children 19
CYB 18
Danjeon 208, 227

Danjeon Breathing	227
Dark energy	152 ff., 200 f., 207, 222
Dark matter	152 ff., 200 f.
Darwinism	26 f.
Database	36, 38
David South	130
David versus Goliath	170
Days of Darkness	117, 119 ff., 124 f., 137
December 26, 2012	xiii, 36, 47 f.
Deep impact	94, 99, 101, 105, 108, 134
Defoliation	17, 136
Deluge	49 f.
Demons	38, 177, 216, 222 f., 225, 270
Destroyer	15, 31, 35, 46, 49 ff., 98, 112, 123
DEW	132
Directed Energy Weapons	132
Doppler effect	36 f., 112
Duane W Brayton	196
Earth	17 f., 20, 26, 34 ff., 44, 46, 48 f., 51, 53, 65 f., 77, 89 ff., 94, 96, 98, 103, 106 ff., 111 f., 114 f., 117 ff., 129, 133, 135 ff., 147, 154, 163, 178, 187, 194, 196, 198 f., 204 ff., 208, 210, 213, 215 f., 219 ff., 230 f., 243 ff., 255
Earthquakes	17, 114, 118, 136, 163
Eastern Atlantic	97, 101, 134
Ecliptic	53, 122, 133, 136, 138 f., 144, 194
Ed Dames	117, 125, 137, 182
Egyptian	15, 35, 43 f., 46 f., 49 ff., 98, 123, 155 f., 200
Egyptians	15, 35, 46, 49 ff., 123, 155 f., 200
Enchilada	196, 211, 245
Enchiladas	238, 244, 247 f.
English	29, 187
Ephemeris	34
Eruptions	17, 118, 134, 136, 163
Europe	97, 134, 138, 157
Exodus	43 ff., 49 ff., 119, 136
Extraterrestrial	94, 108, 216, 219
FCC	90 f.
Ferrada	34 f., 53, 95, 117, 120, 122 f., 138
Fires	17, 123
Fluoridated water	227
Follow the photon	190, 201, 204
Fountains of the deep	110, 141
Fountains of waters	107 f., 111
Frightener	35
Gaia	66, 198 f., 205, 231, 255

Gas balloon..212
Gaslighting...192
Generation Alpha..72 f.
Generation X..71 f.
Generation Y..72
George Carlin...215
Glastonbury Abbey..45
Global cataclysm...26 f.
God.....17 ff., 22, 24 ff., 29, 57, 59 ff., 63 ff., 72, 81, 87 f., 95, 100, 105 f., 113, 130 f., 134, 150 ff., 154 ff., 158 f., 161 f., 164 f., 170, 178, 184, 186 f., 189, 195, 197 ff., 204, 206, 208, 215, 224 f., 233, 239, 246 ff., 266, 268
Google...25, 33
GPS..90
Graphene...77, 172
Great mountain...93 f., 105, 107 f., 113, 134 f.
Great Winnowing..106, 112 f., 136, 140, 172, 179, 184, 221 ff., 229 f., 243 ff.
Ground Zero and the Obliteration of NATO...95 ff., 100, 105, 135
Guardians of the Looking Glass..87
Guides.................34, 79, 95 ff., 105, 122, 124, 156, 158 ff., 164, 178, 180, 183, 187, 195, 197, 211, 215, 218, 223 f.
HAM...90 f., 147, 257 f., 260
Harold Stark..38 f., 54
Harrington...34
Healthy..21, 23 f., 57, 59, 65 f., 170, 229, 234, 248, 251, 270
Heaven...35, 49, 150, 153, 159, 163, 167, 177, 180, 182, 187, 190, 194, 198, 203 f., 206, 208 f., 213 ff., 220 ff., 247, 249 ff., 256, 263, 266, 269 f.
Hebrews..35, 46, 50, 104
Helion..34, 47, 98, 111, 138
Henry Cowell Redwoods State Park..41
Hercolubus..35
Heterosexual..23, 57, 59, 170, 251
Hillary Swank..40
Hillcrest..232 f.
Holy Bible..43, 45, 47, 49, 104
Hopi..35 f., 111
Human genome..22, 59
Hypertext Transfer Protocol..179
I Am...201 f., 206
Incandescent light bulb..201, 206, 233
Indigo......17 ff., 21 ff., 27 f., 30 f., 41, 55 ff., 69 ff., 80, 82 f., 87, 129 f., 137, 140, 144, 146, 149 ff., 156, 170, 173, 177, 182, 184, 193, 221, 223, 240 f., 259, 261 f., 265 f., 268
Indigo Children...19, 58, 64, 67, 69 f.
Indigo Elder...18 f., 21 f., 27, 58, 64, 71 f., 130, 170, 259
Indigo Mentor...30, 41, 71 f., 75, 266
Indigo path...19, 21 f., 57, 59, 74, 151
Indigo Riselings..19, 57, 72, 266

Indigo way	17, 23, 30, 41, 82
Indigo-E. T. Connection	69 f.
Indigos	19, 21 f., 41, 58 f., 62, 65, 70 ff., 87, 193, 223, 259, 261 f.
Internet	58, 90, 134, 179, 257
Invitro fertilization	24
IRAS	33 f.
Iron oxide	44, 47, 94, 98, 107, 111
J.P. Jones	38
James Cameron	41, 55, 60, 76, 88
Jan Oort	37
Jesus	45, 140, 156 ff., 164, 179, 182, 198
John F. Kennedy	21, 67 f.
Jupiter	33, 36, 53, 111, 133, 139
Karma	65, 210 ff., 224, 243, 262
KH-11 spy satellite	191
Kozai mechanism	51 f.
La Palma	97
Las Vegas	110
Latchkey Indigos	71 f.
Latinos	35
Leica M2-R	238
Lightworkers	248
Lithosphere lock	117 f., 123, 136, 138 f.
Lucifer	216
Lugol's iodine	227
Marines	30
Mark Twain	83
Mars	xiv, 18, 34 ff., 53, 111, 114 f., 119, 124 f., 217, 226, 265, 270
Medicine Wheel	177, 193
Mensan	18 f., 21
Mentor	30 f., 41, 69, 71 ff., 164, 170, 183, 186, 193, 226, 261, 266
Mentors	30 f., 41, 72, 261
Messier 45	133
Meteorites	94, 98, 107
Michael Brown	133
Mississippi River	83, 87
MK ultra	174
Monolithic Domes	130
Monsters	19, 25, 57, 65 ff., 73, 75, 81, 101, 131 f., 162, 169 ff., 186, 196, 208, 210, 213, 217, 226, 270
Moon	34 f., 53, 91, 112, 117, 120, 122, 125, 138, 141, 167, 255
Morse Code	89, 91, 127, 258
Moses	44 f., 104
Mount Graham	53

MRNA...19, 77, 136, 172
Mt. Rushmore...136
Mystery Spot..184 f.
Namaste..206
NASA...33
Native American..69, 177, 193
NATO..95 ff., 100, 105, 134 f.
NDE..81
Nemesis................31, 33 ff., 42, 44, 46 ff., 51 ff., 94 ff., 98, 106 ff., 111 f., 117 f., 120, 133, 135 ff., 141, 144, 231, 257
Nemesis Constellation..31, 36, 42, 49, 51, 94, 107, 136, 139, 144
Neptune..xiii, 133
Nibiru..xiii, 34 ff., 47 f., 53, 117 ff., 134 f., 137 f.
Nikola Tesla..197, 221 f.
Nipton...110
Nordic..98, 135
Old Testament...44 f., 104
Oort Cloud...37, 94, 136
Ophiuchus..139, 144
Out-of-body...157, 167, 183 f., 186, 194
Oxbows..85, 101 f., 129, 144
Pandora..41, 61, 198
Paralinguistics..175
Pedophiles...213
Peggy Lee..200
Percival Lowell...35
Perihelion..47, 95, 98, 111, 133
Perpetual Genesis.......................................iv, 150, 167, 189 f., 193, 196, 269, 274
Phaeton...53
Pharoh...45
Phoenix...16 f., 21, 234, 236
Phosphorus...94, 107
Pineal gland..226 f.
Pioneer 10...33
Planet 9...35
Planet Nine..133
Planet X......................................16 ff., 31, 34 f., 37, 43 ff., 47 ff., 53, 69, 103 f., 111, 118, 133, 137, 139, 155
Planet X 101: Who, What, When, Where, Why and How...133
Planet X System..................xiii, 31, 33 ff., 42 ff., 49, 51 ff., 111, 118, 123, 126, 138 f., 141, 144, 266
Planet X Tribulation..16 f., 34, 36, 47 f., 145
Pleiades...133
Pole shift..................................98, 117 f., 122 ff., 136, 138 ff., 144, 184 f., 222 f., 230, 255, 259 ff.
Popcorn..22, 67, 73 ff.
Prana..207, 227

Premonitions	22, 163
President Trump	136 f.
Primary colors	59
Project Looking Glass	87
Propaganda	35, 82, 133, 200
Prophetic dreams	22, 181
Pseudoscience	58
Purge	222 f., 229, 243, 245, 247, 251
Pushmi-pullyu	200
Q and Anons	213
Queen Mary	85
Radio Free Earth	48, 89 f., 127, 145, 147, 196
Rainbow	56, 59 ff., 63, 76, 244
Rebecca	195
Red bandannas	84
Red Dragon	35
Red Kachina	35 ff., 111 f.
Redemption	199, 208, 210 ff., 224 f., 230, 247, 250 ff., 254, 262
Redshift	36 f., 112
Redwood trees	41
Reincarnation	151, 184, 194, 199, 208 ff., 214, 221, 230, 244, 268 f.
Remote Viewing	118, 179 f., 182
Reno	181
Return to Creator	199
Return to God	199
Revelation	xiv, 38, 43 f., 47, 79, 83, 85, 87, 93 f., 98 ff., 103 ff., 108 f., 113, 266 f.
Revelation 8	38, 43 f., 47, 49, 90, 93 ff., 97 f., 100, 103 ff., 110 ff., 117, 119 f., 123, 131, 134 ff., 267
Revelation 9	38, 96, 98, 103 f., 106, 135
Revelation River	79, 83, 85 ff., 101, 113, 129, 131, 144, 149, 266
River Pilots	83
Robert Reiland	170
Rome	100
Rowena	195, 203
Rtificial intelligence	219
Rumble	75, 121
Russia	29, 96 f., 134
Russian	29, 97, 180
Sabot	174, 178
Sand blows	141
Santa Cruz	41, 184
Sarah Kaplan	133
Satan	131, 216, 245 f.
Satellite	33, 51, 90, 191, 257

Schreibersite 44
Scrolls 50
Secondary color 59
Serapis Bey .... 217 f.
Seven Sisters 133
SG Anon 75
Shawheylu .... 41 f., 63, 126, 229, 231, 233 ff., 239 f., 254, 262, 270
Sidney Poiter 252
Signs .... 37 f., 70, 114, 136, 176
Sky Harbor Airport 16
Social media .... 25, 48, 74 f., 88
Sol .... 33, 37 f., 98, 107
Soul and a spirit 205, 207
Soul-scaring 212
Southern Skies 36, 136, 141, 144
Spike protein 172
SPOT 80, 83, 150, 153, 230
Star Seeds .... 65 f., 220 f.
Star Trek 27, 73, 144, 150, 155, 213, 221, 240, 244
Subatomic .... 152 ff., 164, 201 f.
Sun .... 17 f., 33, 36 f., 48, 52, 60, 101, 112, 119 ff., 133, 136, 141, 163, 167, 169, 191, 194 f.
Supreme Court 197
Survival "R" Us 187, 250
Surviving the Planet X Tribulation .... 34, 36, 47 f., 145, 147, 277
Susan Shumsky 130
Taurus 98, 133
The Days of Darkness 117
The Great Awakening 131, 169, 259
The Great Book 45, 113
The Jab with Marshall Masters 77
The Kolbrin Bible .... 15, 43 ff., 49 ff., 69, 93, 98, 112 f., 120, 123, 155, 160, 221
The Mystery Spot 184
The Plan .... 156, 161 ff.
The Washington Post 133
Theory of Everything 153
Titanic .... 88 f.
Torah 45, 104
Tsunamis 17, 97, 134, 141, 163
Tunnel of light 167, 204, 215
Tunnels of light 167, 202, 204, 209, 220, 223
Turrialba .... xiii, 35 f., 48
Turrialba volcano .... xiii, 36, 48
Unvaccinated 21, 23, 57, 59, 77, 170, 172, 251

Vaccinated	76 f., 136, 172
Vaccines	19, 172
Valles Marineris	119
Vatican	53
Venus	53, 117 ff., 122, 137 f.
Vice President Dick Cheney	70, 72, 74
Visible light spectrum	34
Visions	22, 104 f., 163
Void	65, 149, 152 ff., 156, 162, 173, 189, 199, 201 f., 204 ff., 213 ff., 222 f., 229, 231, 243 ff., 251, 254
White Hat	74, 131, 137, 161, 163
White House	70
William	104, 123 ff., 195
Win-Win plan	253
Win-Win Survival Handbook	47 f., 77, 102, 114, 145, 147, 165, 182
Winter Solstice	95, 98, 118, 144
World War III	80, 161
Wormwood	49, 103, 107 f., 110 f., 135
Yeshua	198, 204, 209, 223, 245, 251
Yoshihide Kozai	51
Young's Literal Translation 1898	93, 106 f., 109 ff., 119, 206, 208
YouTube	25
Yowusa.com	25, 37, 77, 87, 155, 163

www.ingramcontent.com/pod-product-compliance
Lightning Source LLC
Chambersburg PA
CBHW082112230426
43671CB00015B/2674